2820

2810

2800

Belt Line

2790

2780

7

2770

8

Pool (Res)

9

6

2760

4

3

1

2750

2750

D

OB

5

2B

2

2A

HC

2740

2730

W

S

N

E

Graveyard Peaches

Books by Celeste De Blasis:

The Night Child
Suffer a Sea Change
The Proud Breed
The Tiger's Woman

and

The Swan Trilogy
Wild Swan
Swan's Chance
A Season of Swans

GRAVEYARD PEACHES

Celeste De Blasis

A California Memoir

St. Martin's Press
New York

Design by Dawn Niles

Library of Congress Cataloging-in-Publication Data

De Blasis, Celeste.
Graveyard peaches : a California memoir / Celeste De Blasis.
        p.   cm.
"A Thomas Dunne book."
ISBN 0-312-06362-8
1. De Blasis, Celeste—Biography—Youth.   2. Los Angeles Region (Calif.)—Description and Travel.   3. Ranch life—California—Los Angeles Region.   I. Title.
PS3554.E11144G7   1991
813′.54—dc20
            [B]   91-18131
                                                          CIP

First Edition: November 1991

10 9 8 7 6 5 4 3 2 1

With thanks to all the guests who arrived at the ranch as strangers and became friends; And to the "Help"—Freida, Louise, Mary, Petie, and so many others—who became special parts of our lives.

ACKNOWLEDGMENTS

When I write historical novels, I often spend more time on the research than I do on the actual writing. While working on *Graveyard Peaches,* I discovered that even in the recording of personal memories, there are facts to check. References such as "that was the year we got new saddles" will not do. I asked questions such as, When was the concrete barn built? Did the sign on the back of the last Santa Fe Chief say VAYA CON DIOS or ADIOS? When was the last run of the train made? On and on.

Lila and Gordon Gossard and Dorothy and Leonard Henderson helped with local and ranch history; Nancy Nilsen and the rest of the staff of the Victorville Branch of the San Bernardino County Library ferreted out all sorts of odd lore; Carol Rector fixed the approximate dates for the artifacts found at the early-man site at Oro Grande; and Chard Walker shared his railroad expertise. Anna Slavick and Nancy Nilsen did the proofreading.

However, relatives who have been closest to the

ranch's history were the best sources for much of the information, and I plagued my mother, Jean De Blasis, my aunt Donna and uncle Joe Campbell, and my cousins Craig and Scott Campbell (their brother Kemper escaped my grilling only because he lives in Ohio). The process was sometimes amusing, sometimes sad as everyone tried to remember the exact dates and shapes of milestones passed in our collective lives.

History slips away from all of us unless it is marked before generations fade. When my brother died, the best, and often the only, witness to our shared childhood was gone. In my mind, I still ask him, "Do you remember when . . . ?" And a week after this book was finished, Uncle Joe died. He was a man of acute intelligence and memory. With his death, an important voice in the ranch's oral history was stilled.

But even with the losses, much of the past has been saved because of the many people, family and friends, who are good storytellers, and I thank all of you for sharing your memories with me.

CONTENTS

Graveyard Peaches

PROLOGUE
GRAVEYARD PEACHES

A couple of summers ago my mother called to ask if I wanted some of the peach crop. "There're so many, I don't know what we're going to do with all of them."

I accepted the offer, assuming she meant fruit from the trees in front of her house, and she said she'd send some down the hill in care of Michael.

Michael is one of the most organic of my friends. He tolerates human beings to a certain point, but he much prefers the company of his bear-sized dog, Becker, and the quiet of the country.

He was as excited as Mother about the generosity of Nature. He was also more specific. "The trees over there are so loaded with fruit, the branches are bending to the ground." He underscored his words by taking a few sample peaches out of the bag to show me.

"The trees over where? I thought these were from Mom's trees."

"Oh, no, the raccoons took hers. These are from the graveyard."

My hands were stretched out to take the peaches, but at that clarification, they snapped back. "Yetch! I don't want graveyard peaches! What a disgusting idea!"

This struck Michael as a funny rejection, and at first he couldn't believe I was serious.

"Take them away! I don't want to touch them, and I certainly wouldn't eat them."

He was thus convinced that I meant it, and he took the peaches off to distribute to more tolerant palates. But the morbid fruit was to haunt me. Freida, who used to cook for our guest ranch, showed up at my door with a pie: "Why, I never seen such a crop of peaches! Your mother sent over sacks and sacks of 'em. I've been makin' pies all day, and I thought you'd like one."

Under normal circumstances, I would indeed have liked it. I'm not much of a dessert eater, but Freida's fruit pies are of the old school, rich with the taste of summer and wrapped in pastry that's always perfect and decorated with a leaf and branch design to let the steam escape.

I didn't want to hurt her feelings, so I accepted the pie with thanks. As soon as she was gone, I wrapped it heavily in foil, as mad people wrap their heads against signals from outer space, and that night I took it to a barbecue given by a friend. As I handed the pie to the hostess, I felt obliged to explain that while the dessert was one of Freida's originals, the peaches were of grim harvest, and I didn't think anyone should be lured into eating them without knowing the truth.

The hostess, intelligent, sensitive woman that she is, agreed, and the reaction of others gave me a new philosophy: There are a lot of ways to divide people in the world (more seem to divide them than unite). There is the most basic "good guys/bad guys," to lines determined by gender, race, custom, geography, religion, and education; but I believe I've discovered the ultimate and least prejudicial division. It is between those who will eat graveyard fruit and those who won't.

PROLOGUE

That night at the party, there were a few more people who ate the pie than those who wouldn't (after all, it was one of Freida's pies), but the ones who wouldn't had the same visceral reaction that I did, complete with vivid images of peach tree roots worming through the earth in search of nutrients from the human dead. A few people said, "Oh, that doesn't bother me," on first hearing where the fruit had come from, but then a secondary reaction set in, visible in the sudden clenching of their features, "Never mind, I don't think I want any pie after all."

Confirmed graveyard-peach eaters do not hesitate. They chomp away without reservation. They do not care what the peach trees have absorbed to attain such bounty. They would probably, were the taste sweet, eat baked Venus flytraps without a shudder, and I would not like to be on a life raft with any of them if rations were running low.

However, I am convinced that there are many more people on my side than of the other because, if that were not so, crops would regularly be planted in and harvested from graveyards. As far as I know, most of the world does not do this, and the accusation of cannibalism of any degree remains a dandy way to insult one's neighbors. In a time when I so often find it difficult to fit entirely into any of the many standard divisions, it is a comfort to know that I belong to such a vast group, a group that has no barriers of race, gender, or creed.

Last summer Michael reported that the peaches weren't as good as they had been the year before. "They're a little fleshy," he said, belatedly recognizing the dark humor of his serious agricultural observation. I didn't eat any of that crop either.

Though I will not eat the fruit, that does not mean I can't enjoy the ferocious blossoms in the spring.

Besides serving its most obvious purpose and besides producing peaches, the graveyard has long been our dragon at the gate. The main road into the ranch is, at its northern end, the road to the cemetery.

If you wish to be private, having a graveyard along your main entrance is a good way to do it. Despite the care lavished on what are now called memorial parks, most people don't visit them anymore often than they must.

When I was a teenager, it was a test of courage to go into the place at night. Luckily, this was a case where sexism played a welcome role, as girls were not required to pass this test of valor.

That a cemetery lies close to the ranch makes an odd kind of sense. The ranch has long been a place of contrasts, of joy and sorrow, gain and loss. The road, the railroad line, and the Main House run fairly close to north-south, but little else about the ranch has ever proceeded on an even course.

A hundred miles northeast of Los Angeles, and one mile south of the town of Victorville, the ranch is in the "high" Mojave Desert; the altitude marker near my front porch says 2700 FEET. The Mojave River runs through it.

Its history as a cattle ranch began in the second half of the nineteenth century. It was the major spread for a large area because other ranches used it as a shipping point for their cattle. Its brand, the "hashknife," was well-known. The cattle business was still in operation in 1924 when my maternal grandparents and their law partner, Andy Sorenson, purchased the 4,000 acres from a client. The man had hoped his son-in-law would make a success of the land, but he hadn't. My grandparents and Andy immediately divided the place, the grandparents drawing the new boundaries and Andy in turn having first choice. The Verde Ranch became the North Verde and the South Verde. Andy chose the 2200 acres of the South Verde because the grazing was better for livestock; my grandparents were pleased to get the 1800 acres of the North Verde because the land was more varied, more beautiful.

4

First purchased as an investment, the ranch quickly appealed to my grandparents as a country home, a place to bring their children away from Los Angeles, where the grandparents practiced law. There were old buildings on the ranch, but the central part of the Main House was begun in 1927 and finished in 1929. The world changed for almost everyone in 1929 with the crash of the stock market, and by 1931, my mother and her two brothers were living here full-time, though their parents still practiced law in the city. By 1932, those Californians who'd had money to travel in luxury to exotic, faraway places now needed a closer—and more affordable—retreat. The first paying guests appeared then, which turned out to be the beginning of the guest ranch, a business that would continue until 1975 and would host people from all over the United States and from Europe.

During much of this time, the ranch continued to be a working ranch. The beef-cattle business went on until 1955; Arabian and Palomino horses were bred and raised commercially from the 1930s to 1951; there was a dairy until 1970. Field crops were planted and harvested, and poultry was fattened to be served for Sunday dinners at the guest ranch. I and my brother David were raised here, as were our cousins, Kemper, Craig, and Scott.

Most of the ranch buildings are against the hills and fit so well that they appear to have grown from the landscape. The Main House looks as if has been in place for 150 years. It was designed by John Byers, an architect who specialized in the Monterey style, an imaginative interpretation of the wedding of the Anglo influence and Spanish Colonial houses, a union that occurred mostly in Northern California in the 1800s when New Englanders arrived and added their own shapes, such as pitched roofs and second-story balconies, to adobe buildings. But John Byers did his best known work in the 1920s.

The adobe bricks for the Main House were made on

the ranch, and the tiles for the roof were hand-shaped, molded over the thigh, in Mexico. Great timbers support the roof and the porch, and the floors are mahogany or tile. The primary living room is two stories high with an inside balcony running along the back wall, giving access to a little suite of rooms and to the attic. The balcony is reached by an inside, open-step stairway on the south wall and from the outside by a parallel staircase.

A labyrinth of dining rooms and living quarters was added over the years and wanders west, north, and south from the main living room, yet the house remains so harmonious, it seems to have been built all at once.

The Main House is one of the few places I knew as a child that has not seemed to shrink now that I am grown.

Innumerable meals have been shared in the Main House. There have been countless hours of discussion and debate. There have been weddings, funerals, birthday parties, poetry readings, concerts, dances, political rallies, and charity drives. New Year's Eve, Easter, the Fourth of July, Thanksgiving, and Christmas Eve have been celebrated for decades there. Generations of families and thousands of people have come and gone. Far more than the cemetery, the ranch has become my sacred ground, holding the traces of all that has been celebrated and mourned in it. Once shaped by human hands, it has since then shaped in one way or another the humans that have been sheltered by it.

When I was a small child with an insular view, I thought everyone lived as we did; I didn't realize how eccentric the place and the people were until my experience broadened. I remember going to stay overnight with a school friend. I came home in shock.

"They don't say anything at the table except 'Pass the salt' or 'Pass the ketchup,'" I reported. "And they don't say much away from the table either."

My mother tried to explain that a lot of people were like that, that the ranch just happened to be a place where

6

people liked table conversation. That made sense, but none-theless, it was the beginning of my recognition that ranch life was different.

The natural configuration of the ranch has long kept it hidden. I used to imagine that there was a magic wall around it that made it invisible. Because we are so close to town, the main road is really just an extension of Victorville's "C" Street, but it gives no warning of where it is going. Past the cemetery, the hill is steep going up along the western flank of the Narrows, a high jumble of rocks that channels the Mojave River from both sides as it flows north, not south, until it disappears into the desert. The Mojave is a quixotic river that flows underground along some of its course, though the portion that travels through the ranch has always been aboveground, forced upwards by the Nar-rows. And when you crest the Narrows, the surprise of the ranch is there, an oasis cradled on the western side by hills. Looking east from the Main House, the view is spectacular. Desert quickly gives way to green country: meadows, ponds, sloughs, and forest until the horizon stretches to desert again where the old boundary of the ranch used to be. From there, you can see across the desert to distant hills that change color all day as the earth travels, sometimes soft gray, sometimes bright pink to deep purple and blue. Even the most accurate paintings of this landscape look false, as if the pieces fit only through the eye and brain and heart, not through someone else's brush.

The green land is rich with wildlife. Hawks hunt the long days, and owls the nights. Skunks bustle homeward at dawn after nocturnal feeding. Beavers build dams wherever they can find sufficient water. Coyotes trot the meadows even when the sun is high, and cottontails and jackrabbits burst from cover. The bobcats, kit foxes, and weasels were always elusive, and their numbers are much diminished now, but with patience and luck one can still see them occasionally. Sightings of mountain lions used to cause great excitement, but now the wild land is so surrounded by development that there is no way for the lions to get here.

The ranch lies in the path of one of the major flyways for migrating birds. More than two hundred and fifty species have been identified here, and it is not unusual to see forty or fifty in a single fall or spring morning.

Many species stay here the year around. The red-tailed hawks and the great blue herons are my favorites, the hawks for their slow sailing watch over all, and the herons for looking prehistoric. They can stand four feet tall; and with their blue-gray, color-of-twilight plumage and their huge wingspan, with their necks pulled in as they fly and their croaking cries, they create the illusion that the earth is forever newly born.

The view from the hills is open and vast, as it is from the shore of a sea, but here, there are spaces of silence. Just at dawn and just at dusk, everything stills; even the wind usually stops its singing, a stately pause to mark the passage from darkness to light, from light to darkness.

As the crow flies, this place is about seventy miles from the Pacific Ocean; as a man walks or rides or drives a wagon, it is much, much farther than that, separated by mountains and by areas that were once inaccessible. These conditions have kept the human history of the region prior to the twentieth century to a minimum, but even so, various peoples did pass through. In addition to the vanished tribes, Native Americans of the past few centuries are known to have frequented the area, including some who escaped control of the mission fathers over the mountains and killed some Spanish soldiers in their bid for freedom. Utes captured wild horses to sell, as well as to "liberate" some that weren't so wild. Even Willie Boy was here early in the century. He was a Paiute Indian who lived for a while in Victorville and worked on the ranch. He made history in 1909 when he led lawmen on a five-hundred-mile chase across the desert, this despite the fact that he was on foot and they were on horseback. Robert Redford played a good sheriff in the movie *Tell Them Willie Boy Is Here,* which was sympathetic to Willie Boy, played by Robert Blake. Local history is not so kind. According to that version, Willie Boy, after being refused permission to marry Lolita, the Indian girl of his choice, murdered her father, kidnapped her, and, in the process of fleeing from the posses, shot the girl, leaving her body behind. He also severely wounded a deputy Sheriff, albeit in self-defense. In both versions of the story, the posses eventually caught up with him only to discover he had committed suicide.

The Spanish expeditions that passed through during the eighteenth century were followed in the nineteenth by trappers and scouts such as Jedediah Smith, John C. Frémont, and Kit Carson, and then by more organized bands of settlers, including some Mormons who felt God had intended them to travel beyond Utah. Most of these were headed for California's inland valleys, rather than the desert itself, but river land meant fodder and water for livestock. One of the buildings on the ranch, the Red House, was a hotel for travelers, and the man who built it, Mr. Brown, had the toll rights to the Cajon Pass, which leads through the mountains toward San Bernardino. In exchange for collecting the tolls, Mr. Brown was obliged to keep the road as passable as possible.

And as noted before, toward the latter part of the last century, the land was a cattle ranch with attendant rights to water holes across the desert that enabled the driving of the cattle without having them die of thirst. The old bunkhouse where the cowboys slept and the thick-walled creamery still remain.

The discovery of gold, silver, and copper in the region also influenced the community, enough to make it worthwhile for a rail line to be built. This in turn fostered the growth of Victorville and other small towns, a process that was responsible for the settlement of much of the nation

9

beyond the eastern seaboard. Victorville's original name was Victor, for Jacob N. Victor, the construction superintendent of the Santa Fe railroad's push through the Cajon Pass. As more people arrived, vast cattle grazing lands became smaller farms, orchards, and turkey farms. Soft mining—cement and lime—took the place of hard mining when the metals ran out.

Not far from here is an archaeological site. It was uncovered and explored several years ago and then it was carefully reburied so that more could be learned from it at a later date when knowledge and technology will have advanced enough to make preservation more certain than it is today.

The estimated age of the artifacts is from four hundred to eleven hundred years old, but the prints uncovered in the lower stratum are judged to be six thousand years old. The site is not far from the river and was marshland all those years ago. The tracks of the animals that gathered there to drink, feed, and hunt were embedded in the mud. They hardened and lasted like plaster molds and were covered over by layers of protective earth. I saw the ones that the archaeologists had uncovered. There were paw prints of various small mammals, and there were prints of larger mammals, a human family, the footprints of a man and of a woman, and those of the child who had walked between them.

No human bones were found, but ornaments and tools from later ages were, and among those were a crystal drill and dainty carved beads decorated with a floral pattern. The drill was made to be functional, probably to make holes in plant materials and animal hides, but it was also fashioned to be beautiful. It was carved from quartz, and it catches and refracts the light as if it were a jewel. Nothing has ever made me feel the continuity of the best in humankind as keenly as I did when I held that crystal drill in my hand—small, exquisite, shaped equally for beauty and for use.

Closer to home, only a ten-minute walk away from my doorstep, the rocks of the Narrows hold their own mysteries. There are petroglyphs carved there, records of maturation rites and of belief in the power of the sun. There are metates where grain was ground into meal. There are dark shadows from ancient fires.

Some places are sacred ground. The part of me that wants scientific proof for everything shies away from this, but the part of me that saw those footprints, held the carved crystal, and has wandered the Narrows and this river valley believes.

I know that all things change with time. Civilizations once rich in life often leave no more than faint traces, which can be translated into only imperfect accounts of what was. Even stone is finally worn away.

I know about change, but I do not accept all of it gracefully. In the mid-fifties, 400 acres of the ranch that lay across the river were sold. The 1800 acres of my grandparents' original holding became 1400. Then in 1968, 800 acres were sold to the state to become a regional park. This was all of the land across the tracks, most of the fields, and all of the forest. I was heartbroken even though the sale was the only way to preserve the land. At the same time, the South Verde was plowed under and resurrected as a jumble of houses around an artificial lake. Every day that I am home, I walk on the park land, but it is not the same. A shortage of funds and staff prevents the park from being cared for as it deserves to be.

In the eighties, the remaining 600 acres were reduced to 172 as the back hills and the southern desert space were sold. This sale is far worse than the park. Someday there will be buildings all along the hills behind us and out on the desert. But there is no way around it. For all of its beauty, this is marginal land for farming and ranching, much of it

11

totally unfit for cultivation; it could not generate enough profit to offset the taxes and maintenance costs.

We are doing everything we can to save what is left, but I have no doubt that the cemetery and those peach trees will be here long after traces of the ranch as it used to be are gone.

My cousin Scott, who is an honest man and a lawyer, says that books ought to be about something. That seems reasonable even if it is not as widely held a view as it used to be.

This book is about the ranch, about growing up on it in a way that was in many respects more reminiscent of the nineteenth century than of the twentieth. The nuclear family had little place here. It was a world of many generations, of friends and strangers, some of whom became friends, of famous and ordinary people mixed together. It was a life where the nonhumans, creatures both wild and domestic, played their own roles on the ranch stage, a world where the ranch itself was often the boldest player and dictated the course of the play.

Sometimes it was joyful, sometimes sad, but it was always, always more like *Through the Looking Glass* than "Leave It to Beaver."

In *Through the Looking Glass,* the White King says, "I shall never, never forget it!" And the White Queen replies, "You will, though, if you don't make a memorandum of it."

This is my memorandum, before I forget. This is my revenge on the longevity of the graveyard peach trees.

FAMILY
TIES

Chapter 1

A GO-AND-GET-A-SHOVEL RAIN

In third grade, my friend Charlotte said she was going to visit her grandparents.

"Both of them?" I asked.

"Yes, of course, Grandma and Grandpa," she answered.

"They live together?"

She nodded, looking more puzzled by the second.

"Well, are they older than fifty?"

She thought about that for a while and decided they were so old, they must be over fifty.

"They can't live together then," I told her. "Once people are fifty, they don't live together anymore." I had the force of experience behind this pronouncement, and since Charlotte was rather timid, I'm sure she believed it, at least until someone in her family straightened her out. Or maybe she discovered that her grandparents weren't fifty yet.

I saw my father's parents so rarely, I didn't think of them as grandparents. My real grandparents, Kemper and

Litta Belle Campbell, were my mother's parents, and by the time I really knew them, they had long since ceased to live together.

Grandma was very gregarious; Grandfather disliked crowds of people intensely, a situation not helped by his deafness, though it was family legend that he would turn off his hearing aid when he was bored with the company. Grandma came to think of the ranch as a place to live forever; Grandfather thought of it as an investment that ought to be sold.

They married in 1916, and they had three children, Kemper Jr., born in 1918; Jean, my mother, born in 1920; and Joseph, born in 1925. Kemper died three years before I was born. He was a pilot in the Army–Air Corps and was slated to go overseas. Instead, due to mechanical failure during bad weather on a night flight, the plane crashed into the side of Cheyenne Mountain. My mother was waiting for him. She had gone to Pueblo, Colorado, in order to drive back his car. Instead, she brought home his body on the train. The North Verde ranch became the Kemper Campbell Ranch in memory of him.

Kemper was the golden child for my grandparents. First born and male, he was by most reports funny, brilliant, and charming. He went to St. John's College at Oxford in England, where he was the youngest student to enter—and from a rural high school, no less—there since John Stuart Mill. My mother and Uncle Joe still remember him with great affection. I think their hearts are very kind to do so, for they, particularly my uncle, grew up very much in his shadow. Though Joe always had his material needs met, his parents let him learn early on that there was no way he could ever match his older brother, and it was my mother who raised him, who gave him love and attention.

The domestic situation was not eased by the fact that the children were moved to the ranch full-time in 1931, during the Depression, while their parents continued to

16

practice law in Los Angeles for a couple of decades after that, returning on weekends while the children were young. There was always a paid staff to care for them, but there was more than financial cost in that, particularly for Joe, who was considerably younger than his siblings.

It was a necessity of the time because their parents' careers were a hundred miles away—not here—but certainly all would have been better had Grandfather and Grandma been in harmony with each other. But they were far from that. They were both intelligent, ambitious attorneys and they seemed to have worked well together, but both were from families where affection was not given easily, and Grandfather came from a tradition of men who did not consider fidelity a necessity in marriage, at least not for the males. Once Grandma accepted that Grandfather was unfaithful, she seems to have gone to the opposite extreme, believing as a point of pride that no woman could have said no to him, so I really don't know how many mistresses Grandfather had. I do know that despite the acrimony that characterized much of their marriage, Grandma retained a sense of wonder that such a dashing and handsome man as Kemper Campbell had married her. That is surely the saddest thing about their relationship.

Whatever was going on between them, they stayed married in name, the main reason being that when one was ready for a divorce, the other wasn't, and vice versa, and my grandfather remained a part of his children's and his grandchildren's lives until he died.

In the time of my memory, he lived at the Jonathan Club in Los Angeles, a "men-only" establishment then. Because he was red-green color-blind, Grandfather had a chauffeur who would drive him to the ranch on Fridays and take him back to the city at the end of the weekend.

His quarters on the ranch consisted of a large bed/sitting room with its own bathroom, which in later years had a glass shower door etched with the figure of a graceful nude—a gift from his children. The adobe walls of the room were thick, the tiled floor deep red, the ceiling high beamed, so that it is more like an audience chamber than a bedroom. Persian carpets and heavy wooden furniture added to the atmosphere.

Calling on Grandfather was like going to see the Emperor of China in some other age. The routine was always the same. I would knock on the heavy, metal-studded, blue-painted wood door.

"Who is it?"

"It is I, Grandfather; it is Celeste." Our exchanges, even through thick paneling, were formal.

"Come in, Child."

In the next part of the ritual, I would try to work the wrought-iron latch, but I never could manage it. That latch didn't yield its secret to me until more than a decade after my grandfather's death.

"Grandfather, I cannot open the door."

"Ernie will open it for you."

Ernie, who acted as gentleman's gentleman as well as chauffeur, would then open the door for me, and the audience would begin.

"How did you do in school this week?"

"Very well, Grandfather, except in penmanship," I would answer, or variations on the theme. Grandfather would reiterate the need for studying hard and doing well before he asked me about any ranch adventures that might have livened the week. Then he would present the money sock. During the week in the city, he dumped his pocket change into a sock, and I, as the oldest grandchild, was given the privilege of receiving the gift and sharing it with the others. No one ever administered a trust with more care. There were my brother and I and then the cousins as they were added to the family, and I counted those pennies and the occasional nickels and dimes repeatedly and divvied up the change under the strictest self-regulation. If there was

18

change left over, it was saved until the next money sock; I did not charge banking fees for my services.

By the time I knew Grandfather, his thick wavy hair was silver. His eyes were an electric blue. He wasn't like anyone else, this impressive, nearly mythic personage who wove in and out of our lives. His voice was beautiful, and though the piano concerts at the ranch ranked very low on my list of things to do, near the top were the poetry readings Grandfather gave in the living room of the Main House. His voice would roll out to fill the room, and every word was given its full life. I didn't know until I was an adult that it was Grandma who had chosen the verses for the readings.

In his public life, Grandfather was prominent in politics and in the law. His voice exists on a recording at the University of California, Berkeley, and he was associated with many of the power brokers of the state. Locally, he helped protect the Mojave River from destruction, and he and Grandma threatened to take the case to the Supreme Court when the school system tried to send my Uncle Joe to one school and his black friend to another, though both of the little boys lived on the ranch.

He was, by most accounts, an overly demanding man for whom to work. Heavy rains on the ranch are still called "go-and-get-a shovel rains" because Grandfather, if he heard that it was storming on the desert, would call from his comfortable quarters in Los Angeles and direct various family members and workers to get the shovels and dig out the drainage ditches. Sometimes he sent telegrams, always directing others to expend effort. But none of this mattered to me; these were not the things I knew of him.

I was ten years old when he died. We always chose Christmas gifts that didn't have red or green. I had gotten him a desk organizer. I thought it very elegant, something that would fit comfortably in a place called the Jonathan Club. It was one of those circular devices that slip around on their own little turntables with compartments for small

19

office supplies. It was covered with fake leather, embossed with gold.

The gift was returned to me because Grandfather had died before it was delivered to him. It is difficult to explain how profound that was. As small and insignificant as I now understand the gift to be, at the time it was, to me, the ultimate in grown-up sophistication, equipment for someone who had a real desk and important issues to consider every day—matters that required paperclips, stamps, staples, and the like. Suddenly this belonged to me. It was absolute confirmation of death, certainty that I would not see Grandfather again.

His funeral was the first I remember attending, and it was horrible. It was held at the famous Forest Lawn, where copies of old masters' artwork mix with death and where bodies are kept in "slumber rooms." Grandfather's casket was open and we had to file past it. He didn't look at all like himself but rather like a hideous wax doll.

I recall odd little details, the light trying to come into the shadows of the place, picking up all the dust motes while outside a mockingbird was singing hysterically of life. I remember the rage I felt when some old biddy assured my mother that the children were only crying because the adults were. "They really don't know what's happened," she said. I wanted to scream that she was the one who didn't know what had happened, that she hadn't lost anything while we had lost something very, very important. But, of course, I said nothing at all; I was a well-behaved child, and at the very least, Grandfather would have expected proper behavior at his funeral.

I'm sure that that service was conducted with all of the rituals and trappings required to salute the passing of a man of standing, but it made me certain that it was not the kind of ceremony I would want to mark my death. And in fact, over the years, funerals in the family have left the realm of the morticians' handbook and have become a matter of mourning, celebrating, and remembering the dead with the music, words, and ideas they themselves loved.

My grandmother lived for decades after Grandfather died, and she never remarried. She had so much to do with raising me that I knew her on a far more personal level than I knew Grandfather. I was still very young when she retired from practicing law to live full-time at the ranch, so she was a permanent fixture in my landscape.

She was a bizarre blend of Auntie Mame, Queen Victoria, and God. Hers was the egocentricity of an infant. I don't believe she was ever convinced that anyone else on Earth was as fully realized as she. And from that perspective, she felt not only entitled but also obliged to pass judgment openly and with alarming frequency. Any woman who dyed her hair red was on the road to moral ruin, if not already at the destination. Anything anyone found to do after midnight was bound to be evil. She once announced that she was grateful that none of her children or grandchildren were left-handed, bald, or prone to bed wetting, all sure signs of degeneracy. Fortunately for us, she did not list nearsightedness, dental problems, or allergies in the same category.

Born in 1886, she grew up in Illinois, coming to California with her family when she was just old enough to have taught in a rural school for a bit. It was a hazardous duty, as some of the students were older than she, and most of the farm boys were much larger and resentful of having to attend classes. She was very glad to go west. She recalled the smell of orange blossoms as perfume of paradise when she stepped off of the train.

She was valedictorian of her law school class at USC in 1913, a time when few women were in the profession. She was the first female deputy district attorney in California, and she taught torts and real property at USC for four years and medical jurisprudence at Loma Linda University for thirty years in addition to practicing law.

Her sisters were likewise unique. Lura, the youngest, was an orthodontist, and the middle sister, Lola, was an accountant. Their mother, Ida, was fierce in her determination that they be independent and able to earn their own livings. Ida had been a tent preacher, earning a good amount, when she met David Hibben. I have the letter that Ida's father wrote to David, explaining in the most circumspect way he could that it was possible for a married couple to enjoy physical bliss without conceiving a child. But Nature's drive to perpetuate the species is more than a match for good intentions, and Ida became pregnant almost immediately after the wedding. That put an end to her preaching, to David's plans to attend college, and thus to their mutual hope for a better life.

I don't think I would have liked Ida much, though I can understand what drove her. David was a dreamer and not that good a provider. Grandma used to describe her background as "poverty honestly come by and decently maintained." Ida must have felt that the family's well-being depended entirely on her practicality matched against David's bemused approach to life. But her attitude affected her children deeply, particularly the two oldest. It made them capable and independent, but it also made it difficult for them to express or accept love.

Grandma remembered her mother with affection, and she took care of both parents when they were enfeebled by age and illness, but she never had any doubt that her own birth had been a disaster for her mother. Lura was spared much of this because she was not only the baby but was frail as a youngster, often allowed to stay home from school and be coddled as the other two girls were not. It seems a pretty direct reason for Lura's being so different from her sisters. She was a much softer personality, openly loving and tolerant in ways her siblings could not manage.

The only thing that gives me pause when I think of Ida is that the full names she gave her daughters were Litta

Belle, Lola Dell, and Lura Nell because she loved poetry. I find the names pretty awful, but they do show a softer side, I suppose.

Added to the other stresses of Grandma's background were the intense and joyless religious beliefs that dominated those days in Illinois.

The family were old-style Seventh-Day Adventists, waiting in the early years of Grandma's childhood for the Second Advent. They believed it was so imminent that they had specific dates, which, when passed without Armageddon, were changed to a few years hence. With the Lord due to descend in judgment at any moment, it followed that frivolity of any kind—dancing, personal adornment, reading novels, for example—was to be shunned. Grandma never forgot the Christmas she received a book on the life of Christ rather than the roller skates she had wanted, and she never ceased to resent the visiting ministers who had been fed all the good strawberry preserves and other delicacies.

As strict Adventists, the family was vegetarian. Once, however, a pheasant was dashed against a telegraph pole during a snowstorm, and David, who didn't care much for the restricted diet, insisted, over Ida's objections, that the bird was obviously a gift from God and meant to be eaten. I think I would have liked David, and my mother and uncle say he made a wonderful grandfather despite all of his shortcomings as a husband and provider.

Great-Aunt Lura had long since ceased to belong to the church by the time I knew her, which surely accounts further for the gentle tolerance she showed to almost everyone. The church she had left not only believed that the earth could be no older than five thousand years but also taught that only the chosen were going to heaven—and that the chosen were an absolute number, eleven thousand at one point, and, at that time, encompassing no black people, let alone Roman Catholics and such.

Great-Aunt Lola was always devout and still is, at 101 years old. I am grateful that she has mellowed somewhat with age, but I know she has always considered my branch of the family scandalous. When my mother gave her a copy of *The Proud Breed,* my first historical novel, Aunt Lola kept it locked in a closet for a year because she'd heard it was a dirty book. But the book was released from darkness and claimed as a family product when at a meeting of the Republican Women's Club the members started talking about the book as one that many of them had read and enjoyed.

I have never been very close to Aunt Lola, but I do remember the wonderful things she made for my doll's house, the chair covers and rugs. I know she tried to love the odd, young outlaws that came into her small, tight world. For years she gave all of us magazine subscriptions for Christmas, though I'm sure she did not approve of many of the choices. For her, that was very liberal.

Grandma's belief system fell between those of her sisters. She never fully gave up her early tenets, but she had a fragile relationship with the church. At least once, and possibly twice, she was "churched," thrown out of the organization, for unsuitable beliefs and questions, but in later years they courted her return. She occasionally accompanied us to the Episcopal church, but she said she couldn't become an Episcopalian because her knees couldn't take the calisthenics of all the up and down—sit, kneel, stand, etc.—done during a typical service and because she didn't know the hymns as she did the ones sung in the Adventist church.

She was quite sincere in her beliefs, but they were her own. She didn't think anyone could really believe in an eternal hell or a God who would create such misery. She loved the literature of the Bible and knew it very well, but she distrusted those who subscribed to the literal interpretation or interpreted it for their own ends. For instance,

24

though she disapproved of drinking, she was quite sure, given the time and circumstances, that Christ had changed the water into wine, not into grape juice—the official church line—at the wedding. And further, she thought the authors of the Book of Revelations must have been crazy, drunk, or stoned. Nor did she think God cared whether she ate pork, shellfish, or any other reasonably edible substance. She did not consider fancy sauces reasonably edible, but she also did not assume that God had any objection to them.

I found some of her beliefs rather peculiar. When my middle cousin Craig grew a beard, Grandma said he looked like Jesus. Craig is blond and blue-eyed.

"How do you suppose Jesus could have gotten Nordic coloring, born as he was of Jews in the Middle East?" I asked.

"Well, Jesus is blond in a lot of church pictures," she replied, "and besides, only his mother was Jewish."

The most obvious legacy of Grandma's religious upbringing was that absolute conviction that she had the duty to pass moral judgment on everyone else's actions. There was no gray for her, only black and white. However, while she claimed the right of such pronouncements, she did not think the same privilege should be extended to the government or made into law. She maintained that the government's only duty was "to protect me from you and you from me, but not me from me nor you from you." She lived through the time when marijuana was legal to when it became illegal, and though she did not approve of its use, she approved far less of the government's criminalization of it. She also considered laws against suicide foolish, though she thought people who jumped off of buildings ought to be careful not to land on those below.

She never hesitated to take on the government when she thought it was in error, believing absolutely in Burke's admonition that "the only thing necessary for the triumph of evil is for good men to do nothing." And she believed that the government was surely capable of evil were it not checked by its citizens.

One day, butcher knife in hand, Grandma barred a health inspector from the ranch kitchen. The Health Department was insisting that the ranch was a public restaurant and therefore subject to all regulations, including the one most violated at the ranch—the height of kitchen cabinets. Ours were low enough to allow a tall dog to pee into them. Grandma maintained that the kitchen served only registered ranch guests, and that in any case, she never, ever allowed dogs of any height in the kitchen. The butcher knife was in her hand because she'd been doing some chopping when the inspector arrived, but she didn't put it down, and he didn't return.

On the other hand, she also believed in my favorite of all of her quotes: "It is not worth the lather to shave an ass." I don't always succeed, but I try to remember that it is not worth the energy to protest when no change or improvement is possible.

Grandma was formidable enough when I knew her, but she was sixty when I was born, and had been even more of a Tartar in her younger days. She ran the ranch as if it were a reform school. Given her character, that isn't so surprising, but it is astonishing that so many people put up with it and came back for more. Some of the guests were even nostalgic for the early days and remembered with delight what fun it was to hide whiskey and beer at the bottom of the pool and out in the artesian well and to plan cocktail parties on the sly. She particularly hated the local saloon, the Green Spot, and a man who had been coming to the ranch for years told me that he had actually crouched down behind the bar when word spread that Mrs. Campbell was in town.

"I was a grown man, an adult," he mused with wonder, "but I hid like a schoolboy just in case she passed by and looked in."

When the Green Spot burned down, Grandma was one of the first spectators. Given her love of fires and her hatred of the bar, we were glad we knew where she had been when the fire started.

Even the Hollywood notables who visited the ranch during the thirties and forties played her game. When John Wayne and Ward Bond were here during the war, perhaps for the filming of *Tall in the Saddle* somewhere in the area, they stayed out much too late by Grandma's standards, but they left a peace offering of a huge beefsteak on the piano, so they weren't scolded. Meat was rationed, even on cattle ranches, at that time.

The famous often received special treatment. In deference to her passion for privacy, Greta Garbo had only to walk out of her door and down the stairs to find a horse saddled and waiting for her, so that she would not have to mix with everyone else down at the stables. And when she was outside, other guests and residents stayed in. When part of *Lost Horizon* was filmed in the desert and some of the cast and crew stayed here, the rooms were measured to make sure that Mr. Colman got the largest one; Grandma thought this was a bit excessive, but she didn't object. Sometimes the noblesse oblige flowed the other way. When Greer Garson was at the ranch in 1945, she was gracious despite the fact that Grandma called her Gar Greerson. Ms. Garson had a good sense of humor. She discovered her own picture in a frame for sale at the local drugstore.

"I always wondered what they did with these photographs," she said as she purchased the frame to send to her husband as a joke.

"You just throw that picture out, and put what you want in the frame," Old Doc Bowers, the store's proprietor, instructed her. He never made the connection between the woman in front of him and the photograph, and she did not enlighten him.

Groucho Marx came with his family in the early thirties. He tried out new jokes to test people's reactions. Grandma thought he was mildly funny, though she didn't care much for the behavior of his children. Her feelings about Harpo were not as kind. After a sojourn with his family in 1941, he left his harp, and Grandma had to wrap and ship it to him. That experience left her with a prejudice against any guest who left belongings behind.

Grandma must have liked Henry Fonda and Pat O'-Brien. They were here in 1936 while filming *Slim,* a nearly forgotten movie but one that Mr. Fonda included as one of his favorites. Though it has been lost since her death, among Grandma's belongings was a photograph of her with the two actors. She was swift to throw away anything that no longer interested her, so it is a tribute to the charm of the men that she kept that picture.

Writers were also honored. J. B. Priestley visited in 1935, and he mentioned the ranch in *Midnight on the Desert:*

> The main ranch house on the Mojave Desert had a fine big sitting room, with a wooden gallery and rafters, adobe walls hung with pictures, and an enormous brick open fireplace. Here we would sit up late, lounging at ease, after my day's work. All this I remembered, while the memory of many pleasant things, the mountains in the afterglow, the picnic suppers at the ranch, the good talks we had, was already ghostly.

Herman J. Mankiewicz worked on the script for *Citizen Kane* at the ranch in 1940. John Houseman was one of the small group with him. Mankiewicz's leg was in a cast due to it having been badly broken in an auto accident. In 1988, when John Houseman died, Frank Mankiewicz, Herman's son, wrote a fond piece about Houseman for the *Washington Post.* In it he related how his father had thought that "the desert" they were going to was Palm Springs, where alcohol and gambling were both readily available. The discovery that the destination was the "high" desert and Mrs. Campbell's dry ranch emphasized how serious Houseman was about the script. If Mr. Mankiewicz did manage to take a drink while he was here, it could only have been with the complicity of his companions and without my grandmother's knowledge.

People could also receive special treatment for being distinguished artists, musicians, jurists, or teachers, but everyone else had to worry about being above or below the salt, the measure of status being whether one was invited to sit at Mrs. Campbell's dining table rather than at one of the other tables or even farther away, in the upper dining room. And Grandma was not above unseating people when those of greater interest came in a bit later. This was one of her most distressing tyrannies, and deeply embarrassing to the rest of the family.

When the third generation was in place and when enough of us were eating at the Main House, we often ate in the family dining room, and that was a relief. It meant not being on show for the guests, as we often were, and it circumvented Grandma's picking and choosing who could or could not dine with her. A full house was fifty-two guests, though in a pinch and with families willing to share close quarters, we could accommodate sixty—that gave Grandma much too wide a choice.

She was a skilled raconteur and loved having an appreciative audience. She envisioned the intellectual life of the ranch as being a continuation of the tradition of salons presided over by witty grandes dames. In fact, it was often like that. But I'm certain that many people who sat at the other tables were very relieved to be there instead of caught under Mrs. Campbell's eyes.

She seemed like a tall, imposing woman, but she was only four or five inches over five feet (if asked, she claimed five feet eight inches). Until she was very old, she was heavy-set and carried herself like an empress. When arthritis attacked her spine in her fifties, she pushed herself up against the wall every day until she was straight so that her spine fused in a rigid line that made it impossible for her to slouch. Her ancestors were mostly English with a little French, but there was also a family legend about being related to Pocahontas through the English connection, and Grandma's picture would fit easily into the annals of American Indians. The bones of her cheeks and brows were starkly defined; her nose was an arrogant blade; her lips thin; and she had eyes so dark, they were nearly black. No wonder people preferred not to cross her.

It was much better to be male rather than female if one wanted her favor. She suffered from what has been called the Queen Bee Syndrome. She made her mark in a male-dominated profession, but that did not cause her to want to help other women; it made her think they'd better be as tough and smart as she was if they wanted to go as far. She relied on women within the family and outside of it for certain kinds of support, much as a ruler depends on ladies-in-waiting, but she reserved most of her praise and respect for men. And many of them courted her shamelessly, not romantically, but intellectually with a touch of the gallant. In the presence of some of these men, she was almost girlish, as Queen Victoria was reported to be. I resented it, but it also fascinated me, even as a child, that such a transparent exchange of flattery could be so satisfying to both sides.

There were a few women who commanded her respect, however. One of these was my aunt Donna. She was working in Boston when Uncle Joe met her while he was attending Yale University. But Donna Pollard was originally from Maine, and possessed, as she still does, a full measure of that steadfastness Maine produces.

When Joe called home to announce his intention to marry, there was a pause over the line, and then his mother,

30

my grandmother, asked, "Is it anyone you know?" This has since become the standard response to announcements regarding marriage. And though Donna was in her twenties, my grandfather called her "the child bride of India."

Donna confesses that her first encounters with Grandma were so terrifying, she was afraid she would faint. Grandma would fix her with those ebony eyes, and all coherent thought would flee Donna's head. She barely said two words to her mother-in-law in those early days. But subtly, Donna staked her claim to her own life here. She is small, slow-moving, and soft-spoken with the Maine accent still in her words. Yet everyone defers to her. When David and I were small, we were more afraid of having Donna angry with us than of anyone else. Even Grandma came to fear her.

Donna's secret weapon is that she is seldom angry with anyone about anything. She is so easygoing that when her temper does flare, it is like having a volcano erupt in a flower garden. We depend on her to be calm in the middle of this volatile pack. When she forsakes that calm, she shakes everyone's center.

For years, the normal drill was for immediate emergency measures at the first flash of her dark eyes or tightening of the jaw. But as it turned out, this was guaranteed to make her madder. Finally she demanded to know why everyone tiptoed around and avoided her instead of standing and fighting.

"Even you, Mother," she said to Grandma. "What do you think I'll do if I'm angry?"

"I'm afraid you'll leave us and go back to Maine," Grandma confessed.

After a shocked pause, Donna laughed at the idea and pointed out that she'd lived here longer than she'd lived in Maine and that her life, her family, was here now. But Donna knew what an avowal of love that was from Grandma.

31

Had Grandma's character been composed only of prejudice, judgment, tyranny, and favoritism, she would have been unbearable, but all of it was leavened by a marvelous sense of humor and an astonishing degree of sensuality, though she would never have defined it so.

No one could tell a story about her failings as well as she.

Despite her cavalier attitude toward women, she did risk arrest when she followed Margaret Sanger's lead and passed out information about birth control, though such literature was forbidden by the law. But when it came to giving the vote to women, Grandma took part in a public debate, her argument being that women were not fit to vote. She spoke first, going on at some length with intelligence and eloquence. Her opponent was a man who listened intently and waited patiently for her to finish. Then he got up and asked, "Ladies and gentlemen, do any of you think this woman is unfit to vote?" With that, he sat down. When women got the right to vote, Grandma admitted that she was ashamed of the effort she had made to prevent it. And later, she was instrumental in obtaining for women the right to sit on juries.

Grandfather had already been in practice for a few years in Los Angeles when Grandma came to work in the office in 1913. She left the practice to serve as a deputy district attorney from 1916 to 1918, but after that, she and Grandfather practiced law together until they closed the office in 1950.

Los Angeles was a lot wilder, in the literal sense, in the early days of this century. Once as Grandma was crossing the street, she felt something crawling up her long skirt. She grabbed the wriggling body and ducked into the ladies room of the bus station where she released a large lizard that had caught a ride. No one saw her shake it out of her skirt, so she left the lavatory and found a seat outside where she could listen to the chaos that ensued when other women found the reptile in the bathroom.

Grandma insisted that by the tradition of English law, on which our law is based, a jury, no matter what the specifics of the law or the instructions of the judge, did not have to find anyone guilty if they did not believe in the justness of the law alleged to have been broken or in the penalty for breaking it. She cited the case of the jury in England centuries before that had found a poacher innocent even though he had killed one of the king's deer because his family was hungry. Likewise, she did not approve of the law being enforced to what she considered an illogical degree.

One day she drove through a crosswalk in downtown Los Angeles on her way to work. She went through it while there were still pedestrians in it, but they had passed her vehicle. A policeman stopped her and gave her a ticket. She bought a newspaper, drove around the block, and parked at the crosswalk, quickly tying up traffic for blocks behind her as she calmly read the paper.

"All right, Lady, what do you think you're doing?" the policeman demanded, recognizing her from their previous encounter.

"Officer, since I parked here, the crosswalk has never been empty. Someone has either been entering or leaving it. I am just waiting until it is clear."

"You win," he said and tore up the ticket.

Unlike the rest of the family, Grandma loved funerals—the more traditional, the better. She regarded them as grand social events, and she wasn't too picky about who the deceased was. If there was any excuse to go, she went. Once, while the family was still living in Glendale, near Los Angeles, she led an entire funeral procession astray. It was on its way from the church to the cemetery, and Grandma pulled into an alley in order to make a short detour to her house. But then she realized that a long line of cars with their lights on was behind her, following her lead.

When a local dairyman died, she went to his funeral. She didn't know him personally, but she thought she ought to do the good deed of attending since she was sure he would have a very small turnout. She came back in some distress. Not only had the Southern California Portuguese community come to the funeral en masse, many of them had arrived in newer Cadillacs than hers.

I believe Grandma bought her first Cadillac in the 1950s. In my memory, that is all she ever drove. She thought of Cadillacs as unmistakable status symbols, and she drove hers with pride.

She was generous with her automobiles, lending her car to any family member who needed it, and she never issued warnings with the loan, unlike her policy of "with my money goes my advice."

My brother nearly lost the privilege for all of us. We were going to the beach for a few days, and David had a license plate holder that read: HONK IF YOU'RE HORNY. He decided to put it on the Caddy before we left. I didn't think it was a great idea, but he promised he'd remove it when we got home. He didn't. Grandma drove around with that sign on her car until a local busybody called her and asked her if she knew what the sign on her car meant.

Grandma was enraged, particularly because in the interim she had gone to speak to a church group in Whittier, a group that had wanted to hear the words of this great lady of law and literature. She had parked right in front of the church.

She knew David had been driving the car, but she did not want to believe that her beloved grandson had committed such a crime. She went on a rampage, searching for some other culprit. A friend of David's lived on the ranch and had gotten into enough trouble with my brother to be a likely target. She invaded his rented quarters and confiscated the worst thing she could find, a wooden sign that read: ILLEGITIMATI NON CARBORUNDUM. She didn't understand exactly what it said, but the *illegitimati* sounded dirty enough to her. Actually, the rough translation is, "Don't let the bastards get you down."

David was out riding while Grandma was on the warpath, and my mother intercepted him to warn him that the list of suspects was dwindling down to him. David, a splendid rider, nearly fell off of his horse laughing.

Grandma found no sympathy from all of us. When questioned, I told her that yes, David had put it on the car, but I didn't see that it was a huge problem, though it might have been a bit unwise. Further, I felt it was funny and that anyone who didn't think that was pretty dull.

The matter was resolved for one reason: Grandma could never stay angry with David for any length of time. He was her son Kemper born again; and he was very ill at the time, despite his valiant continuation of daily life; and all in all, when she thought again about the incident, it must not have seemed so important. However, she never did see the humor of it, though the rest of the family relished the story, the best part being that Grandma had, before knowing about the license holder, wondered why so many people had honked at her.

Grandma drove a lot longer than she should have. The family kept hoping that the DMV officials would refuse to renew her driver's license, but they were no match for her. She would dress up and go to the office and they would treat her as if God had smiled on them to send such a dignitary to their humble establishment.

It was a very touchy subject. Southern California is a bad place to be without a car, and there is the matter of stripping an elderly person of his or her independence when the license and the car are taken away. On the other hand, we were terrified that Grandma would kill herself or someone else.

One of her driving adventures involved destruction of federal property. As she told it, it was simply a matter of her wearing uncomfortable shoes. She was wiggling her toes, or trying to take a shoe off, and she hit the gas rather than the brake as she was trying to exit the post office parking lot. She made the proper and heroic choice to hit a wall rather than bump the car in front of her into traffic. The postmaster had been entertaining a guest from out of town. Looking out of the window, he had seen Grandma get in her car and start out. "There goes one of the smartest women I know," he said.

At that point Grandma hit the wall. The visitor said, "Oh, what makes you think so?"

Uncle Joe happened to be driving by at the same time. He was quite sure Grandma might have left the scene of the accident had she not had such an audience. Her excuse was that no one, including herself, had been hurt and she had a dental appointment and planned to come back and explain. She had to concede that that might not be such a good plan when damage, however slight, had been done to federal property.

The first things she gave up were night excursions to McDonalds, one of her favorite places to eat. She confessed she had ended up in Apple Valley a couple of times because her night vision wasn't so good anymore. Apple Valley is not only in the opposite direction from where she should have been headed but it is the community across the Mojave River from our Victorville, and getting there involves going over the Narrows bridge. The fact that she had traveled this dangerous stretch of road without knowing it until she fetched up at a big market in Apple Valley was appalling.

We owe a great debt to our optometrist, who also happens to be a friend. When Grandma went to have her eyes checked and her glasses adjusted, she confronted him, wanting support for her driving.

"I can see perfectly well to drive, can't I?"

"Well, if you are very careful, you might be all right in town," Dr. Nassif told her, "but I don't think you ought to drive on the freeway anymore."

Grandma thought about that for a while and then she announced that she was giving up driving. "I don't know anybody who lives on the freeway, but a lot of my friends live in town," she said. "I'd hate to kill one of them."

It was a great relief to all of us even though it meant she was more dependent on us than she had ever been before. With her last Cadillac, she hadn't even learned to adjust the seat buttons, so if one of the family borrowed it and returned it without readjusting the seat to its prior position, Grandma would drive around barely able to see over the steering wheel until she found someone to push the right buttons for her. One morning I passed her on the top of the ranch hill, but the only way I knew it was she was that I recognized the top of her head.

As Grandma grew older, she planned adventures, saying she needed things to look forward to even more than she had when she was younger. She took whichever women were available with her. We went as ladies-in-waiting in exchange for having the costs of the trips paid, but the duties were light and the journeys great fun.

The arrangements with the grandsons were somewhat different, and she didn't plan trips for Uncle Joe or my father, which was certainly wise of her. Though she took my brother and my cousin Kemper to Tahiti, she sent cousins Craig and Scott off to Europe without her. I think the Tahiti trip convinced her that traveling with teenage boys required too much energy.

One of my trips with her and with my mother was due to the publication of Grandma's first book. She had always wanted to write a novel, but she could never remove her overlord's voice from the narrative, nor could she escape from an exaggerated Victorian morality that made her characters seem foolish in the twentieth century. However, her nonfiction was charming—tart and tender stories of her life and her law practice. She was just short of her seventy-seventh birthday in 1963 when Simon and Schuster published the first book, *Here I Raise Mine Ebenezer,* and she wrote three more after that. She went to New York to appear on the "Today" show and to make various other publicity stops.

We stayed at the Algonquin Hotel because that was where the famous literary "Round Table" of such notables as Alexander Woollcott, Robert Benchley, and Dorothy Parker had met; Grandma wanted to stay there despite the fact that the meetings were long over, the principals long dead.

When Mom and I discovered that the plumbing wasn't working too well and that doorknobs tended to fall off, it was so much like the ranch, we felt right at home.

There were two things in particular that Grandma hated to spend money on—shoes and food. She bought her shoes at an outlet, and while we were in New York, we ate at the Automat as often as Grandma could manage. She liked simple food and couldn't see any point in paying for fancy sauces. While she was being entertained by the publishing world, Mom and I slipped away to good restaurants, keeping a sharp eye out for fear Grandma and her host of the day might end up at the same establishment.

Actually, the Automat food wasn't bad. But the same could not be said of Grandma's discount shoes. They looked fine, but they often hurt her feet since she was willing to put up with that for a bargain. Over the years she used lamb's wool and various other substances for padding, but nothing was quite satisfactory until she discovered the secret.

"My shoes aren't hurting my feet anymore," she told me one day as I was on my way through the Main House.

"Well, that's good," I said.

"Aren't you going to ask me why?"

"Okay. Why?"

"Because I'm using angel food cake instead of lamb's wool. The vanilla works much better than the chocolate because it's softer. It's too bad we have angel food cake only on Sundays; it gets a little too hard to use by Wednesday or Thursday."

"Grandma! That's awful! You'll be followed by a trail of ants," I told her, but as far as I know, she kept using it as long as the cakes were served on Sundays, but, fortunately, not on our trips.

Being known as such a formidable woman had its drawbacks as well as its advantages. I think Grandma sometimes felt as if she were trapped behind the facade, always having to be strong and in control. On a journey, she became someone else entirely, dependent, hesitant, as if these were traits she thought very feminine and which did not fit with her usual image. She would profess herself baffled by how the hotel plumbing or drinking fountains worked, how room service could be summoned, how dining or theater or tour arrangements could be made. Suddenly she was unable to choose what to wear or how to dress properly without the handmaidens fluttering around to assist her. It was a game, but a harmless one, and each played her part.

The best trip we ever took was on a canal in England. We were on "narrow boats" specifically designed to use in the canals in their heyday before railways took over commercial shipping. The boats are seventy feet long and only seven feet wide, so accommodations on board are cramped. But we managed. It was spring in England, and hawthorn and laburnum trees framed the way in blossoms. I saw an English kingfisher, an enameled dart of brilliant turquoise and rust so different from the much larger, blue-gray belted kingfisher we have here; and I finally understood the Gerard Manley Hopkins line "as kingfishers catch fire."

Getting on and off the vessels was difficult, so

Grandma never went ashore once she had boarded, but she did cross from the "motor," the one with the engine, to the "butty," the one that was towed. It was necessary because the dining and lounge facilities were on one vessel and most of the sleeping quarters on the other, it made us very nervous when Grandma made the crossing, but she didn't seem to have any worries about falling into the canal.

That spring day, three English friends joined us (Grandma; my mother; Aunt Donna; Trudi, a friend from home; and I) on the voyage (as did two English women we had never met but who have remained in touch through correspondence ever since); one of those friends, Monica Halford, was only slightly younger than Grandma. They had known each other since the thirties, and though they had not seen each other often, theirs was one of those special friendships that does not need constant reassurance.

When the canal trip was over, they said good-bye to each other with such dignity and love, I could hardly bear it. They both knew there was little chance they would ever see each other again. The distance between the west coast of the United States and England was just too great. Monica, who had been a ballerina in her youth, was still quite spry, but she had suffered for years from hearing loss and an ear problem that made flying difficult, and though it was never stated, it was clear that Grandma knew this would probably be her last trip to her beloved England. They did not weep in parting, but the rest of us did.

They never did see each other again, but I think that mattered more to me than to them. They had made their peace with age and loss, and they kept in touch by letter until Grandma died; until then, Monica was one of the few female friends whom Grandma treasured.

Nor did Grandma allow saying good-bye to Monica to spoil the few days we spent in London after the canal trip was over. As we were packing for our morning flight, she announced that it was just too depressing to spend our last night in the city fussing over our luggage. She wanted to go back to the little pub where we'd had supper one evening. This was a rather startling suggestion from someone who frowned on liquor and had tasted little of it in her life, particularly given the nature of that pub. It is very small and frequented mostly by the tradesmen from nearby shops and by the doormen and servants who work in the gentlemen's clubs along Pall Mall. After a full day of the stifling decorum, the servants go to the pub to relax and to drown their fatigue in multiple pints. It was packed full and rowdy, but Grandma's venerable age cleared a little space for us, and we sat crammed together in a corner, happy to be there since so many people were standing.

It was all very cheerful and English, and Grandma went so far as to have an Irish coffee, having already been corrupted by a glass or two of ginger wine on the narrow boats. She was sitting there, smiling benevolently with the red flags of Irish whiskey brushing her cheeks, when a man wove his way through the crowd. He was small, neat, and round in his three-piece suit, and he tipped his derby hat as he addressed Grandma. He had eyes only for her.

He was a bit the worse for wear due to the pints he'd enjoyed, but finally I realized that he was not speaking Gaelic, and I understood what he was saying.

It was difficult enough to persuade Grandma to wear her glasses and she would have nothing to do with a hearing aid—an unfortunate prejudice since she missed much of what was being said as her hearing got worse—and watching her as the Englishman spoke to her, I was sure she didn't know what he was saying. "Yes, yes," she intoned, nodding and smiling her best Queen Victoria smile, typical signs that she couldn't make out the words.

"Best to you and good evening, ma'am," the little man finished, tipping his hat once again and weaving away.

"Grandma, what do you think he said?" I asked.

"Well, he asked if I was from the Mummy Room of the

41

British Museum, didn't he? I'm very old, so I can see how he might think that," she answered.

"My God, Grandma! That's not it at all. He said, 'Ma'am, didn't I see you at the British Businessman's meeting this morning?' "

I hope the little man didn't hear our shrieks of laughter and think that they were at his expense.

The last trip Grandma planned was to Carcassonne, a walled city in southern France. She got the idea from the Gustave Nadaud poem about a man who always wanted to go to Carcassonne, a metaphor for the dream that is never quite realized in a lifetime. The last lines of the poem are these:

> That night the church bells' solemn toll
> Echoed above his passing soul.
> He never saw fair CARCASSONNE.
> He'll never see fair CARCASSONNE.

Grandma never saw fair Carcassonne either. She had planned the whole adventure, but died before the trip began. She had considered that possibility and had instructed that we go even if she could not, so we did, seeing the city for her.

Grandma remained remarkably acute to the end of her life, but there were little lapses, though not in her sense of humor.

When the guest ranch closed in 1975, Grandma moved into the rooms above the Main House living room, leaving her apartment, also in the Main House, vacant. This coincided with my finally earning enough from my writing to afford the rent for a place of my own. There were a couple of other units available at the time, but the Main House apartment had the best view and the most light. (During much of the guest ranch era, there was a population of twenty-five to thirty in permanent rentals—various houses,

42

apartments, and rooms. Since the guest ranch's closing, with conversion of some of the guest quarters into self-sufficient units, the permanent population of the ranch has increased to thirty-eight.)

I went to Grandma and told her frankly that I would like to move into the apartment, but that since I worked at home, I couldn't do it unless she could respect my privacy. She assured me that of course she could, but it was a struggle for her with sometimes annoying, sometimes amusing results.

At one point, she nearly drove me crazy by parking her chair on my porch, right in front of my office window, so that my view of the ranch had her head squarely in the middle of it. I hadn't rented the back unit yet, so I had no back door, and by keeping watch on my porch, Grandma could monitor my comings and goings. Despite the boldness of this ploy, I know Grandma understood how obvious it was since the big patio is on the other side of the Main House living room.

Another of her strategies was sidewalk patrol, which involved her wandering back and forth past my place, peering in the windows. I countered this by having one-way glaze put on the glass. It wasn't only to Grandma-proof my quarters; it was also because there is quite a bit of normal traffic on the sidewalk, and working with passersby peering in was difficult.

One day I looked out to see Grandma prowling past. I went back to work until the mail truck squeaked by. When I went out back to collect my mail, I found Grandma trimming the pyracantha hedge, a perfectly innocent meeting. She had lost track of her "scissors," so I found them for her. They were lethal-looking pruning shears. We chatted for a bit, and then I went back to work.

A while later the phone rang. "I know I shouldn't be bothering you, but I was worried. I went past your apartment this morning, but I couldn't see any lights on or hear any noise, and I just had to check to see if you are all right."

"Grandma, I saw you out at the mail box."

"No, you didn't. That was Mrs. Evans." Mrs. Evans was one of the tenants, about my height, but blond and about thirty years older than I.

"I assure you it wasn't Mrs. Evans. It was I."

"No, it wasn't. I know the difference between Mrs. Evans and my own granddaughter," she insisted.

I felt as if I had fallen down a very deep rabbit hole indeed. "Grandma, if that wasn't I, how do I know that you lost your shears and that I found them for you, hung up on a branch above your head? How would I even know that you had been back there unless I'd been there, too?"

There was a long silence, and then reluctantly, she conceded, "I guess it must have been you."

Shortly after this episode, she called me at night. I was still working and tired, so it took me a moment to focus on what she was asking.

"Do you see light outside?" she asked, and since it was after nine on a moonless night, I immediately assumed that there must be a fire or a plane crash.

"Just hold on! I'll go outside and check." I raced out but saw nothing. Completely baffled, I picked up the phone again. "It's pitch dark outside, just as it should be. Where did you see the light?"

"I didn't," she said. "I thought I was going blind." She paused, and then she asked, "What time is it?"

"About nine-thirty."

"At night?"

"Yes, that's why it's dark."

Another pause. "Well, now I understand what happened. I fell asleep. Then Freida called. We talked, and after that it seemed that I'd been asleep all night. I did my exercises, made my bed, and I was hungry for breakfast. Then I noticed how dark it was, and I thought I'd lost my eyesight."

With that both of us started to laugh, and I asked her if she needed cereal or fruit for her night breakfast. She declined, explaining that she was going to tell her stomach it was mistaken and would have to wait until morning.

Not all of the passages between us were so amusing or so easily resolved. She was a much better grandmother for young children than for older ones. It was a paradox that she could teach the young to explore the world and learn, and yet, when the independence she cultivated began to be obvious, she could not accept it. Even when we grandchildren were fully grown, she wanted to choose our friends, what we wore, what we did, what we thought. But the first lessons were too well taught, and each of us went his or her own way.

Then, when she was very old, there were times when I felt as if she wanted to be me. She wanted a jacket like mine, a this, a that like mine, she wanted to wear the same perfume; and she wanted more of my time than I could give her. I saw her every day, but that was not enough; she resented any time I took from work in order to be with friends, since she thought that time ought to have been given to her.

Most of all, she still hoped to be a novelist, wanted my agent and publisher to be her own, and could not understand why they wouldn't automatically publish the manuscript she was offering. I had not used any of her publishing connections when I started out—I couldn't see what use they could be and didn't want to do it that way in any case—but I did ask my agent to read Grandma's manuscript. It was very gracious of my agent to do it, but her verdict was the same as mine, that the work was unpublishable. The whole business was both aggravating and sad, and it went on to become embarrassing when Grandma pursued her object further by writing to one of the book clubs that had published my work. In her letter, she told them she was my grandmother and that she was sure they would be interested in her book because of that. The poor editor who received that letter replied as generously as possible, citing the secondary market aspect of book clubs. I was mortified.

Sometimes Grandma was so difficult and demanding that dealing with her was infinitely frustrating. But I have never forgotten that some of the most precious things in my life came directly from her.

I was so young when she taught me to read, I do not remember a time when I could not. I asked her once how old I was when she taught me, and she said, "Oh, I should have known that children can read much earlier than anyone thought. You couldn't read by yourself until you were about two and a half." No wonder I can't remember being without that skill.

She read to us, holding us on her ample lap so we could follow the words. And in those exercises, she read the classics: *Winnie the Pooh; Wind in the Willows; The Five Little Peppers and How They Grew; Toby Tyler: or, Ten Weeks with a Circus; Beautiful Joe; Black Beauty;* and on and on. The only one my brother and I couldn't stand was *Little Lord Fauntleroy.* We thought the little boy in it a perfect sap for wearing velvet knee breeches and curls.

But she also had a system of rewards for reading exercises of a different sort. She would buy two copies of children's readers, and would cut the words out of one and make flash cards, so that the child could learn all new words in the books. She taught the old-fashioned way. She worked through spelling, phonetics, and meaning, and she maintained that no word was so long or formidable that it could not be broken into smaller parts and understood. She loved the language, she adored books, and she could think of few things worse than being unable to read.

Grandma had a system of reward for learning new words from the readers. For every new word recognized, we got the choice of a penny or a little candy (the ones I best remember were M&M's). Perhaps her grandchildren weren't as bright as she thought since each of us in turn chose the candy over the pennies instead of taking the money and saving it for a bigger supply of sweets. Then again, our parents frowned on using pocket money for candy that was bad for our teeth, so perhaps it was better to grab the forbidden when it was offered.

When the Dr. Seuss readers began to come out, in time for my cousin' lessons, Grandma rejoiced. She had always hated the "Run, Spot, Run" books, and she found the Seuss books perfect for teaching the flexibility and fun of English, or "almost" English.

I know Grandma would not have called herself a sensual woman, but in basic ways she was. She loved this piece of earth with a passion that never faded. The gardens she planted here still bloom. Even when she was in her nineties and her knees were too stiff for kneeling, she spent hours sitting in the flower beds, working the soil, weeding, pruning, and planting. And when I planted a little garden in front of my apartment, she kept track of what was growing there.

She could identify countless wild plants, too, and, intrigued by the idea of survival on the bounty of the land, she tested it periodically. Before my time, she went through the tedious process of putting up dandelion wine, not real liquor in her mind. But when it was supposed to be ready for tasting, she discovered that the handyman had helped himself to the brew, finishing it off over the months when it should have been aging.

Some of her wild-food experiments made me nervous. She made pie out of black nightshade berries, insisting that they were a lot like blueberries. It took much convincing, but I finally persuaded her that those berries at certain stages contain too much solanine to be safe. Actually, I think she only gave up because the pie didn't taste very good anyway. And in her defense, in some areas the berries have been cultivated as a blueberry substitute, though authorities disagree on the safety of them.

More frightening was the wild-mushroom period. She remembered the joy of collecting and eating morels when she was a child in Illinois. But my botany teacher in college had put the fear of God into his students by telling us that it was suicidal to pick and eat wild mushrooms in any area where poisonous ones existed unless one was a highly trained expert, the problem being that most harmless mushrooms have lethal counterparts that differ only slightly. He cited the cases of poisoning that occur every year in areas where people gather wild mushrooms, even among people who have been foraging for years. He also pointed out that as little as one quarter of a mushroom of certain species can kill a fully grown man.

I kept producing this data for Grandma to no avail, though she did not insist that everyone else eat the fungi. Then I tried another tack.

"Have you thought of how embarrassing it is going to be if after such a long and distinguished life, you kill yourself with a wild mushroom? Can't you just see the headlines in the newspapers?"

It was a sneaky appeal to her vanity, and it worked.

Grandma kept close track of all the wildlife on the ranch, but the birds were her special delight. She took me birding from the time I was tiny, and it is still a major joy in my life. I take my binoculars and field guides wherever I travel. She used to admit the oddity of the hobby and of the apparel, particularly the battered hats affected by birders. How surprised she would be now to witness the status that birding has acquired—so lofty a position in social activities that millions of people confess the addiction.

She demanded exactitude. How big was the bird? What were the wing and beak shapes? What colors and distinctive markings or lack thereof did it have? Where was the bird and what was it doing—near the marsh, in the field, in the desert, ground feeding, perching on a fence?

It all seemed so basic and sensible to her and to me that we used to laugh at some of the reports that untutored guests used to present to her, hoping to curry favor. They never saw ordinary birds, always insisting they had spotted something so exotic that research in the field guides would indicate that such birds only existed in a small rain forest in South America or some equally remote locale.

One woman claimed that she had seen a magnificent specimen on the Play House lawn (the Play House is a little one-room adobe built by my mother's generation, the site of many celebrations, including the one for the end of World War II, but in my time a rental for people who are not claustrophobic). The woman also insisted that the bird had three legs, which made the whole thing suspect, though I could understand since I'd once added an extra leg in a drawing of a killdeer, probably using the tricycle principle of balance. Despite this, Grandma was intrigued because some of the other details—long legs (even if there were three), for instance—made it seem as if this might be a shore bird gone astray.

I'm sure the woman wished she'd never brought it up once she was being questioned by Grandma. During the interrogation, the legs were lessened to two and the length diminished; the iridescent coloration was noted; the body shape refined; the beak and behavior explored. There was no doubt about it. The bird was a pigeon, the identification later confirmed by the return of the fellow with some companions.

But sometimes the birds were rare, and Grandma and I welcomed sightings with the same fervor shown by UFO buffs who see lights in the swamp.

For a long time, she wanted to see a verdin, and she traveled to various locations in the Southwest in hope of sighting one. When I found one in the back garden, I was, remembering the pigeon incident, reluctant to claim the credit. I told her that I'd seen this small, quick gray bird with yellow head and throat and rusty shoulder patches, but that it probably wasn't a verdin because it couldn't really be, could it?

Grandma had more faith in me than I had; after all, she had trained me. Together we found the verdin in the garden. We never saw a mate, but the male had built its spherical nest in the tamarisk tree. Grandma read somewhere that male verdins aren't all that domestic and have bachelor getaway nests stashed along their feeding routes. Maybe the verdin reminded Grandma of Grandfather; in any case, she was very fond of the species.

She and Great-aunt Lura took my brother and me to Yosemite one summer in the days when the park was still very wild and not overfrequented by tourists. We drove on a cliff road, and I saw my first osprey, looking down on him from above. But the bird Grandma really wanted us to see was the water ouzel, now more commonly called a dipper. She knew where a family raised their young along one of Yosemite's streams. She'd first seen the birds thirty years before, and she was certain their descendants would still be there. They were, of course. They would not have dared to disappoint Grandma. The water ouzel isn't very colorful, being mostly slate, and the shape is like that of a large wren, but its behavior is magical. It not only dives into the water; it is specially adapted to walk along the bottom of streams as it feeds. In the clear waters of Yosemite, we could see it strolling among the pebbles.

When it came to birds, Grandma made an exception of "Not by appointment does one meet delight," a rule she often quoted for the purpose of getting us out of school for some sudden adventure.

The teaching of the names and habits of the wild things was constant. On Saturday mornings, she would take the grandchildren and often the tenants' children out on the ranch to Pelican Lake for a picnic breakfast. I used to feel sorry for our parents, who were not invited. I was grown before I learned how grateful they had been for the gift of Saturday mornings without children underfoot.

I cannot remember a single disciplinary problem on those outings, the idea of misbehaving with Grandma being simply out of the question.

We packed all the supplies in the ranch car, usually some form of station wagon, and drove out to the lake. Once there, much of the equipment was loaded into a rowboat kept there, and those of us who could swim were allowed to row across the lake while Grandma walked along the dam with the younger nonswimmers.

I have one piercing image of her from those mornings. She was still quite broad then, and the early-morning sunlight glowed on the borders of her and in the silvery white of her hair pulled back with combs and knotted in a bun. A basket that hadn't fitted into the boat hung on one side of her, and her other hand was clasped by Scott, the youngest of the cousins. He was small, and the contrast of silhouettes was vivid. She walked at the slow pace set by his short legs. It is the perfect picture of a grandmother.

We gathered at the point of land that held our fire pit, and we all helped prepare the feast. I expect I'd turn up my nose at the food now, but then it was the best meal of the week. We had bacon or ham, eggs, and hash browns—all cooked in a cast-iron skillet, so that there was usually a sprinkling of ash and sand mixed in and everything tasted smoky. Sometimes, as an added treat, we had doughnuts from the local bakery, the sweetness of the glaze providing an added attraction for the insects that joined us.

Weather permitting, we swam in the lake, but this was a precarious business, not from any strong current or the like, but from a parasite that, when conditions were right, would burrow into the skin and cause furious itching. It was a harmless attack, but very uncomfortable, and when that

51

happened, Grandma would rush us all home, always with the instruction to take a bath or shower immediately and to use plain soap—a remedy that never failed.

I confess that as I got older, the risk of the itching outweighed the pleasure of swimming in the muddy water, and I gave up that part of the routine, though the boys never did.

The whole time we were at the lake, Grandma was teaching us, though it never seemed like that. She pointed out the trees, shrubs, flowers, and always, always the birds.

She often babysat for my brother and me, and those evenings were as adventurous as the Saturday picnics. We read and were read to and were allowed to make great creative messes of papier-mâché on the big dining room table in the Main House. Best of all, Grandma would show us how we could cook things such as potatoes in their skins and eggs in their shells in the embers of the hearth. We weren't required to eat all of these usually charred offerings, but it was fun to taste.

She was very patient at answering questions, but she did not think learning was without danger. On the patio on a summer night, because I was counting out loud, she asked me what I was doing.

"I'm counting the stars," I told her. "I've figured out that I only have to count one fourth of the sky, then multiply by four, and I'll know how many stars there are."

"Don't do that," she said. "I knew a man who tried to count all the stars in the heavens. He went crazy and ended up in an insane asylum."

Maybe that is why I never took astronomy, but I heard just the other day that the most stars one can see with the naked eye in the night sky is 5,776 or thereabouts. I wonder who did the counting. And I wonder how much of the feeling of harmony with the night sky I lost when I learned that that patch of sky visible over the ranch at night was not all of the universe or even of this galaxy.

Grandma believed that school was important, but that other things were, too, and that school should never preclude interesting or enjoyable events, so it was not unusual for her to allow us to miss school now and then when we were in her care. She covered this by quoting, "When joy and duty clash, let duty go to smash."

In 1953, my parents went to Europe for three months, leaving Grandma in charge. I was seven, David five, and Grandma sixty-seven. She told us she was too old to chase after us all day or to worry about where we'd gone, so she was willing to pay us each ten cents a day if we would report to her regularly about where we planned to be and what we were doing. If we failed, we could have to pay her. Ten cents a day was a fortune, and aside from one lapse from David, we collected our wages easily.

David had been missing for long enough for Grandma to panic by the time the foreman found him down near the front gate, invisible from the Main House because the bushes were taller than he.

"That's going to cost you ten cents, young man!" she told him.

"I wasn't losted, you were," he protested tearfully, and he charmed Grandma into paying him for that day, too.

At the end of those months, Grandma took us on the train to New York and then to the airport so we could wait for our parents' flight to arrive. But the plane was out of contact and missing for five hours (this in addition to the interminable number of hours that transatlantic flights took in those days). Long afterwards, Grandma admitted that she had thought they were surely lost and that she was going to have to raise two young children, despite her advanced age. My response to the crisis was to buy a St. Christopher medal with some of my earnings, though I'm not sure how I thought that would help Mom and Dad since I was on the ground holding the medal and they were wandering the sky. In any case, with or without the saint's help, the plane finally came in after battling headwinds and detouring here and there.

Grandma could not really have been called domestic in a general sense. Her ideas about it were best summed up by her oft-repeated, "Nobody ever went blind looking through a dirty window." But the domestic things she enjoyed doing she did well. Her hooked and braided rugs and needlepoint chair covers were colorful and skillfully done. And her cooking, despite experiments with wild plants, was superb, not for fuss and fancy, but for plain and delicious dishes with basic country roots and disastrous results for dieters. Thick-crusted bread; apple dumplings and apple pies; sugar cookies the size of saucers; buckwheat pancakes of the old-fashioned kind, dark and lacy; dishes with wonderful names such as finnan haddie and toad in the hole; a dense meat pie that could make pub owners in Britain weep for the recipe (this dish was best served with Cousin Ilott's home-cured dill pickles); cream sticks, finger-shaped twists of baked dough tasting something like slightly sweet, beaten biscuits; on and on, and including only a few things I didn't like—rhubarb pie, gooseberry pie, and mulberry pie. The mulberry pie was made from fruit picked in the back garden. Don't try it; when cooked, mulberries reduce to something resembling juice on beard shavings.

Almost everything she made was unique (usually in a good way, according to my palate), labor intensive, and time-consuming to prepare. Grandma food. She could knead bread dough in enormous amounts for so long that my own wrists and hands would ache watching her. But she had broad hands, wrists, and arms. Grandma strength. She used no written recipes, though she welcomed anyone who wanted to watch her cook. As a result, the family has a collective though faulty memory of how most of the dishes were produced. I've come close to the buckwheat cakes and bread, but that's about it. I wish I could make her sugar cookies.

When each of the grandchildren went off to college, receiving a box of these cookies in the mail was a great treat. Once a box sent to me got lost, and instead I got a load of Adventist Bible pamphlets in Portuguese. It struck me funny, so on my Sunday call home, I told my mother about it.

"Grandma's been doing missionary work, would you believe it?"

Mother didn't. "That doesn't sound like your grandmother at all."

"Well, the box is addressed in her handwriting," I pointed out.

When Mother called her about it, Grandma was not amused. She suspected a postal conspiracy. Her theory was that someone at the local post office knew about her cookies and had stolen them, substituting the pamphlets. Though the postmaster had just recently gotten out of the hospital after a bout with pneumonia, Grandma called him that very night at home. He assured her that none of his staff would stoop so low, but he promised to investigate the matter. Eventually, the truth was known. The box had been sitting out in the rain with other packages at some intermediate shipping point, Springfield, Missouri, I think, and when the labels had come off, the clerks had put them back on as well as they could, which in the case of my sugar cookies and the Bible pamphlets wasn't very well at all.

When that batch of cookies finally arrived, they were still edible, unlike the first shipment I'd received at college. I'd bragged about the treat that was due, and as soon as the cookies came, I'd doled them out to my friends, telling them they would never taste a better cookie in the world. One face after another glazed over as they sampled them, and no one had anything to say to my, "Aren't they wonderful!"

When I tasted one, I understood why. Grandma had accidentally used salt instead of sugar. Fortunately, her reputation and mine were redeemed when the good batch arrived.

Grandma might have been a plain cook, but she was also innovative. When she ran out of cake flour, she used ground-up cornflakes or some other cereal. When a devil's food cake fell right before an important dinner, she shored up the sunken middle with left-over brownies before frosting the whole affair, and turned a potential disaster into a triumph.

Aside from her loathing snakes, she was the least squeamish person in and out of the kitchen that I have ever known. My grandfather had stocked the ranch with bullfrogs with legs big enough to eat. (That was in the days before people noticed that introducing foreign species to an area too often results in the decimation of native species.) Frog-gigging expeditions were a regular summer activity, as close to big-game hunting as I ever got. I couldn't do it now if someone paid me, and I didn't do it very well then, but on this particular night, we had bagged nearly forty frogs, and I got the worst of a bad bargain. The boys said they'd pith the creatures if I'd do the rest of the cleaning. So there I was with forty brain-dead frogs in the back kitchen of the Main House.

Cleaning required cutting the legs off at the saddle and then peeling the skin from the legs. I was furious, disgusted, and near tears when Grandma floated into the kitchen in a yellow peignoir to see what the commotion was about.

"Those damn boys left me with all of these to clean," I sniveled.

"I'll be right back," she said. She reappeared within seconds with her gardening shears.

Still dressed in the peignoir, she cut and skinned frogs, doing two or three to my one, until all of them were done.

After the fact, Grandma understood some of her shortcomings as a mother. Her children had always been well cared

56

for, but often not by her, particularly in the case of her youngest, Joe. I'm not sure Grandma ever fully accepted how profoundly her and Grandfather's favoritism toward their firstborn son, Kemper, affected the other children, but she did know things hadn't gone quite right. I think she saw being a grandmother as a second chance, though she recognized the unique features, maintaining that the only job of a grandmother was to indulge the grandchildren and to enjoy their company.

She was nearing her ninety-fourth birthday when she had a stroke. She called me, and at first I didn't recognize who it was, the voice was so garbled. Then I knew what had happened.

Mother, Aunt Donna, and I sat with her during the hours it took to secure a hospital bed. Her speech was slurred, and one side of her body affected, but once we were there, her fear eased. And she did not mind being in hospitals; indeed, she liked them because it meant people would come to visit. A few days after she had been admitted, she seemed to be improving so much, Donna and I discussed what adjustments would have to be made to make Grandma feel in the center of things since it was doubtful she would be able to get around on her own anymore.

In truth, Grandma was just holding on until all the grandchildren had checked in either by phone or in person. My cousin Kemper and his wife drove up from Los Angeles and visited with her on the final evening. She was coherent, cheerful, and very glad to see them. All of us had been accounted for. A few hours later, she died.

But she is with me still, when I write, when I read, when I garden or cook, when I walk out on the ranch and hear the birds singing. Whatever problems she and I had later on, when I was a child, she was both a safe harbor and a guide to the seasons and the rhythms of the earth.

Chapter 2
THAT, MY DEAR, IS SAVOIR FAIRE

My mother has a Christmas bell. When the string is pulled, it plays "Silent Night." Or at least it tries to play it. The bell was made in Japan, and the song has sudden quick steps and discords, which make it sound as if it would be as appropriate in an Oriental temple as in a Christian church. The bell itself is neither elaborate nor precious; its charm lies in the foreignness of the music. Every year we are enchanted anew by the way it makes us listen so carefully.

If only my father could have understood the principle of the bell.

He was the son of Italian immigrants, raised in the Little Italy of Philadelphia, and he did not speak English until he was five or so. There was enough prejudice against Italians so that when he and his sisters went to school, their lyrical Italian names were immediately Anglicized. "Remo" became "Ray," but it was only the beginning of a long process of transformation.

In some vital ways, my father's parents were atypical, though surrounded by all of the expected trappings of an Italian family. My grandfather, Pelino, was a skilled carpenter, but he was also a self-proclaimed *suvversivo* who took my father to march in a parade protesting the executions of Sacco and Vanzetti. I did not know until after Pelino died that he had known most of the great Italian poets' works by heart. The last time I saw him, I was quite sure he didn't recognize me. We sat side by side on the couch in his house. He was watching an old Western, and I thought I would exit the room as soon as possible.

Then he turned to me. "Ah, Celesta, that Dolores del Rio, she's some cute chickie," he said, and I decided there wasn't much that had slipped from his mind.

Dad never said so, and he always defended his father as a man beleaguered by a badgering wife, but I suspect his father's definition of love was "a ready hand." Dad once said that in his neighborhood, fathers beat their sons until their sons grew large enough to knock them down.

My grandmother, Mariannina, had the courage to come to America, but her nerve failed her after that, and she was always afraid. She spoke little English, and I never had any sense of her beyond the woman who was constantly cooking and who would vacuum under you while you were still at the table.

While Dad was growing up, almost all of his neighbors attended the Catholic church, but not his parents. My grandfather was atheist, as well as a *suvversivo,* and my grandmother had been propositioned by a priest in Italy, which she took as a sign that God didn't want her in his church.

Surely the peculiarities of his background made it harder for Dad to see the positive aspects of Italian culture. When we were children, he would not speak Italian to us. He didn't want us to be immigrants' children. More important, he did not want to be an Italian. He wanted to be an American, or perhaps an English gentleman, but surely not an Italian.

I think it is impossible to overestimate the effect of this kind of prejudice on a child. There seem to be only two possible responses—to be deliberately ethnic, clinging to all the old ways in defiance of the surrounding culture, or to reject one's roots entirely. Few first-generation Americans seem to have found the middle ground that would allow selecting the best from the old and the new.

When he was still a young man, my father discarded all the easy give and take of emotion that characterizes most Italian families. He gave up the ready laughter and the relief of tears. In their place, he cultivated the repressed nature of the strong, silent male so beloved in American films. He also set out to become a cultured man. He read endlessly; he learned about music, literature, art, and food.

He was a very handsome, intelligent man, and at his best, he was charming, funny, and erudite. He was tall, well built, and had wavy black hair, dark eyes, and chiseled features, even to the cleft in his chin. Whether in Levis or tweeds, he looked as if he'd just stepped out of *GQ*. I have a picture of him taken when he was about nine years old, and even then, he was elegant.

He became the myth of what he thought an American man ought to be, but he lost precious things along the way; most of all, he lost the sense of who he really was. I think he was always afraid someone would see behind the sophisticated facade to the Italian street kid. He never seemed to understand that he *was* the sophisticate he had modeled as well as the street kid, and that that was just fine.

There was a grim sadness about him much of the time, and his only outlet was in ferocious bursts of unreasonable rage, often fueled by alcohol.

I loved him, and sometimes, I hated him. He was treacherous ground for a child. Just when things seemed to be going well, he would pick a fight, cursing us all for imagined shortcomings. Often he used music as a weapon during these seizures, playing set pieces on his stereo at top volume so that the entire house would vibrate with the thunder of this other voice. To this day, I still hate almost everything Rachmaninoff composed and have left concerts when his music was being performed.

Fatherhood was not a comfortable role for him. He really didn't know how to parent. I don't think his father and mother had given him much to go on since they seemed to have had their hands full with adjusting to life in a new country, though they managed, despite the pressures, to raise three daughters and a son.

My brother and I reacted to our father in what I now know were predictable ways. I was the oldest and female, and so I tried to be the perfect child in order to make things better at home, a course of action doomed to failure. My brother did not feel the same sense of responsibility. He drifted in his own space, not paying much attention to either parent.

Dad really didn't have much to do with our daily routines, but he was determined about broader aspects of our lives, as if he were a brilliant though irascible professor of the universe. He wanted us to be well educated and widely traveled; he wanted us never to feel as inferior as he had. That process included concerts, plays, and elaborately researched trips; it also addressed details such as which utensils to use for which dishes at mealtimes.

One night Dad was teaching us the proper way to cut meat when his veal cutlet flew from his plate and clear across the room. David and I nearly suffocated trying not to laugh.

Years later, in the more sophisticated setting of Au Pied de Cochon in the old Les Halles of Paris, Dad was pouring wine. He was perfectly sober at the time, but he was also fighting the need for glasses. His arms were not long enough anymore to permit reading maps, and pouring wine into a glass was far more demanding than that.

"Dad, you're not hitting the glass," I whispered nervously.

He didn't miss a beat. He kept pouring until the entire bottle was absorbed by the tablecloth. Then he put the bottle down and said, "That, my dear, is savoir faire."

That trip to Europe when I was fifteen and my brother was thirteen happened because my father had bought and then sold some land in town. Though there were many other things he could have used the money for, Dad financed the trip because he thought expanding our horizons was more important than easing the daily grind of pinching pennies from ranch land that never produced quite enough income.

Dad was in his element on trips he had planned, though he could be intolerably rude when others were in charge of the itinerary. When he traveled under his own direction, he left his demons at home and showed extraordinary patience.

We were standing in St. Mark's Square in Venice when a pigeon bombarded Dad. David and I waited for an explosion of temper, but Dad didn't say a word. He took out a handkerchief and cleaned off his head as best he could, and then he disappeared for quite a while. When he returned, he had a straw hat for each of us.

Things were on much shakier ground when anyone tried to organize my father for an activity in which he did not wish to participate. This included most holidays, especially Christmas and New Year's Eve. He always turned ugly on one or the other. As I grew older, I used to wish he'd explode on Christmas Eve so that New Year's Eve wouldn't be a matter of waiting for the shoe to drop.

Sometimes his reluctance was funny. Once, Mother couldn't find a babysitter for an evening when she was supposed to go to her bridge club, so she left Dad in charge.

He was probably appalled at the idea of having to entertain us, so he took us to the movies. David and I had a marvelous time. I can't remember what the feature was, but the other film was some sort of geographic study that included lots of footage of bare-breasted native women. This was new material in our limited film experience.

One Christmas a local shortage of ethnic-looking girls led to my being chosen to play the Virgin Mary in both the Episcopalian and the Catholic holiday programs. Mother insisted that Dad accompany her to the Episcopal program. The church was very quiet as the story was being done in a series of tableaux. When the time came for my scene, during which I gazed down raptly at the flashlight wrapped like a baby, my father said in a stage whisper, "My God, Jean, I didn't even know she was pregnant!"

Sadly, my relationship with him grew more difficult as I grew older. Adolescence is a strain on both children and parents in most families, and if the family is dysfunctional to begin with, the tension can be crippling. When one is very young, one's family seems normal no matter what is going on, because small children make few judgments or comparisons. But later on comes that shock of reconciling with a wider view of everything, including one's family.

I don't think Dad changed; I did. More and more I felt I had to be an adult, to somehow act responsibly in the face of the chaos he generated. And there was the added problem of the world outside the family and the one inside colliding.

In high school, father-daughter celebrations were important social gatherings. It was usually the mothers who had the most to do with school life, so special events were planned to involve and to show off the fathers.

The Father-Daughter Banquet of my junior year in high school was like a riptide. I knew from the beginning that I ought not to get involved, but the pull was irresistible. I was asked to help stage the event, and I enjoyed the work and the camaraderie with the other students, but all the while, I was pushing aside the knowledge that I had a living father and was expected to attend the dinner with him. Looking back, I'm sure he would much rather have refused the invitation, but he was caught in the tide, too, a treacherous confluence of currents external and internal.

I made repeated, nervous inquiries of my mother. "Do you think it will be all right?" "Do you really think Dad ought to go to this?" etc.—all coded phrases meaning, "Do you think he will behave?"

Mother was the wrong person to ask, and I should have known that, but I still shared some of her eternal optimism and denial.

I had a new dress for the occasion. It was drop waisted and made of flame-red chiffon, so that the skirt floated when I walked and would swirl when I danced—dancing being the activity planned for after dinner. I thought it one of the most beautiful dresses I'd ever seen, let alone owned.

Despite Mother's continuing assurances that everything was fine, I knew by the time Dad and I left for the banquet that we were headed for disaster. Dad had had quite a bit to drink, and he was gearing himself for trouble.

Even now, nearly thirty years later, I can't be amused when I remember that evening. He called one of the adult advisors a "silly bitch," one of his milder epithets for women, but more than enough for the occasion. He rearranged the carefully planned seating arrangements. He disparaged the food and cursed the music. Actually, he cursed just about everything and everyone within range in a voice loud enough so that only the very deaf could have missed it. I was so mortified, I was paralytic, firmly caught in the tide. Everyone else was, too, for while many stared before they looked away in embarrassment, no one said anything directly to him, not wanting to become a target for his wrath.

My friends had known before that night that I had a

"difficult" father. Some of them were afraid to knock on the door and would wait on the porch rather than risk facing Mr. De Blasis. But this public display of meanness left no room for prevarication. And, typically, as children do, I felt I was somehow to blame for his bad behavior. It took me years to understand that I was the only one who thought that, and far from blaming me, my friends and teachers considered the whole incident nothing more than a show of bad manners by a boorish man. Some of them undoubtedly had similar problems in their own lives. The fact is that no one needs to borrow anyone else's troubles for more than a few seconds.

Sometimes I think the vividness of my memory of that awful night would have faded had I not been wearing the flame-red dress. It became the technicolor for that nightmare. But there were other reasons for remembering. I had detested my father's orgies of temper for a long time, to the point that I deliberately stayed away from knives and refused to learn how to handle guns for fear I might do violence to him—I do not underestimate the rage that children can feel. But I had retained a Pollyanna view that somehow all of that would stop, and we would become what I thought of as a "normal" family.

I ceased to believe that on the night of the Father-Daughter Banquet. I had good times with my father after that, but I never again fully trusted him. I realized he was emotionally handicapped and could not be depended on to behave in a measured or sane way for long stretches. In a way, it added an extra sweetness to the times when he was calm, humorous, and kind. But it also gave those times a sorrow, a sorrow from the knowledge that they would not last, could vanish in the instant under a cloud of rage.

My response for a long time was to placate him, to try to change the subject or to back down in an argument, anything to avoid the mood swings. But eventually I ceased to do this, too, because I learned that his shifts weren't in response to other people, but boiled up from within. I started to stand my ground, and though I think it annoyed him sometimes, I also believe he respected it. Nor can I blame my prior attitude entirely on my father. Little girls are taught to nurture and cajole, to do almost anything rather than confront a male. And little girls who do that grow into women who do it, but with the women there is often a tinge of contempt toward men who can be manipulated by guile. It seems to me a nasty system that injures the integrity of both genders.

The closest my father and I ever were emotionally was when my brother was dying. Dad was tormented not only by the daily exposure to David's suffering and his own inability to ease it, but also by visions of his inadequacy as a father. He remembered the little boy who had gotten up before dawn, dressed, and waited, hoping to be noticed and invited along on a fishing trip with the men, but who had instead been ignored and left behind. He remembered too many occasions like that, and he said, "My father did so little with me, I didn't know how to do those things."

The things he had done—the trips out on the ranch in the Jeep when we were little, the brusque but thorough training he had given David in the use of firearms and tools, the journeys to exotic places—did not mentally outweigh his despair.

He reached blindly for the religious faith he had never had, and found only darkness in the idea that a God should exist who would inflict such terrible pain on a young man as David was suffering. I stayed up many nights until the early hours of the morning, listening to his grief, listening to the love he could not speak.

The closeness we had then did not last. It died with David. Dad and I settled on a neutral ground, a place of intellectual give and take that left the heart outside but was nonetheless important to both of us. He was widely read, and he liked discussing ideas; he was and I am of the "almost everything is interesting and worth knowing" school of thought, while my brother was and my mother is of the linear type—information is only interesting if it is needed for the matter at hand.

The intellectual ground was not new between us. Despite the fact that he called women "bitches," "ball-breakers," and worse, he always expected me to do well academically, and he out of everyone in the family believed that there were no limits to what I could do. When I was still very young but interested in subjects as diverse as art and science, he brought me two very special gifts from trips back East. He brought me a painter's box stocked with pigments I could never have afforded on my own. I still have that case; it is of such quality that hinges and all function as well as ever. And he brought me a microscope that opened a window on a teaming world of tiny life. I wish I still had the microscope and had not passed it along to younger children. I'd like to see if life has evolved in the murky horse-trough water.

When I graduated from college, I had a lot of plans, but I was so tired, just getting out of bed in the morning was a big chore. This and some other peculiar symptoms did not seem normal for a twenty-two year old. I found out I have lupus, an immunological disease that can cause a wide variety of problems, from minor to lethal. Suddenly what others might have wanted me to be didn't seem nearly as important as spending my time, long or short, being what I wanted to be, a writer. I spent a few years at jobs that took too much of my time and energy to leave anything for writing. When I decided I needed a year to try to write a novel, it was my father who said I should try it, not wait until I was sixty years old and then mourn what might have been. Surely he was speaking of himself. He had tried his hand at mechanical engineering, farming, aeronautical engineering, stockbroking, and selling real estate, but he never found anything that consumed his intellect and his passion.

He and Mother agreed that I could live and eat in their house for that year. I continued to do odd jobs, but my basic needs of shelter and food were provided. And I wrote my first novel.

Once, as I wandered through the house trying out names for characters, Dad turned to Mom and asked, "How much does she charge to haunt a house?"

There is definitely a loony side to writing novels, to losing oneself in the conjuring of an imaginary world, but it never seemed as strange to my father as to Mother and the rest of the family. And it was Dad who read the first books in manuscript form, before anyone else except my proofreader saw them. He was a good reader, a good critic, and we came as close to easy harmony as he could manage.

After publication of the first novel, *The Night Child,* I was able to rent a place of my own on the ranch. This was a great relief to all concerned, but it meant that I couldn't observe Dad reading the manuscripts but would have to wait until I received a call. We developed a ritual not unlike the one I had had with my grandfather, except that it was less formal. Dad liked the first two novels, short mysteries, but he knew a bridge had been crossed with the completion of the first of the historical novels, *The Proud Breed.*

He called me after he had finished reading it, and I went to see him. "This is a wonderful book!" he said, and then after a long pause, he added, "How did you learn all of this?"

By "this" he meant not the details of California's history in the nineteenth century but the sexual aspects of the book, mild as they were compared to others being published at the time.

"Wouldn't you worry if I didn't know those things?" I asked, and with a grin he conceded the point, nicknaming me, "my daughter, the porno queen."

When he had finished *The Tiger's Woman,* we had another interview. Again he praised the work, but this time he asked where a missing, original page was. It was evidence of what a discerning reader he was. He was right: I had replaced the original page. It dealt with the killing of the chief villain, and I had judged the first version too violent, but Dad said, "No, by now your readers want that son of a bitch torn into little bits; they need to know he was punished."

I handed him the original. He read it and nodded, "This is it! This is the way it ought to be." That page, not the rewrite, went to press.

He had a final comment, "I hope your Aunt Lola never reads this," and we both laughed at the idea of Great-aunt Lola's reaction to a story such as *The Tiger's Woman,* which deals with a woman's offering of her body in exchange for protection against an evil much greater than the bargain.

But despite Dad's often rough talk, he had a streak of Puritanism, which while not as wide as Aunt Lola's, was surely there. That is undoubtedly part of the reason he found it so difficult to deal with a girl child. I think it is always difficult for fathers to adjust to the fact that their daughters are growing into women, and for my father, who had married into a world so different from his own background, there must have been few familiar markers. The sisters and girlfriends of his youth were not part of the WASP establishment and did not go to college. They had jobs, not careers, and their basic obligation in life was to stay in the neighborhood, marry, and cater to their husbands and children. Dad had made a major adjustment in marrying my mother, and while he wanted the kind of life her background represented to him, I don't suppose he fully considered the reality of having children who were so fully a product of that background until we had arrived. I suspect we must have seemed very alien to him in many ways. And so, he kept his distance in one way, but in another, in the intellectual sense, he encouraged the difference.

So niggardly with emotional sustenance, he was always

generous in other ways. I doubt he consciously considered it, but it was an effort to make up for his inability to offer his heart. He never did anything so spontaneous as to bring my mother flowers or to say he loved her, aloud, with witnesses, but he learned to give her lovely things for birthdays and Christmas even though there had been no tradition of this in his family. And there were gifts to us, his children, as well, and trips and meals in restaurants, often given when he could ill afford them and always in sharp contrast to the Spartan habits he had regarding buying anything for himself.

I was not supposed to get a car until I graduated from high school. It was to be a bribe from Grandma for not smoking. But Dad thought it was stupid to wait. I was a good student and responsible. And I was certain to be going off to college where I might not be allowed to have a car. On my seventeenth birthday, Dad handed me a set of keys, and I found a bright red Tempest Le Mans outside. I enjoyed that car immensely, and it gave me marvelous freedom until I went off to college. I am glad I remember it as vividly as I do the red dress.

Dad was also generous in an intangible way that was ultimately more important than the material gifts. He allowed me and my brother to seek nurturing from other trusted men who became substitute fathers. Never did he convey any jealousy. Perhaps he was relieved that they could offer what he could not, but our enthusiasm for these people must have hurt now and then.

I wish I could report that our relationship improved as both of us grew older, but it didn't. Dad hated the signs of aging. He despised the problems with teeth, eyes, and ears and everything else. He thought the term "Golden Years" was the worst oxymoron yet, and he called retirement homes "Limp-Dick Villages." He grew more cranky, solitary, and unpredictable.

The last trip we—he, Mother, I, and a couple who are

70

close friends—took together was a disaster. I love England and Scotland passionately and had done much of the planning for what we would see, but Dad, who had chosen the accommodations and had been there before and therefore had no excuse in ignorance, refused to be charmed by any aspect of those countries. He behaved like an ugly American, a species he had always detested. There were brief passages of laughter and light, but most of the time he was in a foul temper.

Some final tie broke in me during that trip. It is always a risk to share something that is particularly beloved with another person, no matter who that person is, friend, lover, sibling, or parent. If the gift is rejected, the wound is deeply personal.

Within a few months, Dad was diagnosed as terminally ill. Our last direct conversation was as sad as much of the rest of our relationship had been. Because he was spending his days mostly reading and sleeping, I had been purchasing books for him for several weeks, thinking they would make good Father's Day gifts. Mom and Dad hadn't been traveling anywhere except to the clinic where Dad was being treated, but I said to my mother that while I realized Dad wasn't up to much, I could surely take them out to dinner for Father's Day. Looking a bit embarrassed, Mom told me that wasn't possible because they were going to Los Angeles for the weekend, to spend Father's Day with Dad's nephew and his wife.

We all had dinner with friends during the week. I gave Dad the books and his card then. He opened the books, read the card, and said, "You know I never wanted children anyway."

"I know," I replied. "You've made that very clear."

I suppose he meant it to be a joke. My mother has always maintained that Dad wanted children more than she did, though I never saw any proof of that. If a joke, it comes under the heading of most inappropriate humor and timing.

They went off for the weekend, but on their way home, Dad's health failed, and he was rushed to the hospital.

I kept faith until the end, insisting that he be allowed a painless and dignified death, which we had discussed so often while David was dying and afterwards. I helped to plan his memorial service, but all the while, I felt a strange distance from all of it, and finally I realized that I had already done most of my grieving long before. I had grieved for the constancy and kindness I could never find there, for the bond that had never been.

I do not miss the temper tantrums or the verbal abuse. I do not miss the intractability of a father who never said, "I love you," or "I'm proud of you," directly to me, not even when he knew he was dying. But I do miss the brightness of his mind, his critical sense about books, his willingness to discuss all sorts of things when he was in the mood. I miss the flashes of humor. Most of all, I miss the faith he had come to have in my abilities as a writer. Somehow, he alone of the family understood the terrors and the joys. Maybe it was because he never clearly defined his own dreams. Or perhaps he just lost them along the way.

When I was fourteen or fifteen, my mother tried to teach me to drive. At the time, the ranch car was a gray Rambler station wagon that attempted to amputate feet as people got in or out. The driving exercise turned into a screaming match. I abandoned the car and my mother on a gentle slope. At least I remembered to set the parking brake.

After the age of ten or so, my relationship with Mother was difficult. I resented being called upon to be an ally when she and Dad were fighting yet being relegated to the role of a child when I dared suggest she ought to divorce him. I resented being treated as a familial appendage, as she had been treated, as if daughters existed only to be dutiful, conventional, and pliable handmaidens while sons were a special gift from Providence, expected to do little else but exist in their own light. I resented having my problems and concerns trivialized as if they were a cartoon exerpt from "Emmy Lou." And most of all, I resented the complacent judgment that I was "just like my mother" and was expected to be so. Mother and I both knew early on that this was not true, whatever the spectators said.

We both hate doing dishes, routine sewing, and various other domestic chores, but these are hardly important similarities. In temperaments, psyches, interests, political beliefs, artistic tastes, in so many ways, we are radically different. And perhaps the greatest difference is generational.

I suspect a lot of my contemporaries would have a hard time describing what our mothers were like when we were young, what they were like as people, not just as mothers. For white, middle-class, married women, there was a code of behavior, and most of them appeared to adhere to it, no matter what they were feeling inside. On the surface, they seemed interchangeable. God only knows what was going on inside of them, particularly in cases such as my mother, who had a full-time job outside of the home. It is a measure of their collective distress that so many, in retrospect, recognized their dependence on the drugs, uppers and downers, so casually prescribed by their doctors.

Even as a child, I knew my mother was often in a state of near panic. Looking back, I can understand why. She was in charge of a business that demanded attention twenty-four hours a day. If the cook didn't show up to provide dinner for the guests, or if the plumbing quit or one of the horses foundered, Mom was the one who had to marshal whatever aid was needed. My aunt worked with Mother, but she and Uncle Joe kept their lives much more separate from the guest ranch than we were able to do, and Donna went home at the end of most days. It made sense because Mother was the one who had the power and made the decisions, which meant she also carried the responsibility. Grandma was still the figurehead, but Mother did the work.

And at home, she had two children and a demanding, temperamental husband who liked ranch life but not the guest-ranch business that provided it. He was more than a little jealous of the time and attention the business took.

I don't think Mother expected her life to belong to herself in those days. She had started out as a caretaker for her brother Joe, and her caretaking chores just increased as the years went on. She was only eight when she asked her mother if she would inherit her things if her mother died. Grandma thought this a greedy question and told her that yes, she'd receive some things, jewelry and such, but not everything.

"Oh, I don't mean that," Mother said, "I want Joe."

Mother's parents and her brothers were brilliant by any measure, and so was she, but in a much less assertive way. She graduated from high school and went to school in France at only fifteen. Then she graduated from college at twenty-one, but none of that seemed to count. She grew accustomed to taking the path of least resistance, of fading into the woodwork in a family where everyone else was forceful and flamboyant.

But she loved the ranch, and she loved running it. By her own confession, she would have been horrified to be stuck in the house all day with two children. I think it is fine to be a housewife if that is what one enjoys and can afford, but it is a dreadful sentence for those who are not suited to it. It is a particular kind of work done in a particular environment, and to assume that every woman ought to be overjoyed with the job is like assuming that every man ought to want to be a house husband.

Being the child of a working mother is surely different from having one who stays at home all day—not better or worse, just different. Knowing that Mom had so much to do outside of the house gave David and me an extra measure of independence at an early age. And I often felt more like a parent to my mother than a child, but I suspect this stemmed from the specifics of our personalities and the volatility of her relationship with Dad rather than from her job.

Though Mother worked, the office was close even after we'd moved out of the Main House itself in 1951 to the house my parents built on a nearby slope, and while we were young, we were never left alone. I don't know whether the times were so different, the screening process so careful, or the fact that Mother and Dad were nearby if not always in the house was the key—whatever the reason or combination of reasons, my brother and I were never abused by any of the people who cared for us. We had a couple of babysitters who were a bit odd. My mother swears that my belief in Pasteur's theory of the germ cause of disease, a theory she still seems to doubt, comes solely from "Mackie," a sitter who was overzealous about cleanliness. David and I did not notice that Mackie was strange, but we did think there was something off about the woman who called peanuts "goobers," not common speech in California, and who tried, without success, to prevent us from staying up to see an eclipse of the moon.

But despite having help with us—including, when we were small, Grandma—Mom usually seemed just at the breaking point. And the socially shy, academic overachiever child that I was then was surely not going to do anything to make her burden worse. I behaved and kept to myself. I read and wrote, escaping the chaos with orderly words. I am sure that some writers come from calm, "normal" families, but most seem to be cast up from turbulent familial seas.

Dad's larger-than-life, roaring personality simply took up too much of the domestic canvas for Mother to be painted vividly. She was a shadow figure, pale and fragile. The only thing she seemed sure of was that she loved my father and was willing to do anything to keep him in her life.

She changed after my brother died. I think it was sheer, desperate defiance. She had been a "good" girl all of her life, always doing and being what others expected of her, but it hadn't done any good, hadn't kept the people she loved safe. First her older brother had died in his twenties, and now her son had, too; and two years after David's death, the guest ranch closed, so the job she had done for decades was finished.

There is something to be said about accepting the randomness of life, the flood that so often washes away even the most carefully made plans. It was as if after years of trying to stop all the leaks in the dam, Mother just let the wall break and went with the river toward change.

She could have drowned, but under the panic of years, under the confusion, there was a strong swimmer, a strong woman. It was amazing to watch her take charge of her own life. She went out and got a job in a local real estate office, in addition to managing the transition of the guest ranch to permanent rentals, and then she got involved in local politics, not only winning a seat on the city council but also serving as mayor and as mayor pro tem.

She began to do remarkable things on a regular basis, things that would have been unthinkable for the self-effacing person she had been before. She made speeches and held her own in debates over the town's future. She went up in a fighter jet with no qualms at all, reporting afterwards that streaking over the desert and mountains had been a marvelous experience. She greeted visiting dignitaries and officially opened new businesses within city limits.

So much changed, it was as if she was reinventing herself, though perhaps it was more a case of the person who had always been in the shadows stepping forward into the light. She even began to dress differently, in bright, deep colors and in styles that still suit her very well.

She worried about Dad's reaction to her political life,

but didn't let that stop her. He grumbled sometimes, called himself the Prince Consort, and didn't go to many political functions, but basically, I think he was quite proud of Mom even if he couldn't fathom her patience with the demands made on her time. And while Mom would have preferred to have her own escort to the various receptions and functions, her newly born independence allowed her to go by herself or in the company of fellow politicians.

Even with her new priorities, Mother's love for my father did not change; it remained the central force. When he fell ill and died several years ago, she was devastated. But the mourning was not as it would have been before. In the interim, she had learned to love herself as well as him, had learned that her own wishes, her own survival were important. The sorrow of losing a husband of forty years was deep, but she didn't drown this time either. She went on.

Had she died first, I have no doubt that my father would have followed soon after, one way or another. Dad seemed to be the dominant one, but he had few connections to the world except through her. She had long been his sole provider of comfort and of social contact with other people.

Society, particularly that of Mother's age group, does not like widows. An extra man is always welcome, but an extra woman isn't. It is a measure of Mother's appeal that she is welcome at the gatherings of a large variety of people. She is interesting and interested in other people, and her calendar is so crowded, it makes me tired just to think about it.

If anyone had asked me when I was a teenager whether or not I loved my mother, I would have insisted that I did, but I would have qualified it inside, admitting that I didn't know her very well, understanding that loving and liking can be very different.

Our personalities and outlooks are so different, we could easily have drifted further and further apart. We could have been polite enemies, bound only by duty. Instead, we have become terrific friends. I cannot name a woman I love, like, and respect more than I do her, and my friends, who have no obligation by blood, are so fond of her, some of them regard her as a substitute mother and draw the comfort from her they cannot get from their own families.

There are things we cannot talk about, a bridge we will never cross. And my mother's life and mine are separate. Because we both live on the ranch, we make a constant, conscious effort to respect each other's privacy. But we keep in close touch. We have many friends of assorted ages in common; and we often plan trips together. We have a grand time when we travel, something we have done together since shortly after my brother's death. It is a way of meeting on neutral ground without encroaching on each other's lives.

I would highly recommend her to other historical novelists as the best of research assistants. I know of no one else, male or female, who would be so patient with my determination to see absolutely everything in any locale that is going to figure in the novels. I plan the itinerary, she drives, I navigate, and we laugh a lot, sometimes in near hysteria.

While I was doing research for *The Tiger's Woman,* I wanted to see Cape Flattery. It is the furthermost northwestern point of land in the contiguous United States, and it was an important landmark for sailing ships into the last century.

We were unwelcome Anglo visitors on Indian tribal land that was well posted with signs warning that we were now under the jurisdiction of Indian, not United States, law. I could hardly get out of the car and explain to the Indians that we hadn't come to peer at their lives but only to see a remote jag of land. We drove on and on in our rented car. The sun was going down, and the road was getting worse with every bumpy mile. Several carloads of young men passed us, their hard, set expressions giving clear indication of what they thought of Anglo women wandering on their land. No one at home knew where we were, and Mother confessed afterward that she could hear my father cursing when he heard of our demise in the wilderness, but she didn't give up. I did. Finally I said, "I don't think this is very smart. I don't think we ought to be here even to see Cape Flattery."

"Thank God!" she said, as she turned the car around, but she would have gone all the way.

The only time she obviously wanted to quit, it was a matter of bears. We had seen a remarkable variety of wildlife, including a black bear, in Yellowstone before going on to Grand Teton National Park, but moose were still on my list, so I planned a dawn walk around Jenny Lake.

It was a splendid dawn, the light rising slowly to paint the jagged peaks of the Grand Tetons across the lake, the elk bugling in the distance. It was autumn, and the summer crowds were gone. There wasn't another soul.

I set off down the path with Mother trailing further and further behind, her soft lament floating through the still air of morning.

"What if we do meet a moose? What if it is right on the path?"

"It won't be. It will be in the water," I called back.

"What if it isn't?"

"Then we step off of the trail."

"What if we don't see it until it's right there?"

This was a reasonable question since the foliage was dense, but I assured her that it would make enough noise so that we'd know it was there. I sounded confident, but my own doubts were beginning. Moose are very large.

"What about bears?"

A mad moose could surely do as much damage as a bear, but bears, not moose, are one of my primal fears. When I was a child, I dreamed of a grizzly bear out in the pasture, killing horses. The dream was in vivid color and realistic detail until I tried to run and my feet turned into anvils that struck sparks on the ground. I know where the nightmare originated; it came directly from a stuffed grizzly bear in a natural history museum. It was nine feet tall; its head was massive; its teeth and claws unbelievably long and lethal. And the nightmare had been reinforced by a trip to the Canadian Rockies in the summer when grizzly bears were snatching people out of sleeping bags and off of golf courses in both the United States and Canada.

The funny thing is that I like bears. I admire their skills and the sheer undulating power of them. And I believe they won't bother me unless I bother them. The problem stems from the definition of "bother." My ideal definition is that I could only bother a bear by deliberately provoking it. Unfortunately, bears may consider it provoking to be suddenly confronted by a human on a narrow trail.

Mother's voice had been quite steady while she was inquiring about attack by moose, but when she'd moved on to bears, there was a definite quaver.

Grizzly bears like water when the salmon are running, but we were at a placid lake, and I had read the sign that said "most" of the bears were on the other side of the lake, but to be careful about surprising them, just in case they were on this side. Add to that the fact that we had already been indoctrinated by the cautions in Yellowstone and by the visible fact of garbage pails that are built like vaults to protect gold, and by my own experience of abandoning my preferred walking trail in Yellowstone because of the sudden appearance of a CAUTION, BEAR sign that turned out to refer to a grizzly, not a black, bear. That particular bear had been airlifted to a remote section of the park a couple of times, but she knew where she wanted to live, and came back. The compromise was to remove the people from her path rather than to relocate her again, and I heartily approved of that solution.

I also approved of my own determination not to provoke any bear anywhere. Mother's "What about bears?" sang louder and louder in my head, and I rounded foliage-shrouded corners evermore slowly, while Mom fell further and further behind.

Finally, she admitted defeat, bugling as stridently as the elk. "Celeste, let's go back to where there are more tourists!"

I collapsed. I laughed so hard, a bear could have harvested me as easily as ripe blackberries. There we were in a national park that often has traffic to rival Los Angeles at rush hour, but we had the universe to ourselves, that miraculous situation most tourists long for and never achieve, and we couldn't wait to get back to "civilization."

By then I was a full participant in the moose-bear conspiracy theory, and we scurried back to the car as fast as we could go. (I feel obliged to add that on our last day, leaving early on our way from Jackson Hole to Bozeman, Montana, we saw moose and other wildlife aplenty, including the pronghorn antelope who have apparently been hired to greet visitors at the northern entrance to Yellowstone.)

This year my mother will be seventy years old, "three score and ten," as the Bible says. She looks younger now than she did twenty years ago. It is as if the changes and discoveries she made worked out from the inside. It is not a subtle difference, and it is not solely my judgment. I've had many friends ask if Mom has had a face-lift—she hasn't—and most cannot believe her age.

When I was a child in Catholic school, it seemed to me that a state of grace ought to confer an aura of beauty and light that is as visible to the eye as to the soul. Now I know that, sometimes, it does.

Chapter 3
MY ONCE WILD BROTHER

The Bridge of San Luis Rey, by Thornton Wilder, has haunted me ever since I read it long ago. Deceptively lyrical, it is a horrifying story of predestination, of disparate people brought together just so they can die when the bridge collapses.

Though a large population of the world believes in predestination, I try very hard to not count myself among their number. It seems so numbing. If the path is set, with all the major markers in place, why bother? It is the perfect formula for inertia.

Having stated that, I must confess that I have my doubts about the freedom that fate allows us. Fate may be identified as anything from gods to genetics—the results are the same, little more than imagined freedom, with the real course unfolding all along. Life in the twilight zone.

Some people seem to be born with a master plan in place.

It is impossible to imagine my brother as an old man; it was always impossible to imagine that.

He was born in 1948, a year and eleven months after my birth. I think he must have been a shock to my mother. I was such a placid, self-contained infant, surely there must have been some concern about whether or not I was slow. In contrast, David hit the ground running and never stopped.

He was certainly a shock to me. While still in a Taylor-Tot, one of those combination baby buggy/baby walkers, he managed to get up enough speed going down the long hall of the Main House to knock me over and cut open my head.

Mother was embarrassed, but she had no choice. She often had him on a lead, like a fractious puppy, when they were in public. It was either that or risk having him dart away forever.

He and I were as unalike as two children could be. I have always liked projects and thoughts to have a beginning, a middle, and an end, always working through to the finish. David had little interest in anything after the initial idea or tryout. The spark fascinated him, but he seldom waited to see if it went out or went on.

I came to feel responsible for everyone and everything around me when I was very young; David was far more detached. If what people were doing did not affect him directly, he paid no attention. Of course, this is typical of first child–second child behavior, and even more typical, I think, when the older sibling is female. Girls were taught, and still are, that they have some special responsibility for pleasing and nurturing the people around them. It is not entirely bad; male children could do with a little more push in that direction, but it can be wearing, and it becomes very complicated in a family that doesn't function too well as a unit. In this case, it must be very similar for the responsible child, male or female. He or she feels at fault for every bad thing that happens. Strangely, there is no corresponding sense of taking credit when good things happen.

Graveyard Peaches

David and I even saw the world around us in distinctly different ways. I've always loved the colors of the earth; David was red-green color-blind, an inheritance from our maternal grandfather. David saw things in linear terms. To me, the ranch is one band of color against the next; to him it was a series of intersecting planes: railroad tracks, field, road, fence, tree, and skyline.

Mother noticed David's color blindness on his first Christmas when he ignored a package wrapped in bright, shiny, red paper, but generally it didn't cause him many problems, except for choosing clothing when he was grown. Once he came home with chartreuse socks to go with a blue suit he was planning to wear to a dance. "Do these go with this suit?" he asked.

"Only if you want to stop traffic," I told him. "That color is the same one they use for warning stickers at night."

"Damn that salesman! I told him I was color-blind, and he told me these were pale yellow."

David had to take the socks back for an exchange, and I was cross with the salesman, thinking he'd been mean, but later it occurred to me that maybe he was color-blind, too, even if he did work in a men's shop.

I have taught myself to use VCR's, food processors, answering machines, and the like, but I have never had a love affair with them. David loved the way machines fit together and hummed. When he was small, this interest had disastrous consequences when he disassembled things only to find that when he put them back together, there were parts left over, parts that no longer seemed to have any place in the works. Not always, but usually when this happened, the machines no longer hummed. He wasn't very old before he knew that all parts had to be accounted for. I suspect this is the way most inventors start their careers.

I do not fully trust machines. I follow directions exactly, use the device only as instructed, and find it easy to believe that an explosion or some other awful consequence might result from improper use. David never had such reservations, not even after he plugged himself into the wall along with the Christmas lights. And he believed that machines were infinitely adaptable. He took Mother's vacuum cleaner down to the swimming pool, connected the hose to the exhaust, and tested it on our cousin Kemper as diving equipment. For this experiment, Kemper was required to tie rocks to his waist so that he could walk on the bottom of the deep end of the pool.

I had visions of Kemper being electrocuted or drowned, or at the very least, of the vacuum cleaner being destroyed. However, between them, David and Kemper proved that vacuum cleaners, or specifically my mother's model, were not sufficiently powerful to work for diving because as the water pressure increased at the deeper levels, the machine started to suck instead of blow, even from the exhaust end.

My warnings of dire consequences always fell on deaf ears. I think I was born feeling obliged to consider that every action leads to another, that every act has some consequence. This was another great difference between my brother and me. David blithely assumed that things would go the way he planned, or if they didn't, he'd figure out some way to avoid complete disaster. And usually he did, though sometimes it was nip and tuck.

He and a friend who was slightly older decided to have a picnic on the pool, in a rowboat. The pool is vast because when the hole was being dug for it, the sides kept caving in, and my grandfather kept saying that was fine, to just make it bigger. David and Mark rigged a card table with a blanket over it in the boat and sailed out into the middle of the pool with a candle for light. As I remember, this was in imitation of life in Venice.

As Mark reported later, it was pretty dark, despite the

candle, but things were going fairly well, if a bit damply, until the candle was suddenly snuffed out by the rising water as the boat sank.

Both boys were good swimmers, but the blanket floated out and then down. It was pitch dark without the candle, so when Mark surfaced, he couldn't find David. He admitted afterwards that he was torn between panic at the loss of his friend and terror at what my grandmother and mother would do to him when they found out what had happened. However, David surfaced at the far end, having swum underwater in order to avoid the sinking boat and other debris. And in the end, since they were safe, the boys got in trouble for using one of the good ranch blankets in such a fashion rather than for having risked their lives.

In another mechanical adaptation, David stole my roller skates to build one of the first skateboards in the valley. Having mastered that, he eventually purchased a manufactured one with heavy-duty wheels. Then he decided he'd try it on the steepest hill in town. Halfway down he realized he was going much too fast to get off without serious injury, so he rode on, shooting across one of the busiest roads, though luckily for him not at a peak traffic hour, finally slowing down a bit and fetching up against some stranger's garden wall. He somersaulted over the wall and landed flat in front of the surprised homeowner who was out in her garden collecting the newspaper.

Since Dad left child-rearing chores up to Mom 99.99 percent of the time, it fell to her to try to do her part to keep David out of danger and trouble. She gave up fairly early on because, she said, it was impossible to imagine what he was going to do next. She was left with the role of bemoaning what had happened long after it had.

Another difference between David and me was that, unlike my aversion to matches—developed after one encounter in the ranch kitchen—he was fascinated by fire and seemed to have the makings of a pyromaniac. Mother read somewhere that the way to break the enchantment of flame was to make the match lighting so routine as to be boring, and that then the child would lose all interest and cease to be a threat to civilization.

Mom put David out on the front porch of the Main House with a full box of kitchen matches, and she instructed him to light them all, one by one. She went back into the office, but after a while, she began to get worried about how quiet it was out there.

Far from being bored, David wanted more matches. He had used the ones he had to build an elaborate village on the sidewalk, all connected by match walkways so that when one match was lighted, it would touch off all the others, one by one, and in a terrific, intricate pattern, too.

Having had one brother old enough to protect her and one young enough for her to mother, Mom was baffled and distressed by the high level of bickering that characterized David's and my relationship. Her vision of what siblings ought to be often made us feel we were unnatural in our wars. Of course, when we grew older, we learned that our way was quite normal for siblings.

Being the older sister was a no-win situation. If I revealed what David was planning to do, Mother would say, "No one likes a tattletale." But if the deviltry went unreported until it was committed, Mother would say, "Did you know about this?" or variations on the theme of "How could you let this happen? You're older, you should be more responsible." These words did not originate with her. These are parent words passed from generation to generation in order to annoy. I think it highly possible that Cain slew Abel right after hearing those words, though that isn't the way the story has been written down.

In fact, I was restrained in what I reported, letting the measure of yielded information be the degree of loss or harm that might result from the action, and sometimes I was too restrained and had to worry about this or that episode.

One that scared me silly was the sword sales. The legend of Camelot had been rekindled in story and song. We were teenagers by then, and David took lead piping from the ranch and pounded it into beautifully crafted, lethal broadswords. He sold the swords to his cousins and to other boys on the ranch for three dollars each. Then he organized tourneys in the woods, not symbolic flourishes, but real do-your-best-hack-at-'em sword fights.

I was too fainthearted to witness these contests. I simply tried to pretend none of it was happening, all the while hoping no one would be killed. As reported later by the cousins, the fights between David and Robert, one of the tenants' children, were spectacular with leaps and split-second duckings to avoid decapitation. The cousins were smart enough to see that they were not in this league and so fought amongst themselves in a less vigorous manner.

To this day, my aunt shakes her head in wonder that her three boys survived childhood with their cousin David. It was not a matter of malice, just one of balance.

David tumbled into the world knowing exactly where he was in time and space. He could run around the narrow top rail of the pool fence without missing a step before diving off of the cabana roof. He became such a superb rider that he scarcely ever had to dismount to pick up a hat or other fallen object or to open a gate. The first day he was on snow skis, he went from the beginners' class to the top of the mountain. On the water, he eventually learned to ski without skis at all. When he got his driver's license and then a car, drag racing was the next logical step, and he did that with the same skill as everything else. Sometimes he raced for pink slips, but he didn't keep the cars the wins represented; it was just a matter of proving he could race to win.

The drag racing was another of those activities that

gave me early gray hairs. I knew David and his friends were doing it, and that it was both illegal and dangerous. But drag racing in rural America has been a rite of passage for young males going back to horse and buggy days. And, in the boys' defense, they were not the sort who practiced the sport on the town's main street, thus endangering everyone. Instead, they chose obscure roads out on the desert.

Not obscure enough, as it turned out. One day my brother and a friend, Ted, were officiating, rather than racing. Ted was perched on a fence post in order to have a clear view of the field for the start, and just as the cars screeched off, he said, "Hey, Dave, isn't that your grannie's car?"

There was Grandma in her Cadillac, proceeding down the road toward the two dragsters who were just reaching Mach speed. One of the cars spun out in the dirt to avoid a head-on collision, but Grandma drove on until David flagged her down.

He confessed that he could not remember ever being so afraid. "Are you all right?" he asked as her window rolled down.

"Oh, yes, I'm fine," she said, "but those young men were driving very fast. They really ought to be more careful."

It was David, not Grandma, who told this story. To Grandma, David was the Golden Boy, the Chosen One to shine again in the space left empty by the death of her son Kemper. Once he had cleared babyhood and had the promise of manhood, there was little he could do to lose favor with her, though the episode of the HONK IF YOU'RE HORNY license plate holder came close.

David was not oblivious to this favoritism, and he was quite capable of using it to his advantage, but he was also basically kind about it. He paid just enough court to Grandma to keep her happy, and he genuinely loved her.

It is typical of him that he was terrified that Grandma could have been hurt in that drag race, but that he did not consider the same danger for himself when he was racing. Back to balance and reflexes. His were so keen, he could not imagine what it was like to be less physically gifted. And he was what is now being called a thrill seeker in the scientific sense, preliminary results suggesting that there are those who feel alive and fulfilled only when they are getting the extra burst of chemicals produced in the body when it is undergoing the stress of challenge and risk.

This was another day-and-night difference between us. I was a clumsy child, and unless I am careful, I am a clumsy adult. I envy those people who sprint surefootedly through the woods and across streams. When I am confronted with a stream crossing via leap or log, my body hasn't the slightest notion of which foot will lead or whether anything at all will follow. My idea of hell is a speed sport that requires dexterity and split-second timing. Snow skiing would have killed me had I let it. The only part of it I enjoyed was when I was sliding on my rear—then, at least, I knew I wasn't going to break a leg.

Despite his athletic prowess, David did not escape injury; it was just that it failed to make much of an impression on him, though he did get to the point where he would clutch whatever part was bleeding and insist that he didn't need stitches. Despite these protests, he was sewed up now and again, and once he broke his arm.

The broken arm came as a result of yet another sisterly warning unheeded.

The black-and-white pony's name was Pepper, and I don't think he belonged to the ranch; perhaps he was boarding there or on loan. Ponies were never favored, though we did have Major, a Welsh pony–Arabian horse cross, for years. Ponies are often pure malice. Perhaps they feel obliged to defend their lack of stature. One of the cowboys used to say he thought it was a great idea to start a child out on a pony because any kid who could ride a pony could ride anything.

Pepper wasn't any nicer than others of his kind, but his attempt to fling David off of the planet was understandable. David was trying to ride him without a saddle or a bridle, and he got on him backwards. All of this was to impress a little girl. David was five then, and no seven-year-old sister was going to dissuade him from performing for his lady love.

Pepper went crazy, bucking and whirling around the small pen until he threw David through the fence. The wood was rotted and gave way; otherwise, David could have broken a lot more than his arm. Typically, he was using the cast as a club before the week was out.

In a perversion similar to perpetuating wisdom teeth, which cause nothing but misery, Nature has endowed the vast majority of little brothers with a hyperactive brat factor. This is evident in their uncanny ability to annoy. It is a talent that is put to use as soon as the boy is ambulatory, and if the sister is lucky, it might stop in two decades, though in some families, I suspect it goes on to the end of life.

David was a master. If we were on a car trip and told to stay on our own sides in the backseat, he would immediately start flopping around so that an arm or a leg or a foot trespassed. If we were sitting close enough at the table, his foot would unerringly locate my chair so that he could set up a steady tapping, smiling all the while as if nothing were going on. He was a perfect judge of what possession was the favorite and would have it taken apart or broken in short order. The only things that remained relatively safe were my crayons. There his color blindness came in handy for me because my favorite colors weren't in his range. Unlike our mother, who noticed so early, I wasn't really aware that he was color-blind until we'd colored together for a while. Then, looking at the random colors he'd used for trees and such, I announced my finding.

"I am not!" he protested.

"Yes, you are, else you wouldn't have made those trees purple."

He thought about that for a moment and then said, "It isn't because I don't know the colors, it's because I can't remember what name goes with what color."

It sounded so logical, I believed it for a while. And in any case, since he broke any crayons he used, it was comforting to be able to hand over the darks, the browns and such, while being selfish with the reds, pinks, and greens. But the crayons were the only part of our joint universe that I was able to control. Everything else was open to his predations—closets, drawers, etc. And it was worse when the time came for secret diaries and boyfriends. I had to go to such lengths to hide the diaries, sometimes I couldn't remember where my current cache was, but he always found it.

Occasionally the boyfriend betrayals were not his fault. Boys of my age were larger than he, and they knew all about little brothers. In eighth and ninth grades, I had crushes on a succession of classmates. One of them, Bruce, managed, with the help of some friends, to corner David, threaten his life, and thus get a word-for-word account of how much I liked Bruce and what I thought was cute about him. I still remember that those assets included enough height so that I didn't tower over him, a good sense of humor, and a working brain. It didn't hurt that he was also nice to look at. David's information came from eavesdropping on my phone conversations with girlfriends and other such unimpeachable sources, and though he protested that he had to tell them, I was sure he'd done so with great relish. I still blush when I think of Bruce, but at least we remained friends until his air force father was transferred and the family moved.

There are very odd aspects to little brothers' teasing. One is that while it is obviously based on the trespassing of a most persistent variety, which thus stirs up predictable and ferocious feelings of territorialism in the older sister, I have never known an older sister who had the slightest interest in practicing the same art on a younger brother. I wanted my side of the car, my chair, and the privacy of my possessions; I didn't want his, nor did I think there was anything interesting to ferret out in his room, aside from things he taken from mine—I sometimes staged raids for that purpose. Another oddity is that parents almost never acknowledge what is going on.

"Both of you, stop that!" is the universal command when the quarreling reaches top volume. This, lacking all semblance of justice, ranks right up there with, "How could you let that happen? You're the oldest."

Sometimes David and I came to blows, though never dangerously so. It was more a matter of slapping and pinching when we were little. David was not the sort to hit a woman, not even his sister. And the last time I was mad enough to want to slug him, I noticed that he had suddenly shot up a foot or so and was a good deal taller than I.

The one potentially lethal fight we had was when we were teenagers. Our parents were away. I was bent over, unloading the dishwasher. David passed by and couldn't resist the target. He slapped me hard on the rear, and I went after him. We had separate bedrooms, mine with a sliding glass door to the outside, his with a little bathroom that had an outside door. He was clearly going to make it to the safety of his bathroom before I got to him. I still had a handful of silverware, and I threw one of the forks. It hit him on the arm. I was always better at verbal battles than at the physical fighting, so we were both amazed at my accuracy. He turned around and came after me. I had time just to duck into my room and slam the door. Then I heard a strange digging sound. When I peeked out, I discovered he had embedded the fork in the wood.

"Fastest fork in the West," I called and slammed the door again.

The next thing I heard was a hissing noise. He was using insect spray to try to fumigate me out of my room. I slipped out my back door, got my own can of insecticide from the pantry, and went after him.

By then we were both shrieking with laughter, until I noticed that his can was labeled DDT.

"Oh, stop!" I yelled. "That's really poisonous!"

We both stopped, and it only took seconds for us to realize what we'd done. The whole house reeked of insecticide.

"I can see the headlines now," I told him. " 'Two Southland Teenagers Kill Each Other with Bug Spray.' Mom and Dad are going to love this!"

We spent the rest of the afternoon scurrying around, opening every window and door and setting up fans to drive out the stuff. The night was miserable. When we compared notes the next day, we found we'd both been plagued by the same things—mosquitoes, flies, and moths, which had not quite been killed but were drugged and flew like kamikaze pilots, bumping into us and everything else.

Despite our efforts, we had to explain what had happened since Mom's first words on arriving home were, "What is that smell?"

I envied girls who had older brothers. Not only were most of them protective and indulgent, they also had male friends who were great dating material (though that could be tricky if the brother didn't approve of the match). David was not usually protective in this way (witness the Bruce episode) and dating his friends was a very bad idea. But he once intervened, and I think he probably saved me a lot of grief.

Pat (a woman and no relation to the actor of the same name) and Eddie O'Brien were guests who became integral parts of our lives and, having no children of their own, they

94

were wonderfully indulgent with us. Pat is elegant, bright, and funny, and long ago became a role model for me; Eddie adored David as if he were his son. The O'Briens had been spending the summer in Hawaii for decades, and at end of the summer of 1962, we joined them in Honolulu.

David was fourteen, I was sixteen, and we had worked hard for months, doing guest ranch yard and kitchen work in my case, ranch work in David's, to earn enough to pay for most of it ourselves, though our parents contributed toward the food money. Pat and Eddie were staying in the home of friends who, because they had kids of their own, didn't want any children staying there while they were gone—gives you an idea of what sort of children they had. This meant that David and I had to stay in a hotel, and we chose one that was near the beach but still within our budget. The reason we could afford it became apparent as soon as we saw it. It was dilapidated, right down to the roaches, but it was in Hawaii, after all, so who cared?

Along with the roaches, there was a large population of surfers who were as impoverished as we. They were also older and far more jaded. But this was clearer to David than to me. I did not yet have contact lenses, and my glasses were awful. I hated them so much that I took them off whenever I could and just allowed the world to be a blur. This was not harmful with trees or stars, but it wasn't so innocuous with potential dates.

As far as I could tell without my glasses, the guy who asked me out was tall enough, blond, and had a nice voice. For tall, dark, and gawky me, this seemed a great opportunity.

"Are you really sure you want to go out with him? He's pretty crummy looking. He's sort of dirty with a stubbly beard, and he looks sneaky"—this, from my brother who never took any interest in such things, had a galvanizing effect on me. It was enough to make me sure I didn't want to go out with the man, and I didn't.

David and I left the hotel and moved in with the O'Briens, who had decided that their absent hosts could not inflict anything as awful as what might happen to us at the hotel.

The house was near Diamond Head and seemed like heaven after our previous quarters, but it did have its drawback.

At the Bishop Museum, there is an exhibit concerning the vast rat population that has decimated the native fauna since the rats arrived via foreign ships. And on the night that followed our visit to the museum, I heard a tapping going down the hall outside my room. I made sure the doors were closed, pulled the bed away from the wall, and waited for dawn, sure that an eight-foot rat was lurking outside. The rat turned out to have been Eddie, on his way to the kitchen for a glass of water. He hadn't turned on the lights because he didn't want to disturb anyone.

But when Pat and Eddie gave a party, the real thing appeared. Eddie was playing lord of the manor, pointing out the fruit trees in the backyard. And as the guests looked up to admire a ripe guava, a huge rat waddled out, took a bite of the fruit, then picked it, and carried it back into the shadows.

David and I thought the circumstances made this particularly amusing. Laughter colored our days there. David was particularly content because of the surfing. He was as good at that as he was at other sports. He spent as many hours as he could out on the sea, and at the end of our two weeks, he was as dark as the Hawaiian beach boys.

We saved the biggest treat of all for our last night. Having taken care with the food budget before, we had enough to go to the Royal Hawaiian Hotel for dinner. We were all tanned. Eddie and David wore white dinner jackets, and Pat and I wore white dresses.

We were seated near a large party, and one of their number, a young woman who was probably a year or so older than I, scooted her chair back so far in order to eavesdrop on our table that it was as if she were sitting with us instead of her own family.

Just the night before we had discussed this very thing and agreed that when people did that, they deserved to hear a tall tale.

With a wink at me, Pat started it by asking how things had gone on the film set in Rome. Eddie fell right into the game. The girl at the next table nearly fell out of her chair. Only David was without a script.

He had surfed hard all day and was nearly asleep at the table. He let all the fantasies flow over him until Pat asked, "Do you find the fish here as good as it was on the Riviera?"

With that, David perked up and tuned in. "But we never went to the Riviera," he insisted. "We weren't in that part of France."

Pat and I kicked him under the table, which only increased his puzzlement, but he subsided in his quest for truth, and after paying a little more attention, he understood and joined the game.

Pat has been in the fashion business all of her life, and she had directed a fashion show at the Royal Hawaiian a few years before, so when it was time to go to the ladies' room, she was confident she knew the way. Eddie and David stood politely, and Pat and I swept up the staircase, feeling the stares of the girl and various other members of that party as we left.

Pat led us directly into the kitchen of the hotel where the startled staff froze in amazement. We had to cross the landing in front of all the watchers in the dining room to find the facilities.

Though early car trips were long sieges of seat trespassing and squabbling, David and I became good traveling companions quite early, even when we were still fighting frequently at home. I suspect my mother could have done without this particular bond, as one of the very strong things David and I shared was the desire to see every museum and national monument wherever we were. It didn't affect Dad much since he usually left the tourist duties up to Mother, but she used to shake her head and wonder why she couldn't have borne children who were bored with museums after half an hour. And traveling with David meant going to the top of any structure where that was allowed. We climbed to the top of the Statue of Liberty on that awful metal staircase; we saw New York from the Empire State Building and Paris from the Eiffel Tower; we peered down from the Leaning Tower of Pisa into the nuns' backyard; and we stood on the roofs of various cathedrals, though I drew the line at going all the way up in St. Paul's in London for no better reason than that it was one climb to the heights too many.

David came back from the last bit earlier than we expected him.

"They wanted a shilling to go into the ballroom," he reported, "and I wasn't going to pay that to see a dumb old dance room."

We teased him about that for a long time because "ballroom" meant the golden sphere on top of the church. David was thirteen at the time and he was suspicious of anything that seemed designed to get him into an uncomfortable social situation, such as dancing with strangers.

This is not to say that he had any aversion to girls. By then he had already begun to collect an admiring entourage. And he had provided for them when we had gone to St. Peter's in Rome before we headed for England.

We were in Catholic school at that time, and even though we were still Protestant, we had been touched by the mysticism of the church. But St. Peter's was a shock.

"What are those statues made of?" David asked, peering into a glass case under an altar.

"They aren't statues," I muttered, "those are popes under glass; those are their real bodies."

"Jeeze!"

But we were both very moved by Michelangelo's *Pietá* because in those days before madmen started smashing the art treasures of Europe, the *Pietá* was approachable, waiting there in her shadowed alcove.

Pope John XXIII was enormously popular among Catholic schoolchildren and many others, and we got to see him in a "semiprivate" audience, which meant that only half of the world was admitted rather than everyone in creation. When he was carried in on a chair platform, the audience cheered, sang, and wept. It was really quite moving. Then at one point in the ceremony, the pope offered a blessing on religious articles that people had brought with them for that purpose. With that, David dug into his pockets and produced handfuls of rosaries, which he had purchased for all of his girlfriends back at school. (Actually, he and I had a rosary history going back a ways. Covering all bases, we would go to a Protestant church on Sundays but pray with the Catholics during the week, and during one holy season as we were kneeling together to say the rosary one night, I looked beside me and saw that, having misplaced his rosary, he was keeping track on a tape measure.)

Seeing David loaded down with religious articles made me think that maybe I'd better buy a few more for my friends, but I wanted them to have a papal blessing, too, and in the marvelously arcane and obliging way of the church, it turned out that there were special priests in St. Peter's who could give the blessing. In the dark and gloomy corridor of confessionals, I ended up in front of a priest who spoke only Spanish. I held out my statues and rosaries, and he seemed on the point of attacking me with his stick, but it was just an effort to make me kneel for the blessing. The experience was quite terrifying, and I was very glad to get out into the sun again.

This feeling was undoubtedly enhanced by the fact that the ridiculous and sublime seemed wedded together throughout our visit to St. Peter's. Not even the presence of the pope was proof against it. As we were leaving the audience chamber, a masher got behind me. It was my first experience with this kind of insult, but he wasn't subtle. The crowd was packed so tightly, I couldn't get away from him. I looked around in panic and caught my mother's eye. She saw instantly what was happening. She came through the crowd like Moses parting the Red Sea. I heard the man gasp, "La Mama!" before he fled into the crowd.

The last long trip David and I shared was to Europe again in 1970. We went with our parents and Emil and Mary Ann Danenberg, putting through Europe in a VW bus. The men concentrated on where to eat and which dishes to order. David did his share of eating, but he was still game for the museums, cathedrals, and monuments.

When the tour was over, the "adults" went home. I stayed on in England for several months, and David remained in Italy with side trips to even more exotic locales. By then, David had embraced his Italian heritage wholeheartedly, including the aspects that required study.

School had been another field of conflict between us. I was a good student. The neat progression of learning pleased my orderly mind in most subjects, though math bored as well as baffled me at the higher levels. David was very bright, and no student at all. Almost everything about school bored him, and he did as little as possible to get by. He was in only second or third grade when the teacher called my mother in for a conference.

"What would you do with a child who does work like this?" the nun asked.

It was a math quiz. The first problems were done correctly. But then David had obviously decided enough was enough and had spent the rest of the time making the double zeroes into the wheels of various types of vehicles. Some configurations had become airplanes. Math was never difficult for him; the catch was keeping him interested long enough to do the exercises.

Mother didn't have much to say to the nun since getting David to apply himself to schoolwork was an old battle even by then.

There wasn't anything I could do about it, but he wasn't helped by having a studious older sister. Teachers really did ask that unforgivably stupid question, "Are you as smart as your sister?" I'm sure that was enough to put him off studying for a long time, and it certainly made him avoid those subjects that were my favorites—English, history, the biological sciences, and art. That didn't leave much for him aside from mathematics when he cared to finish the assignments, and later on, chemistry and physics.

So he puttered through school and dawdled about in several colleges, taking engineering courses, because, I think, that was what Dad had studied. But David soon discovered that while some of the theories and experiments interested him, the basic dullness of the faculty and students was not to his liking.

And then, quite suddenly, he experienced his own renaissance. Literature, art, and science all flowed together and flourished in his mind. He began to read voraciously, and he wanted to talk about what he'd read. He began to write verse and to execute drawings that were as strong, masculine, and graceful as he was. And Italy was like coming home to him.

In 1970, David was twenty-two years old. He was six foot two, slender but muscular. His dark hair was thick and curly. His eyes were the darkest brown. He had a strong face with prominent cheekbones, brow, and chin, and his nose had been broken, giving it added character. Even from a sister's point of view, I could see that he was gorgeous. Just like my father, he had "it," that indefinable thing that is even beyond handsomeness, some current that electrifies the opposite sex. With amusement, I used to watch women's reactions when he entered a room. To one degree or another, they all melted, from little girls to grandmothers. And he was quite sweet about it. He had a broad streak of romanticism that allowed him to court his dates with style. He was purely Latin at heart, as if the English-Scottish heritage from Mother had not touched him.

It sounds batty to admit it, but when I first visited Scotland, I felt as if I had somehow always been there. That is how David felt about Italy, and when he stayed on in 1970, he looked so Italian and came to speak the language so well that one of his favorite games was to allow American tourists to approach and ask directions in their Berlitz Italian, to which he would reply, "Oh, yeah, the Colosseum"—or whatever—"is just down that way."

He was supposed to be attending the University of Florence, but that lasted one day. Instead, he embarked on his own voyage of discovery. He designed elegant leather pants and skirts for women and made wire sculptures that were so clever, some were displayed in trattorias and the like. He went to a gypsy festival in the South of France, won the shooting contest, enjoyed the prize of wine, and awakened to discover that the gypsies had disappeared in the night. He turned down the offer of a *contéssa* to reside with her as her lover, though he did accompany her to a huge costume ball. He wore the same rough clothing he used when he went riding at home, and he was toasted for being so clever as to fabricate the clothing of a real cowboy. He traveled to northern Africa, rented a dhow, called himself Captain Nirvana, and did a brisk business for a while taking tourists out on fishing excursions that included eating the catch—until local authorities informed him that he was doing too well and therefore could not do it at all anymore because he was a foreigner. He went on a bead safari where he and his friends waited for the "blue men," a tribe of desert nomads, Berbers, whose skin takes on a blue cast from the dye of their robes. These people brought in antique trade beads, originally made in Venice and taken by European traders to Africa to use as gifts and money.

And everywhere David went, he made friends. This had always been an effortless process for him. Part of it was that a day with him always meant adventure, even when he was very young, because he never lacked for ideas about what to do next. Part of it was because he had a keen sense of humor and a great deal of charm. But there was something deeper, a tolerance and kindness that were as strong as the wildness in him. He had never hesitated to be an unpopular child's friend, and he detested social pretensions of any kind. This combination of characteristics drew people to him. Here was this dazzling person who, far from putting on airs, welcomed others to come along. He was the perfect embodiment of his era.

Those were the days of a war that spilled corpses on the television screen every night just in time for dinner, of seeing leaders gunned down, and of one politician after another being caught in one illegal act after another. Those were the days of drugged dreams turning into nightmares and death for too many young people.

But those were also the days of hope, of believing that life could be different, that not all of the old ways that had survived were good ways and not all of the old ways that had vanished were bad. Of course, in a way it was an impossible last effort to turn back the Industrial Revolution that had started in the previous century and seemed to be running away with the world. But for many, it was a genuine attempt to redefine the essentials of being human, what is valuable in humanity and what is not. These are old, old quests, and the answers shift with the centuries and with the variety of cultural experiences, but it is surely better to continually ask the questions and examine the answers than to just plod along on a worn track that may be leading over a cliff.

My parents reacted with annoyance to David's long hair and protests during his college days, but they were among the first of their age and class whom I heard condemn the war in Vietnam. I was still full of the indoctrination of what patriotic Americans ought to be thinking when my parents convinced me that the nonwar was foolish and too costly in lives and everything else. My father, so unpaternal in many ways, went as far as to tell my brother that it would be better were he to go to jail or to Canada than to Southeast Asia. David did not have to make the decision. He was not only color-blind but his childhood asthma had left him with scarred lungs. And if one were in the proper social class, these were enough to exempt one from service. David joined the cultural gypsies, both American and European, as he made his own journeys of discovery.

There was little warning that everything was going to change irrevocably for all of us. David sent a couple of photo-booth strips, which showed him totally loaded on the painkilling drugs an Italian doctor had given him for what the doctor had diagnosed as a back problem. Then, a few months later, he came home, and it was clear that he was seriously ill. Though his stomach protruded, he had lost weight from the rest of his frame and his skin was gray.

Our family physician was a good diagnostician, but he was out of town when David first went to the office and saw an associate. David had been to such exotic places, that doctor suspected liver flukes or some other nasty parasite. The weekend passed, and David went back to the doctor's. This time he saw our regular doctor, who knew instantly what subsequent tests would confirm.

I was home when David came in. "I am dying of cancer," he said very calmly.

"That isn't funny."

"It's true. The doctor says it's inoperable, and I probably have a few months."

The planet stopped spinning and the universe changed

course in that instant. For the next two years, the only thing that mattered to any of us was David's struggle to live. He survived beyond the few predicted months by sheer force of will and by submitting himself to horrific medical treatments that included huge doses of toxic drugs.

Word went out that David was ill, and the modern gypsies came. They left their lives in Europe and in various parts of the United States. They arrived in worn Levis and tie-dyes. They hitchhiked or drove ramshackle vehicles with more rust spots than paint. They came with their marvelous names: Mooks, Kimmer, R.J., Aimée, Mireille, and others. And they joined those of like spirit who had settled here, who also loved David: Rick, Brooks, Clint, Joey, Susan, Becky, Paula, and others. If human beings really do have auras, they formed a light so bright and steady, it must have reached to the furthest edge of the heavens.

Grandma and everyone else fell in love with them because they were love. Whatever their backgrounds and personal idiosyncrasies, they came together to ring David all around, to defy Death on his behalf, and then, when defiance was no longer possible, to celebrate release.

We became the "Tribe." I cannot explain exactly what happened. We communicated without speaking. The divisions between day and night lost meaning. The only measure was what David had the energy to do. If he was up to riding, all of those who could sit a saddle climbed up on whatever horses were available and went with him. If he wanted to party, we partied. If he wanted quiet, silence reigned. He was not selfish in this. In truth, sometimes I think it must have been a great strain to have so many solicitous people around so much of the time. But he was so precious to all of us and we were losing him, so no one wanted to miss time with him.

He seldom spoke of dying. He said, "My business is staying alive; Death will come without any help from me." But he went to the Halloween party the year before he died dressed as Death itself, in black with white bones, and when there were gasps from the crowd, he just smiled and shrugged, "It's all right."

But, of course, it was not. The dying was too hard, too torturous. It erased all the images that had come before. Twenty-three years of normalcy could not stand against those two years of terror. They made six hours on the cross seem slight in comparison. Yet, with all of this, and as thin and pale, as old-young as he was toward the finish, he was still beautiful.

A month before he died, he was best man at our cousin Kemper's wedding. He fretted because he couldn't get his swollen feet into dress shoes. It made me weep. "My God, nobody cares about that," I told him. "It is more than enough that you'll be at the wedding."

He had made sure that Kemper had a suitably wild bachelor party, topped off by a suitably raunchy toast in Italian, but when he toasted the newlyweds after the ceremony, he said, "Health, wealth, long days together—may you have them all." It was infinitely moving to hear those words spoken so steadily by one who had neither health nor wealth and whose own days were nearly gone.

One of the women of the Tribe came to spend the night with him only a little time before he died. Death was in his room by then. I could smell it, I could see it in the shadowed corners. I was not alone. One of his male friends, not given to such fancies, came to me and asked bluntly, "Do you know what's in that room?" And I told him that I did.

This woman who loved David knew it, too. But she went to him anyway, unafraid and offering the best of all gifts, her assurance that the disease had not taken precedence in her eyes, that he was still a vital, desirable male.

Not everyone cared so much about him. It is astonishing and disgusting to see what comes out of the woodwork when someone has cancer. Suddenly the patient is deluged with "help" from people who insist this strange guru or that rare herb will work a miracle. Some of these offerings are made with good intentions, but others are so stupid or so accusatory—if you don't do such and such, you will be punished further—that they are far more harmful than helpful.

David was not immune to these onslaughts, and he did investigate alternative systems, but he was too bright and sensible to accept what he found ridiculous. There was a faith healer who was very popular at the time. She had her own television show and wore floating gowns with angel-wing sleeves while she worked her "cures." My mother and David went to hear her preach. They found hundreds of very ill people being kept waiting in the sun and heat outside the auditorium so that the ailing faithful could be filmed flooding into the place when the priestess arrived.

David decided on the spot that no one capable of that kind of cruel exploitation had anything he wanted. He and Mom went to see the film *Jesus Christ Superstar* instead.

Jesus freaks descended on him, too, assuring him that if he would just believe as they did, all would be well, including him. He was tolerant of them while he kept his own counsel. He believed, but not as they did. Once when he was filling out yet another set of hospital forms, he put "pantheist" in the box regarding religion. That amused him and me because we wondered what kind of chaplain they would send.

A friend convinced him to go to one of those seminars run by a used-car salesman or such turned high priest. It was a system that stole ingredients from all the major religions of the world, charged outrageous fees, packaged the act for weekend consumption, and depended on some of the same techniques I've seen in films of Hitler haranguing the crowds at night. To me, the most offensive part of the doctrine was the assertion that those with cancer or other life-threatening diseases were solely responsible for being ill. After all, how could the system give its followers power if it didn't give them control over Death? It even insisted that everyone, including the babies, who died at Hiroshima or in the Nazi death camps had willed disaster on themselves. This was worse than *The Bridge of San Luis Rey*.

It broke my heart to see David's determination falter in face of this. "Maybe I have done something to be sick. Do you think so?" he asked.

I was so furious, I could have strangled the false prophet with my bare hands. "I think that is the dumbest thing I've ever heard," I told David. "If that's true, then you tell me why trees and dogs and cats and God knows what else get cancer. Do all those creatures will it on themselves, too?"

To my relief, David agreed. "Of course not! I guess that is a stupid idea."

The greatest failure to aid and comfort came from the medical community. And it was the greatest irony because David received treatment at a teaching hospital run by the Adventists, reportedly one of the best places for treatment of his disease. Grandma had taught medical jurisprudence there decades before, and she was appalled at the coldness that had settled over the institution.

I will never forgive that coldness, nor will I ever fully understand it. These people profess to believe so deeply in God and in an afterlife, but I have never before or since seen people so terrified of Death. And the clearer it became that David was going to die, the more they treated him like a pariah. They ceased to meet his eyes or hear his voice. They lost track of his dietary needs, fed intravenous lines into muscles instead of veins, and ignored the conditions they might easily have alleviated while they quailed before their own cowardice. When all that was left that would have helped David was human recognition, contact, and comfort, these were the things hardest to find at that institution.

By the end, David was as steadfastly courageous as he had been throughout, but he and the rest of us had so lost trust in the hospital that we took shifts to make sure he was never alone there.

There were a few nurses who had the courage and kindness that others, particularly the doctors, lacked, and one of them spent several months at the ranch taking care of David so that he need not go to the local hospital emergency room in the middle of the night for pain shots. And there was one doctor David continued to trust—the family physician who had made the initial diagnosis and who never failed to respond with honesty and humanity.

These kind people should not have been the exceptions. They should have been the rule. People who go into medicine believing that they need not be humane because of the stress it might cause them ought to be in some other profession.

The cancer had never been operable, though the doctors had, at the beginning, done major surgery to "get a look at it." They never determined exactly where it had started, though it was somewhere behind the kidneys. By the end, it had gone everywhere and was blocking the bowel, so a colostomy was performed. David had stayed out of the hospital as much as he could, but he died there, while he was still "recovering" from the surgery.

As a final cruelty, as Mother kept watch beside him, he had a seizure in the early hours of the morning and could not speak. He was obviously frustrated and frightened by this, so I lied. "David, you've had a little seizure, and your brain didn't get enough oxygen for a while, that's why you can't talk. But you'll be able to later, when enough oxygen has gotten back into your brain."

That is one of the best, most useful lies I will ever tell. He settled after that, drifting in and out of consciousness. The last person his eyes focused on was Dad. Very softly Dad said, *"Dormi bene, mio figlio."* "Sleep well, my son," spoken in the language of his childhood, the language that had come to mean so much to David as an adult.

Graveyard Peaches

Once when David stopped breathing, Aunt Donna commanded, "David, you breathe right now!" in the same sharp tone she had used to stop mischief when we were children. But she, like the rest of us, knew that the battle was ending.

We were fortunate in the nurses we had that night and morning. After so many who had not cared, these women offered compassion in place of the medical skills that could no longer help.

David did not die in the darkness. The sun had risen, and the Tribe was standing around his bed. The nurse came in. "Oh, no more than two people are allowed in intensive care and only for a couple of minutes . . ." None of us said a word, but her voice trailed off as she understood. "That's all right, then," she said and left.

It was more than all right; it was exactly as it should have been.

Susan was the earth mother of the group, and she had been a source of strength for David throughout his illness, close to him without the complications of romantic involvement. She was stroking his forehead.

"Susan, it's time. Let him go," I said.

She took her hand away; all of us just let go, and David left. It was as simple as that. His breathing stopped for the last time, and it was like a rush of wings, something tangible soaring upwards and away.

When he was young, David had announced that he hated regular funerals—he probably got that, as I had, from our grandfather's service—and that he thought a Viking funeral would be just the thing.

We couldn't do that for him, but we marked our loss as we thought he would have approved. The music was what he had loved, both classical and modern. Scores of people, young and old, came together on the patio of the Main House, under the open sky. Those who spoke had known him; no strangers mouthed platitudes. Wali, the

110

Arabian horse David had raised from a foal and ridden for years, was led out caparisoned in a beaded Indian headstall but without saddle or rider, led in a slow walk to the pasture where he was set free to run across the green earth with the fire of the sun in his chestnut coat.

Only the family, a few close friends, and the Tribe went to the graveyard, but even there, the funeral was different. A friend who was a folk singer sang about thinking of David in all the living things around us, not in death; as he sang, "When you see a white dove flying high, think of him," a flock of white doves passed so close overhead that some people thought they had been released on purpose. They hadn't.

The Tribe gave last gifts, beads and baubles typical of that time, and these went into the grave.

We returned to the ranch and the rest of the people to break bread, drink wine, dance, laugh, and weep under the sun. Our talisman hawk, the red-tail with the notch in one wing, circled above us. He had watched the rides through the forest, the picnics by Pony Pond, the quiet times at the magic meeting place in the small woods at the south end of the pond. It was fitting that he should be watching on that day. I do not believe either our joys or sorrows were known to him. Perhaps he had watched and followed because the stir of our passage flushed out game for him. Perhaps he was just curious at the color and movement below. Or perhaps we had simply become nonthreatening, familiar, reassuring features of his landscape. But for whatever we gave him, he offered more. He gave us the sense of being part of the wild things. He gave us the illusion of a guardian. And on the day of the funeral, he gave us blessing in the memory of all the days of life before Death came.

Despite the many women David had courted so well, he had truly loved only one, someone he had met while in college in Northern California. But it had been a matter of times out of joint, of her wanting to settle while he was still

111

compelled to wander. Eventually, she had married someone else, but she traveled more than five hundred miles to be at the funeral. I took her into David's quarters so that she could see the only photographs he had there were of her. She stood in the middle of the room and shrieked, "You bastard! How could you die and leave me here all alone?" The grief, rage, and love in those words haunt me still. Her life was elsewhere, with other people, but that did not ease her loneliness.

For a long time after he died, I had nightmares in which I urged David to put on a jacket because it was cold, to eat because he was thin, and a host of other mundane instructions, all the while knowing he was dying. I knew it was the last vestige of the older sister fighting against a force no one could defeat, but that didn't make the dreams any less terrible.

At first I tried to reconcile the loss in my mind, tried to make sense of it, and then I accepted that it would never make sense to me, that I would never cease to feel anger and grief over the loss, and that acceptance kept me sane. Part of grief is always selfish. In losing David, I lost the confirmation and witness of childhood. What is important and memorable to children is often overlooked or forgotten by adults who were there at the time. With David gone, there was no other voice to say, "Yes, I remember that, that's how it happened." It has been seventeen years since I have heard that voice; I miss it still. I miss the brother and the friend he had become.

With all of this, I would not have had him live one second longer than he did in such agony. His body failed, medicine failed, but he never did. And it was time and past for the suffering to end.

Before he died, I wrote a poem about him, "My Once Wild Brother." A few lines of it are on his tombstone in the cemetery near the peach trees. The last verses are these:

MY ONCE WILD BROTHER

I shut down my senses
and cry the lie I know is true,
not you, my once wild brother, not you.

The Buddha dies in Asian jungles,
the Irish hunt the Christian dove,
Allah's children kill each other;
the fable continues, "God is love."

But it is only you
I would ask this blind God to see:
my once wild brother, may you go free.

He did go free, and free he still is. He never grew old
or discouraged. His own voice was silenced, but I and all
who remember him so vividly speak often of him, with
laughter, with tears, with love.

RESERVATIONS

Chapter 4

DO NOT STEAL THE BEACH TOWELS

Through all the other commercial endeavors attempted here, the guest ranch kept chugging along. It had been started in the thirties when a few people came to the ranch for a respite and stayed long enough to pay rent. Going to Europe in those Depression days was much more difficult than it is now, and it got harder as fascism spread.

The glamour days of the Hollywood crowd were over by the time I was born just after the war, though recognizable celebrities appeared now and again. And a lot of people who visited were interesting characters, even if they weren't widely known.

The ranch was open all year, but the climate made some months lean. At nearly three thousand feet, there are four distinct seasons, and winter can be very cold and blustery. The best time of year for ranch bookings began with Easter week and went through Labor Day; though it may snow at Easter and fall weekends can be very warm. Some people were aware of that and made those weekends busy, and New Year's Eve was always fully reserved, to the point that many guests made their plans a year in advance.

As the business had grown, various accommodations were added, some part of the Main House or nearby and of the same style, with thick adobe walls, tile or wooden floors, tile roofs, and wood-beamed ceilings. Two buildings past the pool were of a different type, rather low and rambling, with good sitting room on the porches.

Walter Catlett, a comedian, was responsible for the name of one. He had a sly sense of humor, and he helped so much in the building that it was eventually named for him (at the time, many rooms were named after their more famous occupants). There are various accounts, but according to Grandma, he asked her if the building could be called the Cat House, after him, and she thought that a fine idea. Straight-faced, he told her he would be honored. It was years before Grandma learned what a cathouse was, but by then the name was irrevocable.

Handmade quilts covered the beds, books filled the shelves in the rooms, but there were never telephones, radios, or televisions. Guests were expected to entertain themselves and each other without help from the outside world. This was a place for "getting away from it all."

In some families, the tradition of vacations at the ranch went through the third generation. But there was a problem in appealing to this segment of the population because they were only free to travel when the children were out of school or on weekends, so there was a firm line between the times when we, the children of the ranch, could look forward to seeing people of our own ages, and those weeks when young visitors were rare. New Year's Eve was strictly adults only with the exception of the homegrown children. I enjoyed that. It seemed a special privilege to be there.

Meals were family style, announced by the "first bell" fifteen minutes before the meal time, and the "last bell" rung at 9:00 A.M., at 1:00 P.M., and at 6:30 P.M. Lord help you if you missed the final call and tried to wander in later. Breakfast and dinner were served; only lunch was buffet, so tardiness was easy to spot.

Advance reservations were required, and guests' names and addresses were kept on file cards. Grandma, Mother, and Aunt Donna each had access to the corners. If guests had corners cut off the card, it indicated that those guests were too rude, crude, or whatever to be welcome again. Being rude to the "Help" was a sure way to lose one or more corners, as was being too picky or demanding about the rustic accommodations. Actually, I suspect I might well have been the sort of guest who would have been discouraged from future visits. The ranch mattresses were notoriously bad and the bath towels skimpy, but complaints about these defects were not welcomed. On the other hand, the meals were gargantuan and generally delicious, except for the Friday night fish served in deference to the Catholics. Fish had to travel too far to get to the middle of the desert. Even now, in the age of advanced transportation and freezing techniques, fish from local markets can be a chancy business.

The bad fish had its bright side, however. It was the spark of one of the best romances the ranch created. Charles and Kelly had both been married before; their respective spouses had died; and Kelly had a small daughter, a good job at the studios in Hollywood, and no plans to be married again. Charles had been devoted to his first wife, so I don't think he was looking either. But he had been to the ranch before, so on a Friday night, he asked Kelly to dine in town with him, warning her that the fish at the ranch was inedible.

Their marriage endured until he died. When I knew them, they were both white-haired, and they still looked at each other as if the most marvelous miracle was occurring right then, in that instant. It's almost enough to put in a good word for bad fish.

Fish is apropos in another sense. Many of the guests who most loved the ranch were careful never to tell others about it. They regarded it much the same as a private fishing hole, and they didn't want others to muddy the waters, particularly should their referrals misbehave, which would result in the referrers losing corners from their own cards. The idea of having Mrs. Campbell demanding to know why they had sent certain miscreants to the ranch was enough to make many guests hesitant to refer anyone at all. It was worse when they had found a unique niche. In those cases, they felt they were so special, not even their best friends, let alone relatives, could perform so well. It was flattering in a way, but it was deadly for advertising and expanding the guest list.

Still, even with these limitations, over the years thousands of people stayed at the ranch. Some never came back for a second visit, but many returned again and again, and there were those who regarded it as the one unchanging factor in their lives, a place that allowed them to touch some point of innocence and hope in themselves, a way of being safe, childlike when childhood had long since passed.

For the ranch children, the guests fell into several categories. Some guests were just pests, people who returned again and again but complained constantly. However, their complaints were of such a set nature, they didn't lose corners, and no one paid any attention. But in their own way, these specimens were interesting. Ninety-nine percent of the time it was the wife who vocalized the complaints, but I learned that very often this was because she was delegated the task by the husband and accepted it.

At the pool, I would hear the husband say, "We really need more towels," and not too much later, the wife would be in the office saying, "We really need more towels." Or it would be about the food, the heaters, the swamp coolers (loud, demanding hulks of machinery, which were eventually replaced by air conditions), whatever—and the chain of command was usually the same. I came to believe that most of the women were so happy to be away from household chores, they didn't care nearly as much about the details as the men did, but they did think domestic tranquility was their responsibility, even when on vacation.

Some pest guests were parents who were horrified when confronted with the possibilities of trouble available to their children. These were inevitably city folks who probably dealt easily with bumper-to-bumper traffic and muggers at home but who took one look at the open space and the wildlife of the ranch and feared their offspring were going to be lost in the jungle if they weren't watched every minute.

The classic example of this was Annie. She was ten years old, precocious, and bratty. She was intelligent enough to have her rather dull, timid parents completely buffaloed. The father dropped Annie and her mother off and went back to work, planning to rejoin his wife and child for the following weekend.

The first thing the mother asked was, "What are the things that Annie shouldn't do?"

My aunt Donna thought for a moment and then said, "Well, she shouldn't play Ping-Pong before eight in the morning because it wakes the guests who have rooms near the Ping-Pong table."

"Oh, no," the woman protested. "I mean what should she be careful of, so she won't get hurt."

Donna had already taken Annie's measure and couldn't think of anything on the ranch that could intimidate this particular child, though she did suggest that Annie stay out of the corrals.

"What about rattlesnakes?" the woman asked. "Annie learned how to identify them at camp."

"We *never* see rattlesnakes here," Donna told her. She was on firm ground; the last rattlesnake sighting near the buildings had been when David and I were very small, and

121

though we were sure of what we'd seen, the sighting was not listed as official.

A couple of days later, Annie was on the front lawn when she saw a cat stalking something in the grass. She went over to investigate and announced very calmly, "Yep, it's a rattlesnake all right."

It was, probably courtesy of a load of firewood that had been brought in recently, though Grandma said it wouldn't surprise her if Annie had brought it with her.

Domestic or imported, the snake was dispatched by another guest, an elderly man who had been coming to the ranch for years and had heretofore not been viewed as the rugged type. But that rattlesnake aroused primitive feelings in him, and he whacked off the snake's head with a garden hoe.

Though Annie's father joined his wife and daughter for the weekend as planned, they did not return for other visits. I suppose they thought if we'd lied about the rattlesnakes, God knew what other hazards were awaiting their precious child.

One of my most unfavorite type of guest was the cheek pincher. These were white-haired ladies who believed that pinching a child's cheek while cooing was a sign of affection. In fact, sometimes it bordered on abuse; those pinches could leave one's cheeks sore for days. I think this practice was hardest on me and on my cousin Scott. As the first grandchild and the last, we got the bulk of this ill treatment.

The white-haired brigade, even those who did not pinch cheeks, had set things they said to children. At age two or so, I was standing by one of these women out on the patio. I looked up at her and said, "I have a granddaughter just your age at home."

I had heard that so often, I thought it was a greeting, a lengthy version of "Hello, how are you?" This particular woman had a keen sense of humor and reported the incident to my mother.

Some guests were simply stupid. My mother was furious when, after searching frantically, she found me with my mouth stuffed with candy given to me by a guest who had nothing more to say than, "Oh, isn't she cute!" Candy was not a regular part of our diet except when earned in small bits during the reading lessons, and Mother said she was tempted to put a sign around my neck, "Please don't feed the child."

Being involved, however peripherally, in a business such as the guest ranch, was a good way to learn that not all adults are smart enough to be let out on their own.

Behind the long, low milking barn, there was a huge, drafty traditional barn, complete with a hayloft with a rope for swinging. Cats and mice lived in a state of constant war, and birds and bats nested in the rafters. Sometimes I went there with the rest of the gang, but quite often, I went by myself. I didn't like the spiders or the wasps, but in spite of them, the barn was irresistible, like Genesis, dark with the light just beginning, filtering through the holes in the roof and the open stall doors, with life stirring in every corner, so much life that even the barn air was different, so rich it was just this side of explosive. The dairymen kept the newest calves there, feeding them after they had taken them from their mothers, whose sole function was to produce milk rather than to wean their calves over time and hence dry out their udders. Most of the calves were sold, but some were kept and raised to join the milking herd. And the barn was also the maternity ward. Although many of the cows gave birth out in the corrals, if the dairymen noticed labor in time, they brought them into the barn. Sometimes the calf or the cow died; sometimes both did. Life and death were right there.

The dairymen weren't too fastidious. Though they kept the milking area clean, they didn't muck out the barn pens that often. The air was pierced by ammonia and the general organic soup. It's no stretch for me to believe that the primordial world smelled just like that.

Though farm raised, I never lost my fascination for the birthing process. The birth of foals at the ranch was rare by my time, but calves came every spring, and it never seemed less than wonderful to watch the cows produce their exquisite offspring. The cows were so common in their daily treks to the milking stanchions, but they were changed entirely when they gave birth. There was enormous effort, but unless something is very wrong, cows give birth quickly compared to humans, and it is all there to witness. The calf drops out, encapsulated in the birthing sack, still not part of the world, and then the mother's rough tongue baptizes and frees it. The bonding is visible, the calf's first uncertain steps an affirmation of life.

I had enjoyed this communion since I had first been allowed to wander the ranch. The dairymen were used to seeing me and the other children in the barn and would salute us with cheerful words in Portuguese, but one day, some guests took offense.

I was sitting on a hay bale, minding my own business and watching a delivery, when four guests walked in. They were a bit taken aback by the fragrant life that greeted them, but they were truly appalled to find me there, and they talked about me as if I wasn't there at all.

"My God, she shouldn't be here!"

"Maybe her parents don't know where she is." Etc., etc., etc.—more perfectly ridiculous phrases.

Then there was direct communication, and I admit, they lost points by not knowing who I was. "Little girl, you really shouldn't be here."

I was so affronted, I hardly knew what to say, and beyond that, I thought these adults were so stupid, they might be dangerous.

I stood up and faced the chief speaker, a big, white-haired, florid-faced man of the type that appears as the country squire on PBS programs purchased from England. "I live here," I told him. "I always come to watch the calves being born." And then I left.

I hope my right to be there intimidated those people, but I have no way of knowing. I avoided those couples until they left because I thought they were nasty people. I still do. I still think that anyone who believes it unhealthy for children to witness the cycles of birth and death on a farm and thus to learn are nasty people who must shutter the sparrows in the eaves to prevent life from leaking out.

I don't think those people ever came back to the ranch. Doubtless the life here was too bawdy for them.

Some guests were dull or boorish, but many brought glimpses of other worlds and exotic lives with them.

An Englishwoman who stayed for a week was a true member of the Raj. Her late husband had been a colonel in the British army, and they had spent most of his career in India and Africa. In England, her accent would have betrayed lower class origins and none of the "right" schools, but the foreign postings had allowed her to live like a lady surrounded by servants.

She was not as insensitive as she might have been, appreciating the beauty of the far lands and the dignity of the various nationalities. But she had no illusions about the melding of those peoples.

"The Indians and the British were polite enough to each other, but we never really got to know each other. We never really mixed. I'm sorry for that, for there were Indians I would have like to have known better, and Africans, too."

She had a stuffed sausage sort of figure with tiny hands and feet that seemed to be evidence of a smaller body in the past. She wore a brassy blond, tightly curled wig, big beads around her neck, floral print dresses, and she carried a varnished straw handbag. She moved with the dancing lightness some fat people display.

She told wonderful tales of treks through jungles and

125

of sampling dishes quite unlike those found in English kitchens.

"I ate monkey once that I know of," she said, "though it was probably served at other times, and I just didn't guess. It wasn't unlike chicken. But you see, we were miles into the backcountry with bearers and a cook and other staff, and as we were eating, my husband asked how the cook had managed to bring a chicken. Of course, we realized he hadn't brought a chicken at all, and when we asked about the meat, the servants were very proud to tell us it was freshly caught monkey. Quite dreadful to think of eating one of those creatures when one wasn't raised on it, though it really isn't very different from eating poultry, beef, or lamb."

I suspect the basic calm and common sense of her nature had stood her in good stead even though she had lived much of her life away from the culture of her birth. She proved herself strong and capable even during her short stay at the ranch. She was a gifted raconteur, and though Grandma appreciated that talent in men, she was not willing to share the spotlight with a woman, with rare exceptions. She was jealous to the point of being obviously rude to the Englishwoman, but the latter didn't seem to notice, which was the best defense.

A Frenchwoman was not such a cheerful sort, but she was no less fascinating. She carried letters from Sarah Bernhardt with her. The letters had been written to a male relative, a cousin a generation or so back, I believe. Supposedly, the "Divine Sarah" had had a brief fling with this man and had then cast him off, leaving him to go nearly mad with grief and to disgrace his family with his hysterical devotion to the actress.

Actually, I think those letters were genuine, but that doesn't explain why she carried them with her. Perhaps World War II had taught her to travel with saleable items. She had done it before.

I was a young teenager by the time she came to the ranch, and I was very interested in the war. She was anxious to relate the story of her escape, and that she still spoke with a pronounced French accent added to the flavor.

"My husband, he was much older. It was a marriage arranged by my parents. My husband, he had a château off of the coast, on its own island. It was near where the Boche had their submarine pens, so, of course, the officers demanded a good place to stay. I went to Canada with my two children. We brought with us paintings we had cut from the frames at the château, a Gauguin, a Monet, and others. The Canadian officials did not even find them, rolled up as they were in our luggage, and by the sale of these works, I and my children were able to have a new life."

It made sense up to a point, but the husband was missing. I asked about him.

"Oh, but he stayed at the château so that the Germans would not destroy it."

"You mean he was there with the Germans?"

"If he had not stayed, they would have treated the property badly," she insisted.

"Yes, but didn't that make him a collaborator?"

At that, the venom poured out. "Of course not! It was his family home! If he had not stayed, the Boche would have blown it up or destroyed it some other way. And what did it matter what we French did anyway? All those lives lost in the First World War, but it was England and the United States who decided everything afterwards, not France. Why should France have fought at all in the Second World War? It was going to be just the same again, England and the United States taking everything, deciding everything!" she spat out the words. "When the Second World War began, the French army had nothing, not even enough shoes or blankets, and the young men, they were not ready to fight. And the Germans marched in."

For me, coming from a family of Anglophiles whose

English friends had given up appeasement when Chamberlain failed, this was a startling view of World War II. And I never fully understood the Frenchwoman. She did go on to say that she had never been reunited with her elderly husband, though he and his great house had both survived the war. All in all, it is very odd that she would tell me so much. I've never been sure what it was in aid of—the French collapse in face of the Nazi invasion, or her own defection from husband and country? And perhaps carrying the Bernhardt letters was a matter of status, a way to prove that in the country she had come from, she had had some claim to prominence. Then again, perhaps she was totally nuts, the letters were forgeries, and she actually hailed from Kansas City and had acquired the accent in high school French classes.

With guests there were a lot of intriguing questions that were never answered.

Long before the Englishwoman or the Frenchwoman, there was Gwen Polkinghorn. I thought her name alone was magic. In those days, it sounded like an American Indian name to me, like Running Bear or Leaping Deer. In reality, it is a very English name meaning "dweller at a pool of chalybeate water," according to Smith's *New Dictionary of American Family Names*. And Gwen had acquired it by marriage.

To my brother and me, Gwen was a gift. She was frail looking and wispy, with dark red hair and makeup applied as it was in the twenties—the dark outline of red lips, the slim arch of brows. She would have looked wonderful in a flapper's dress, but she had two modes of apparel. She wore either ultrafeminine, drapey frocks with flowing scarves or very businesslike shirts and tailored riding pants. In the 1950s, when I knew her, she must have been in her forties, or perhaps early fifties, though in my mind as a child she was simply an adult.

Despite her delicate appearance, Gwen was tough. She

was the only person, male or female, I knew then who regularly traveled to rugged archaeological sites all over the world. She was a good horsewoman, a good climber, and a splendid guide.

She always arrived with plans for exploration, and David and I greeted her with the sure knowledge that adventures were in the offing.

Once she came during the rainy season and the river was higher than usual, so she went to town and bought a tin bathtub at a junkyard. We hauled it down to the river and launched it. It had several leaks and wouldn't have been very seaworthy anyway. It floated a tiny bit and then grounded in the shallows. It didn't matter. We had a fine time pretending we were sailing off as Gwen pointed out the imaginary sights along the way.

As familiar as the ranch was to me, it was made new through Gwen's eyes. In the rocks of the Narrows, she pointed out metates used by Indians to grind grain, and she found seashells embedded in the stones.

She gestured out over the flat of the desert, over the mountains beyond. "All of this was once covered by the sea, all of it." The story of creation had never seemed more real.

Gwen was a terrific role model because she could appear so elegantly female at one moment and then be all practicality for a march through the bush. And she knew about so many different cultures that things in museums became recognizable because she had talked about them, such as the little glass bottles, iridescent with the patina of age, that Roman women were said to have used to collect their tears when their husbands went off to war, and, a world away from ancient Rome but the legendary equivalent in the western U.S., the obsidian drops called Apache tears.

Gwen's jewelry was as unique as she was, much of it purchased on her travels; so much of it was probably more valuable for ethnic origins and design than for the stones and metal, though that is not a judgment I can be sure of at this distance. Some of it was valuable by any measure, and one ring had a story that has haunted me ever since I heard it.

Eight of Gwen's closest friends were at her house for dinner. One of the guests admired a precious ring Gwen was wearing. I think the piece was new. Gwen took off the ring and passed it to the person who had first noted it. Others in the group exclaimed over it, and it was passed along. Conversation went on. And the ring never came back to her. When she suddenly realized that and asked where it was, no one had anything to say.

My grandmother maintained that Gwen should have announced that she was going to turn out the lights and that whoever had the ring was to put it on the coffee table and no questions would be asked. If the ring did not appear, she would call the police and have everyone searched. Otherwise, every one of the eight would remain a suspect forever, which is what happened.

Gwen was a much gentler soul than my grandmother and was so shocked that some close friend had taken the ring, she was just too numb to take any action at the time. The ring was never found. The friendships were never the same.

There came a time when Gwen no longer visited the ranch. I was so used to people drifting in and out of our lives that I didn't question it. Now, looking back, I know it was because she remarried, and her life changed. She and her new husband settled in New York. As for the old husband, I don't remember him at all, so either she was already divorced or widowed when we knew her, or he didn't come to the ranch with her, or he had no interest at all in David and me and was thus invisible. My grandmother did keep track of Gwen until she died, and other members of the Polkinghorn clan continued to visit the ranch for years after Gwen had ceased to come.

Gwen's talent for making the exotic accessible while enhancing the luster of the familiar is with me still. I suspect she had much to do with the fascination David and I shared for museums; she had sparked our interest in various cultures before we saw the artifacts on shelves. I know she added to my passion for the ranch. Grandma gave me knowledge of the flora and fauna, but Gwen set the land in its wider context, traced it back and then forward again, out of the receding waters and on until ancient peoples came alive as she conjured them.

Gwen's legacy was richer than most, but many guests and tenants left indelible marks on our lives, and most were people we would not have met at all had it not been for the ranch.

Ned Sparks, the comedic actor known for his deadpan expression, retired here with his daughter, Laura. Ranch residents considered it a great coup to make Ned laugh because he was so determined not to. But when mirth did over come him, it spilled out uproariously, as if to make up for all the times he repressed it.

When they first moved to the desert in the late 1940s, Laura said it seemed as if they were going to the Wild West. Her father had given her fine pieces of jewelry, commemorations of this or that finished movie, but she left them behind in a safe-deposit box in the city, rather than risk taking them out to the country.

The safe-deposit section of the bank was robbed, with Laura's jewelry taken in the haul. Much of it was unique, having been specially designed at Ned's behest. Months after the robbery, a close friend of Laura's was at a party when she spotted a distinctive emerald bracelet on a stranger's wrist. It was unmistakably one of the pieces of jewelry that had been stolen.

The friend reported the find to Laura, but nothing was done. Laura was sure that the woman who now had the emeralds had had no part in the robbery. By gift or purchase, the woman believed she owned an honest bracelet.

Jewels are connected with another Hollywood notable, Eduardo Ciannelli. He and his wife, Alma, came to the ranch for years and were close friends of the family. My mother stayed at their house in Brentwood right before I was born in order to be close to a hospital, there being none up here.

Eduardo was from Italy, from a prominent family on the island of Ischia. He was supposed to become a doctor, but he liked opera singing and then acting much better. He became a character actor, popular for decades in film and theater and later on, in television as well. He was a handsome man with dark eyes and hair and strong bones, but he was definitely foreign looking, the cadence of his English was different, and he could easily look sinister—a man one would not want to cross. It was a role he perfected with glaring eyes.

He was the fanatic who jumped into the snake pit in *Gunga Din.* He was countless mobsters who killed other mobsters, policemen, and anyone who got in their way. He was so well-known for this that he and some likewise famous "heavies" got together for an episode of "The Man from Uncle," doing a tongue-in-cheek story about aging gangsters trying to tunnel into the Vatican for treasure. He was, in the tradition of Hollywood's bizarre ethnic casting, a murderous American Indian (and occasionally a noble American Indian) involved in one war after another against the cavalry. He was also sometimes the craven town official or the one on the lifeboat who endangered everyone else.

There was never a clearer case of life not imitating art. Eduardo was the gentlest, most courtly man I have ever known. It was as if he had come from another age. He lived his life with intelligence, courage, and great good humor, characteristics that few of the men he portrayed possessed.

It was pure joy to hear and watch him tell a story, for he acted out all of the parts, his voice changing, his face displaying one emotion after another, his hands cradling, sculpting the words.

He adored Alma, and she him. She was American born, from an old-line New York family, but it was she, not he, who was singled out as an enemy alien at the outbreak of World War II. Eduardo was by then a naturalized American citizen, but Alma was seen as dangerous for having married an Italian. She had never even been to Italy at this point, and eventually the government was convinced of her innocence. Eduardo thought this very amusing, though Alma of course did not.

Eduardo was just as willing to laugh when he was the butt of the joke. Once when he and Alma were staying here, she awakened him in near hysteria, telling him a mouse had run across the bed, touching her hair. Instead of being sympathetic, Eduardo chided her for being so silly. The next day as they were driving back to the city, he reached into his pocket for something and found the mouse instead. The mouse hopped out, more frantic now than he had been in the room the night before, and it is a wonder that the Ciannellis managed to stop the car and let out the unwanted passenger without harm to any of the parties. Eduardo added this to his repertoire of funny stories, and he was always sure to point out how right Alma had been and how the mouse would never have gotten into his pocket had he listened to her.

I believe *The Secret of Santa Vittoria,* filmed in Italy, was the last major film Eduardo did, playing one of the town officials. He died not many days after the film was completed. Alma had died not long before. He had come to say good-bye before he went back to Italy. He loved to bird hunt, and he gave my father a fine over-and-under shotgun. To each of the women, to me, Grandma, Mother, and Aunt

Donna, he presented a piece of Alma's jewelry, telling us to remember her because she had loved us as much as we had loved her.

The jewelry was beautiful—precious, unique pieces he had given to Alma as celebrations of his theatrical triumphs, just as Ned had given jewels to Laura. Grandma's gift was a set of antique mosaic earrings and brooch, the inlay microscopically fine. Gold, pearls, and diamonds adorned these and the pins that went to my mother and my aunt. And I received a double-strand necklace of black-and-white baroque pearls. The rest of Alma's treasures were put in a safe-deposit box in a bank in Italy, to be given to her granddaughter, Caterina, when she turned eighteen.

One week before Caterina's eighteenth birthday, she and her stepmother Genou went to the bank to look at the jewelry Alma and Eduardo had left to their granddaughter. Caterina was justifiably excited about the collection, but before her birthday dawned, the bank was robbed.

In Laura's case, I believe the robbers came in through the ceiling. In Caterina's, they came through the floor. Ironically, it was a scenario Eduardo could have played to perfection in a film. The robbers were, it is said, among the best in Europe, and they came together a couple of weeks before the crime, renting the space next door with the announced intention of opening something innocuous such as a dry cleaning business. It gave them the perfect excuse for renovations—for covering up the tunneling.

Because Caterina and Genou had seen the jewelry so shortly before the robbery, they were able to give very detailed descriptions and to recognize some things that were found, but those were only the refuse, a few rings without the stones.

So far away, we would never have known any of this. It is not the sort of news we exchange with Louis, Caterina's father, and Genou in Christmas cards and other long-distance communications. But we visited them in Rome just after the robbery had occurred.

It haunted me that Caterina would never have her grandmother's treasures, jewels that marked her grandfather's illustrious career. A small step toward a solution was obvious, and Grandma, Mother, and Aunt Donna all agreed without hesitation, so the next time Louis and Genou were in the United States, we gave them the jewelry that Eduardo had given us, and they took it back to Caterina.

Emil Danenberg eventually became president of Oberlin College, but when my family first met him, he was a student at UCLA, a musical prodigy who had given his first concert in Hong Kong at the age of five. He was also a gymnast, and in a fall from the parallel bars, he injured his neck. He went to a chiropractor, who did not realize that a small neck bone was broken, and through manipulation, the chiropractor worsened the condition. Emil began to experience numbness in one hand and arm, especially terrifying for a pianist. Surgeons performed a unique operation on him, grafting bone and restoring feeling to his arm and hand, and his case was written up in medical journals. However, the doctors knew they would not be able to preserve the mobility of his neck. He had a choice of being upright or permanently bent over. He chose the latter, so that he could see the keyboard of the piano; as the years passed, the unnatural curve took a harsh toll on him, decreasing the air capacity of his lungs and putting a constant strain on other organs, muscles, and bones. But as far as I know, he never regretted his decision. Music flowed through every cell; music danced from his fingers.

He was such a brilliant pianist, that would have been enough had that been all there was of him, but he was a Renaissance man. He knew a vast amount about literature,

history, art, wine, food, and baseball. He and his wife, Mary
Ann, also a musician, traveled extensively and lived in
Europe for long stretches. She adored Emil and eased his
way wherever they went, for with the odd, immobile angle
of his neck, such seemingly simple things as crossing a street
could be hazardous for Emil, who could not turn his head
enough to see oncoming traffic.

I wish I could claim that I always knew what a spectacular man Emil was, but the truth is that he terrified me when
I was little. Small and stooped, he wasn't much taller than
I, and he had bright, protuberant blue eyes, a great shock
of black hair, a wide mouth, and a wild laugh. I got him
confused with the trolls I'd read about in fairytale books,
and couldn't understand how the adults could be so stupid
as to fail to identify a troll in their midst. But I took good
care to warn my brother.

"Stay away from him! Trolls eat children."

Poor Emil, it must have hurt his feelings dreadfully to
see us recoiling from him, but time passed, the trolls with-
drew into the mists of the far north country where they
belong, and David and I grew to value the friendship of the
Danenbergs. When we traveled with them in Europe, we
could not have wished for better companions.

Cade, a character in *The Tiger's Woman,* was created
as an apology and a tribute to Emil.

Many people whom we first met because of the ranch became important parts of our lives, separate from the business. If I were to list them all, this would read like the phone
book. But one family became so vital to my life, I finished
the first draft of my first novel at their house.

The McRaes brought their children to the ranch for
years; their son, Peter, is my age; their daughter, Marcia,
my brother's age. But aside from that, the match was, out-
wardly at least, a strange one.

"Big Pete" was from the South, a good ol' boy, and a

career marine besides. It sounds like the perfect recipe for a male chauvinist, never my favorite beast. I probably wouldn't have liked him much in his early, hotshot days, but by the time I knew him well, he had been mellowed by life, by his own kind soul and sense of humor, and by Bonnie, his wife.

Pete and Bonnie easily did what my own family could not. They hugged and kissed and said, "I love you, I'm proud of you," right out loud. They had so much love to give that "Little Pete" and Marcia never, as far as I know, felt any animosity toward me and the other strays who received so much love from Pete and Bonnie.

If ever there was a cuckoo in a wren's nest, it was I in the McRae family. The McRaes are short. Bonnie and Marcia border on tiny, and the men would be considered tall only in southern Italy or Japan. At five feet nine and a half inches, I am a tall woman everywhere with the possible exception of Sweden.

Big Pete and Little Pete were so named only for the fact that one was the father and the other the son. Little Pete is actually taller than his dad, but he is still not quite my height. That should give you an idea of how ungainly it looked when Big Pete hugged me just as he did his own children. But if I sometimes felt clumsy and giraffelike, he never betrayed any unease (though I did have to teach him the difference between the words *big* and *tall);* nor did Bonnie. As far as they were concerned, I was another of their children, as entitled to hugs and praise as anyone.

I still lived in my parents' house when I was trying to finish the first draft of *The Night Child,* and it was very difficult for family and friends to understand that I was in desperate need of privacy—working at home is always hazardous. People who would never think of bothering someone at an office think nothing of barging into private quarters with a "this will only take a moment."

Pete and Bonnie pointed out that they were both out of

their house all day at work and that I would be welcome to the quiet there. They lived in Santa Ana, a city in Orange County, about eighty miles from here. I went, and when my own typewriter quit, the McRaes prevailed on a friend to lend me an IBM—the Rolls-Royce of typewriters at the time and still my measure of success.

From early in the morning until the McRaes returned at night, I typed, writing and rewriting. And in the evenings Bonnie and Peter were there to tell me what a fabulous thing they thought it was to write a book, to tell me that they loved me, to say they had every faith that whatever I wanted to do, I would do.

Some gifts are like rainbow light, so spectacular, so rich in the instant, and so difficult to describe afterwards. What the McRaes gave me and continue to give me is a rainbow of love, every color clear, the arch perfectly defined end to end, over the whole landscape of my life. This is no faint glow. This is love shown and spoken constantly in full color without embarrassment or subtleties.

But Big Pete is missing from the configuration. He died a few years ago, a couple of years after my own father. I was devastated by Pete's death. I could not stop weeping, and I could not imagine a world wherein he no longer existed to give me hugs, laughter, and encouragement. But I have come to understand that Pete had a final gift for me. My feelings and relationship with my own father were so complicated, open emotions so forbidden, that even his death could not simplify the mix of love and antipathy. But when Pete died, it was a straightforward loss, and in mourning him, I was able to mourn my own father.

Perhaps there is always something complicated and mythic in dealing with the death of a parent, a loss not only of the present relationship, but also of all that might have been or should have been, all the child's longings that remain even after childhood has long since ended.

Pete's ashes were left to drift away on Pony Pond as the

sun rose. Family and friends, we stood there with the first light touching us. We remembered Pete, and we saluted the celebration he made of life, first to last.

Like most of our other financial endeavors, the guest ranch turned out to be another case of buying high and selling low.

In 1975, Uncle Joe did the figures on his calculator and proved what we had all suspected by then, that the more guests we had, the more money we lost. It was a combination of factors, but the main one was that Grandma had kept the lid on rate hikes for so long, even by the end, guests were paying only twenty-two dollars a day. That included room, meals, and use of the pool, the tennis court—everything except the horses, and the extra charge for an hour or so of riding was only two dollars. By then it also included the use of beach towels that guests stole with impunity. Even friends stole them.

My mother and I were visiting the home of close friends, and Mom needed a towel for her bath. She discovered a cupboard full of ranch beach towels, with the ranch initials and the year of purchase embroidered on each one. It was a bit like Gwen's ring. Neither Mom nor I said anything, and the next time Mom peeked in the cupboard, the towels had been removed. This was probably a routine our host and hostess went through each time we were coming to visit, but this time, they had forgotten to do it before we arrived.

Grandma had never gotten over her unease with "taking in boarders," so it had somehow seemed less embarrassing to charge rates low enough that money could hardly be the issue.

There was a little bit of Grandma in all of us because we couldn't really imagine doubling or tripling the rates and expecting people to pay them. This despite the fact that dude ranches all over the West and Southwest do just that, many of them operating quite successfully on the theory that less is more and should thus cost more.

It was the end of a way of life, but as many of the guest quarters were renovated to be permanent apartments and the tenant population of the ranch grew, so did the peace and stability of life here. Anyone who has ever run an inn or such knows how constant the demands are; it is far easier to manage long-term rentals.

In the end, though she fully approved of the closing, it was hardest for Grandma because whatever her feelings about needing to rent rooms to survive, she lost her ever-changing audience.

She moved into the rooms off the balcony that over-looks the main living room. I asked her how she could bear to live there, over a room so large it was obviously meant to be full of people but no longer was except on special occasions.

"But for me it is," she said. "When I sit by the fire, all the people who are gone come back again. I can see them, I can hear them talking and laughing. The room is never empty." She was eighty-nine by then.

It is not really fair to judge the guest ranch in the same way as the failed beef-cattle, Arabian-horses and other en-deavors, for the guest ranch provided food, lodging, and a way of life to the ranch families as well as to the guests. And it provided us with a kaleidoscope of humanity that varied the pattern of our days in often wonderful ways.

As the years pass, the people come back in memory for me as they did for Grandma. She was right. The Main House is never empty.

Chapter 5

DON'T QUIT ON SATURDAY NIGHT

The general term for the people who worked on the ranch was the "Help." In particular, those who worked the guest ranch business should have been called the "Invaluable."

Guests expected to have clean rooms, plumbing that worked, and huge, well-cooked meals served on time. These were the basics they were paying for, and these sound simple enough, but, as anyone who has ever run a home, let alone a hotel, knows, providing good service and food day after day is a great challenge that depends on a willing crew.

Some of them worked for the ranch for years, and their lives became entwined with ours. Freida, Mary, Alma, Julie, and Katie were among those whom I knew for a long time, and some of their children are now raising families of their own in the valley.

In those chauvinistic days when I was growing up, no one thought it odd to call these grown women "the girls," and there were other aspects that were right out of "Upstairs, Downstairs." The girls had their own pecking order, always headed by the cook. Next in command was the second cook, and after that came the maids in an order that was internally directed by seniority on the job coupled with actual age. They had an honor code that rivaled the old one at West Point. If one didn't do her allotted work or did something untoward that caused trouble, the others quickly made it uncomfortable for the offender. The crews who had worked together for a long time formed ties and routines that allowed them to function more smoothly than most families, although they could also squabble like family members.

When Freida was head cook and Mary was her assistant, they became good friends, but outside forces nearly caused a rift.

For several mornings, Freida came into the kitchen to find that the tidy place she had left the night before was no longer so pristine, considering egg and shell were on the floor. Since on each occasion Mary had still been there when Freida left, she had no choice but to think that Mary was being careless in her preparations for the next day's meals.

Freida kept cleaning up the mess, but finally she lost her temper, left the mess on the floor, and berated Mary when she arrived. "I'm not gonna keep cleanin' up after you! I leave this place all spic and span, but when I come back in the mornin', it's a mess!"

Mary burst into tears, protesting that she had been leaving the kitchen just as clean as Freida had and that she had no idea who was making the mess.

Freida studied the gooey offense a little closer and thought about it. "Well, look at this! The yolks are gone. I do believe we got ourselves a skunk."

They did indeed. My brother found him sound asleep under the big refrigerator, an unbroken egg cradled in his paws, presumably for a snack later in case he couldn't get to the big wire bin where the eggs were kept. He left via the back door with a little urging from my brother and a broom. Everyone was grateful that the skunk did not find it necessary to spray before he exited.

Some of the girls had fascinating personal histories. One had been married to an infamous criminal who had gone to the penitentiary and eventually to the gas chamber for kidnapping women and forcing them to commit sexual acts. Her comment about him was that "he never done nothing to me," and she never believed he committed the sex crimes. He always denied it, too, though he admitted to being a robber.

She was a big, rawboned woman with the kind of earthy beauty that is scarcely recognized any more in this era of plastic surgery. At the time she was with us, she was married to a wizened old man. I don't know whether he'd been born mean or had worked up to it, but by then, he was a master. They had a clutch of pale children who were terrified of him, and he gave Mischief, a Labrador–springer spaniel who was part of our family, a hatred for the ranch pickup and for other trucks that had similarly noisy engines.

It took us a while to discover why Mischief had developed this sudden passion, but one day David and I heard the dog snarling; we followed the sound to find him crouched, ready to launch himself through the windshield of the pickup in order to get to the man. The man was so terrified, he confessed that he had caught Mischief trying to raid a trash can and had kicked him. Lord knows what the man had done to his children. But here, neither dogs nor children are kicked in order to "be larned a lesson." The mean old man ceased to be the ranch handyman, but his wife stayed on for quite some time. Eventually she left to become one of the first women I knew to drive big equipment and at a much higher wage than she could earn as a maid.

She was that kind of woman, enduring and steady on

143

her course no matter what boulders appeared on the path. But I do recognize that something must have gone very wrong somewhere for her to think she deserved the kind of men she had married.

If one of the maids didn't show up for work, things might have been a little hectic, but they could be managed. When a cook defected, it was much more serious. We used to joke about how much the guests ate, even the very skinny ones. Many of them must have dieted for weeks before they came to the ranch.

One cook spent all her spare time and some cooking time making real estate deals on the telephone, and one evening she left the meal cooking in order to perform with some visiting musicians. It was a trying situation, but at least she produced good meals when she put her mind to it.

I remember Bertha clearly because she appeared as I thought a cook ought to appear: massive, a great mound of a woman who enjoyed eating the food as much as preparing it. But she left under extraordinary circumstances. She did not sing or sell real estate, but with Saturday night lamb chops cooking on the grill, she ran away with the local taxi driver, Tiny. Sometimes very large men are called Tiny, but in this case, the nickname was accurate. He couldn't have been more than a few inches over five feet, and he was thin. He was also married, and several hours after the great escape, the wife, who was built more like Bertha than like Tiny—surely a pattern—came looking for him. She thought he was hiding in the Red House with his lover, though in fact the couple was on the way to Las Vegas. The wife broke down the front door to the Red House, where two of the young maids were living and frightened them so badly, they called the police. I don't know whether the wife ever caught up with Bertha and Tiny, but it would have been a formidable brawl if she had.

I can't recall a cook who forbade David and me access

to the kitchen, though she would have been within her rights to do so. In our defense, we were well behaved and not given to pulling hot pots off the stove. I liked standing on the big galvanized tin canister where the flour was stored because I could watch everything from there. There was one brush with danger from that perch. It put me up high enough to reach the kitchen matches, and one day I experimented by lighting one. The cook watched me but didn't interfere until the flame had just singed my fingers. It sounds cruel, but it wasn't. She didn't let me hurt myself, but she wanted me to know how dangerous matches were. I am still extremely careful with them.

Freida was the last cook who worked at the ranch. She was here for years, right up to the day the guest ranch closed. And not only Freida, but her father and mother worked for us, and her daughter served a brief stint before going on to become a bank officer.

The family came from the north country of Wisconsin and are the most versatile people I know. They have farmed and worked in the big woods, in cranberry bogs, and lord knows where else. And they have the best storytelling tradition I've ever encountered. Even the cadences of everyday conversation have a lilt that beckons the listener.

Fred and Alma, "Elme," were Freida's parents, and I can hear the two of them telling the story in a chorus that turned a disaster into a tall tale.

The camper they used for trips had come to grief, nearly taking them with it.

"Now, I told him to get the flashlight," Alma said, "cuz there was sure enough the smell of gas in there, and it was so dark an' all. But oh, no, he jus' went an' lit that match."

"I didn't smell no gas," Fred insisted, "but it was there all right. Soon as I lit that ol' match, the whole thing went, blewed Elme's socks right off without takin' her shoes."

145

Fortunately, the socks and the roof of the camper were the only losses.

Alma and Fred went on for years together, they and their children and in-laws becoming integral parts of the community. But then Alma fell ill and died, and Fred began to drift in his mind. Everyone made an effort to ease his loneliness, but he had no center without Alma.

For a few years after her death, Fred made an annual pilgrimage back to Wisconsin for deer hunting, and each time he'd say, "Well, this time I'm probably gonna stay back there."

"That's right, Pa, you just settle back there if that's what you want," Freida would tell him, never pointing out that each year his stay in the woods of his youth grew shorter. The last year he went, he hardly had time to get there before he turned around and came back west. Freida understood. Her father was looking for the friends and the peaceful, isolated country of long ago, but he was finding that the solitude had been broken by newcomers and that the old faces were gone.

I was out riding on the ranch when Fred was killed. I waved at both trains, and then as I came to the crossing, I saw that the northbound train was screeching to a stop and that its front engine had the ranch pickup wrapped around it. Fear is such a visceral beast. The mare I was riding suddenly seemed to be two hundred hands high. Climbing down took forever. My brother had been driving the truck that morning, and at first all I could think was that he had been hit. By then there were railroad men on the other side of the train, pacing up and down and speaking into two-way radios.

"We've got a dead man here," one of them said. "We'll need the police."

"Please, is the man old or young?" I called, but no one answered me. And then I saw Fred's old hat, crumpled beside the tracks. He had made the fatal mistake all of us

146

dread—letting one train pass and then crossing without waiting to see if there is another coming from the opposite direction.

I had a Good Samaritan that day. Mr. Jacques, who rented the dairy facilities for his herd, drove up on my side of the tracks, and I told him what had happened. I wanted desperately to go home, but I had the mare to worry about, and I was too numb to consider riding her down along the tracks to cross her where the stopped train wasn't blocking the way.

I didn't ask Mr. Jacques to help. He took one long look at me and took the reins of my horse. "The train is stopped. It's safe enough, so you just crawl on through and go home," he said.

He must have seen the same thing my mother saw when I got home because, despite the chaos that was beginning to erupt at the Main House, the first thing my mother said was, "My God! What happened to your eyes?"

My eyes, usually a dark, greenish hazel, were bright chartreuse from shock.

Everything happened at once as I arrived at the Main House because Mr. Long, the man who cared for the horses at the time, had heard the report of the accident on a police scanner and had called the ranch to see who had been killed.

Freida knew in that instant, and she rushed out of the Main House. "Oh, Daddy!" She wailed the words on a long note of sorrow.

Trite as it sounds, people do show their true colors in a time of crisis, and Freida and her brother and the other members of their family surely did. Though Freida had left the kitchen in order to tend to all the grisly details of her father's death, she phoned back.

"I left the chocolate for the brownies meltin' on the stove," she said.

"Oh, Freida, do you think we're worrying about that now?" I asked.

"But it's such a waste."

I assured her that the brownies would be finished and lunch cooked.

The next call came from Freida's brother who was worried that because Fred had been killed while working for the ranch, the ranch's insurance rates would be raised unreasonably. "It's not fair," he said. "Pa didn't have no one left to provide for, so his death shouldn't be allowed to cause trouble."

We were far more paralyzed by what had happened than Fred's family was. For them, the worst had happened, but that made no difference in their tradition of responsibility and generosity.

The story was not without precedent in their family. One of Freida's grandfathers had raised a bull calf from its birth so that it behaved more like a big dog than a bull. But his sons worried as the animal matured and began to show signs of knowing his destiny.

"It's dangerous," they told him. "It's startin' to act like a bull, pawin' the ground an' such."

"Now, boys, he'd never hurt us," their father assured them, but his sons were not convinced and gave the bull a wide berth.

Then one day while the man was in the pasture, the bull charged and gored him. As his sons carried him to the house, he said, "You'll have to kill him now 'cuz he can't be trusted with anybody if he'd turn on me." He further instructed them to give the meat to the local orphanage, and then he died.

Sorrow and joy, humor and salt—they are woven together in the fabric of the family's lives and in the stories they tell. I think Freida is the best storyteller of them all, and while she worked here, I wheedled them out of her at every opportunity.

When she first applied for a job, my mother asked if she knew how to cook. Freida was worried that she'd only cooked for farm workers and loggers, but that sounded fine to Mom. Unlike one cook who hadn't known the difference and had put veal, beef, pork, and chicken in the same pot to stew on a Saturday night, Freida had been cooking for large groups of big eaters for years, and her pies, biscuits, and brownies soon became so legendary that, in the case of the brownies, guests had to be warned not to snatch stacks of them for later munching.

The story of her grandfather and the killer bull came up after I had a close brush with a bull out on the ranch. The cattleman who had his herds (beef cattle, not dairy) there had too many bulls for the number of acres and cows, all separated by too-flimsy fences. The bulls were evil-tempered and frustrated to the point where they were charging through the fences in their efforts to get to each other and anything else that moved. That might have been all right for the cattleman who was never on foot but always in his truck or on top of his cutting horse, but I was a pedestrian who had grown very tired of being terrorized.

I complained about it to Freida, expecting that, with all of her farm experience, she wouldn't put much stock in my fear, but she not only told the story of her grandfather, she related the tale of her own run-in with one of the creatures.

"I kept tellin' the men that ol' bull wasn't to be trusted, an' that I didn't want nothin' to do with him, but they jus' said I was a fraidy-cat, and they didn't do nothin' about him. Then one day when they was all gone to town an' I was out doin' my chores, that ol' bull got out an' come after me. I held him off with the pitchfork as best I could, but he was jus' too big an' fast. I'll tell you, if there hadn't been that big pile of manure, I wouldn't be here today. I ran around it one way, then the other, an' that bull got so confused, he jus' stood there for a minute, starin' at the manure, wonderin' which way to go next, an' that gave me time to run into the house. Well, I stayed put, didn't even go out to milk

149

the cows until the men come home, an' they took me serious after that an' kept that ol' bull under control."

When Freida and her family lived in the big woods, they knew people of Danish, Norwegian, Swedish, and Finnish background, along with others who were of English and Scottish blood like themselves. There is geographical logic in that. The forested areas of Northern Europe have traditionally produced people trained to harvest the wood for everything from housing to shipbuilding, as well as producing farmers to work the land when it is cleared. When the British Isles exhausted their own big timber, the virgin trees of North America were there to provide masts and planks for the ships of the Royal Navy and for the mercantile fleet. But despite this tie of similar endeavors, Freida's memories of the life there are of separate groups.

Still shaking her head over the sad case, she told me about Peter and Anna, though it had happened decades before.

"They had themselves a nice little farm, an' I never seed a woman work harder than that Anna. Why, she'd be out milkin' them cows no matter what. An' they always had plenty to eat an' all. But then that ol' Peter went an' blewed his brains out, did it in the house, too. Now, I don't know why he done that, to make such a mess in the house for poor Anna to clean up. If he'd done it outside, it would've been a lot easier for his wife.

"Now, Peter was big, an' there weren't no way Anna could haul him out by herself, an' even with her brother helpin', it weren't enough. So they did somethin' that might've been kindee naughty. Her brother went an' got some liquor an' offered it to some neighbors. You see, seems like them Norwegians don't like goin' in a house where there's a dead body, leastways not when the person kilt hisself. So he gets these fellows kindee drunk, an' they help get that body out. But when they come to bury him, they put his feet up where the head usually goes, 'cuz Peter had messed up his face."

Freida paused. "You know, back home everyone is buried facing toward the East, toward Jerusalem. I do wonder if Peter will be able to get into Paradise when he's called."

Freida wasn't going to keep him out because of suicide, but she had her doubts about him getting in backwards.

One of Freida's many jobs had been seasonal work in a lumber camp. Though the women didn't do the actual logging, they handled the heavy equipment used to load the cut wood into freight cars. To work in the camp, a woman had to be married to one of the men.

"Now, maybe we was bein' kindee naughty," Freida confessed (her "kindee naughty" is a phrase that always indicates something out of the way of ordinary behavior). "But we was all married women, an' we didn't mean no harm. It was jus' that we thought of them freight cars goin' way out west, an' we thought of the lonely bachelors out there, so we decided we'd write our phone numbers in them freight cars, just as a joke, to see if we heard from any of them ol' men. Well, now, one of the women, she was a Finlander and kindee sacrimonious an' she kept sayin', 'No, no I can't do such a thing.' " Freida's voice changed entirely to reflect the lilting sound of the Finlander's voice.

"But we jus' kept after her, tellin' her that nobody would know about it at home, cuz' them freight cars were headin' out west. Finally, she went along, an' we all did it, gigglin' like schoolgirls an' writin' our numbers in them cars. Why, do you know what happened? Weren't but one of them numbers ever got called, an' that was the Finlander's number. That car didn't go out west. It ended up about three miles from where she lived. The stationmaster saw the number, an' he knew her. He called her up an' asked her what in the world she thought she was doin', writin' her number where strange men could find it."

Beyond the stories, Freida and I talked about all sorts of topics, and her observations were always worth listening to.

A couple built on lines similar to Bertha's and Tiny's were going to get married at the ranch. Freida and I confessed to each other that we did find such matches odd, though it didn't seem so when the man was very big and the woman small, a piece of sexism that's hard to avoid.

Freida thought about it some more, and then she said, "Well, you know what they always do say 'bout them Banty roosters and them little Jersey bulls." (Banty roosters and Jersey bulls are both small in stature but potent breeders.)

I once teased Freida that if, by some horrible mistake, she was sent to hell, her punishment would be a prohibition against work. I've never known anyone who likes work more than she. Leisure time is an anathema to her. When she goes back to visit the farmland of her younger days, nothing pleases her more than if she can drive a tractor or offer some other help with crops. This provides an interesting mental picture because, unlike Bertha and despite her abilities as a cook, Freida is slightly built, an odd match for a tractor.

She is in her seventies now, but that doesn't seem to make any difference. Over the years, she and her husband, Art, invested in rental properties all over town. When Art died, the burden of keeping the rentals in repair fell entirely to Freida. She and Art had known each other since she was in second grade and he in eighth, and they had shared life and work together for decades. Many widows would have been overwhelmed; Freida dug in and worked harder to assuage her grief and to manage what she and Art had built together.

Freida will hate this if she reads it, but we came to call her Saint Freida for the domestic miracles she performed.

When my cousin Kemper's wedding was threatened by a power blackout on a hot August evening, it was Freida who found the right fuse to run the air conditioners and the wedding music. When the plumbing failed with a full house, it was Freida who solved the problem. If vital ingredients for the main dish were missing, Freida thought of something else to serve. If Freida couldn't fix it, she could hold back the disaster long enough for the repairman or supplies to get here. Saint Freida.

Freida has always given full credit to her mother for teaching her to cook, and I have firsthand experience of her mother's talent, since her parents sometimes babysat David and me. This was always cause for celebration because Alma would make doughnuts for us. Until then, we believed that doughnuts could be obtained only at a bakery. There is always a price for knowledge. Once we tasted Alma's doughnuts, none from any bakery were ever as good.

Like Fred and Alma, some of our sitters were regular members of the Help, while others were hired just to watch us and to care for the house while Mom worked.

The first one I remember clearly was Julie. In memory, she is very tall and stately, though nearly everyone seems tall when one is very small. I do know she was handsome because I can see her face yet, the bones so clearly defined, the eyes big and dark, the skin soft brown. Sometimes she wore kerchiefs tied around her head. This fashion seemed wonderfully exotic to me because I knew no other woman who dressed this way.

Julie was usually calm in her care of us, no small accomplishment given the fact that my brother was a highly active child whose curiosity led him into endless trouble.

One day he crawled under the Christmas tree to plug in the lights. He was holding both of the metal prongs and plugged them and himself into the current. He couldn't let go. Julie was sweeping nearby, and instead of grabbing him

153

and thus becoming part of the circuit herself, she swept him out of danger with the broom.

The only time I saw Julie panic was when David was taking crackers to a little girl who was visiting us. He tripped on the rug and fell, hitting the corner of the piano bench. Blood gushed out of the cut, and there was so much gore, it appeared that he'd put out his eye. What a procession we made, David streaking down the hill toward the Main House, screaming for Mother, Julie behind him, adding her own lament, and I and the visiting friend bringing up the rear. Julie was as relieved as Mother to discover that the cut was above and had not damaged the eye itself.

Julie also taught my brother and me that skin color is no bar to intelligence and love, and later Katie taught us our first lessons about the stupidity of age discrimination.

Katie came to us at a time when she was so desperately needed, Mother still thinks of her as Mary Poppins. Mother was nearly helpless in a back brace from an attack of arthritis, and Katie took over, arriving early and staying late, taking care of us and cleaning even the unseen tops of things.

Katie had bright eyes, gray hair, and the kindest face, but she wasn't being honest. She had been evasive when Mother was filling out the employment forms. To the request for a social security number, she replied, "Oh, I ain't never had one of them."

Then Mother discovered that the totals in the accounts were being confused because Katie hadn't cashed any of her checks and there was still no social security number, though Katie had promised to get one.

Mom started out with mild inquiries but finally had to insist on an explanation. Finally, her daughter, who worked at the guest ranch, came with Katie for the confession.

Katie wasn't sixty-two, she was over seventy. She had lied about her age, and she feared that getting a social security number or cashing the checks would direct the government's attention toward her. The money wasn't the point, anyway. She was working because she wanted to be useful, wanted to be out with other people. And somehow it was managed. She worked for us as long as she could. She called the ranch "the camp." To her, it seemed like a summer camp even in the winter because of all the comings and goings of the guests.

The last time I saw her, she was dying of cancer, and the whole room spoke of how severe her illness was. But Katie was still beautiful.

I rejoice that it is no longer acceptable to cast away someone because of his or her date of birth.

Many of the Help were extraordinarily kind to the ranch children. They were an important facet of the ranch's uniqueness. They expanded our horizons with the experiences of their lives and, in some cases, with their deaths. I am grateful to all of them for making my life so much richer than it would have been without them.

Chapter 6

THE GENERAL HUMMED

After the publication of *The Night Child,* I received a letter from Harry Cross. He wrote that I probably wouldn't remember him but that he and his family had lived on the ranch for some years and he and I had discovered "The Mickey Mouse Club" together when my grandmother had gotten the first television set on the ranch.

Harry was far too humble in his estimation of the traces he had left. He was remembered in vivid color as the commander of our army and in other guises as well. Every child ought to have the equivalent of a Harry Cross in his or her life.

Harry's father was an official at the local branch of a prestigious bank. Mr. and Mrs. Cross were always cordial enough, but I never really knew them, and I always wondered how they had gotten a son like Harry. Harry had an older brother, Jamie, who seemed as reserved as his parents.

It is a measure of how vast small intervals of time are in childhood. Harry was only a couple of years older than

I, but that gave him immense authority, and Jamie was only a couple of years older than Harry, which made him seem as remote as the moon. Jamie certainly had no interest in the activities of the younger children. It was a shock to see him when he dropped by several years ago. Time between us had shrunk, and we had become contemporaries.

Harry's leadership was sometimes shared with Elsido, "Elsie," who was the son of one of the Portuguese dairymen. Most of these people came from the Azores, worked very hard, and then went back with enough money to live comfortably in the old country. But Elsie and his family stayed, eventually moving to Chino, fifty or so miles from here, to own an even larger herd of cows. Elsie's family was strict, and he was doing a man's work long before he was a man, but when he could steal time away, he played with us. He was about Harry's age.

Off and on there were other boys and a few girls who wove in and out of the volunteer army, but basically it consisted of Harry, Elsie, David, and me.

Harry was a stringy-muscled, bony kid with a shock of white-blond hair. He was agile and stronger than he looked. Elsie was not so quick and was much stockier, but he had strength beyond his years, strength acquired by lifting bales of hay and mucking out pens. Between them, they were capable of building great forts, with David and me in charge of collecting and hauling materials.

I envied Harry and Elsie their ability to pound nails and tie knots that didn't come undone. One of the best forts they built was a two-story affair in the little patch of woods at the north end of the ranch, near the rocks of the Narrows. The lower room was not only fairly weatherproof, it had a little altar with a plastic Madonna on it—evidence of our attendance at Catholic school. It was so cozy that the hoboes sometimes used it for overnight stays, leaving behind empty bean cans and such. They were a good class of hobo since they never damaged the fort.

157

The upper floor was a lookout post, reached by a ladder made from forest wood and the rough, fibrous rope used to bind bales of hay and reused by us as a basic material in all sorts of projects.

The woods were dense with underbrush and deadfalls, and we spent hours playing war. Sometimes we fought World War II, and sometimes it was the U.S. Cavalry against the Indians. In this, we were advanced in our views; the good guys were the Indians. We made bows of cottonwood branches strung with baling rope and arrows of sticks, chicken feathers, and points cut from tin can lids. Fortunately, we never achieved enough tension with the baling rope to make the arrows go very far.

Sometimes we even had range wars. I suppose they were over the usual things—water, grass, cattle, and sheep. We hated the imaginary sheep on principle but found the real ones interesting when they were grazing on the mesa land across the river.

With Harry, whatever the war, there was music. He hummed and whistled his own score as he dodged from one tree to the next. When he would deny that he'd been spotted and shot, all one had to do was to point out that it was easy, because of the humming. But he never stopped doing it. The music in adventure movies obviously impressed him greatly.

On occasion, the boys felt compelled to assert their masculinity by insisting I play a standard female role, usually the Red Cross nurse who brought up the rear of the procession. This was hazardous duty because our usual route led through the pasture owned by one of the more ferocious dairy bulls. He was so mean that a chain to trip him was eventually added to the ring in his nose.

The bull would let the first few children slither through the fence, across his pasture, and out, but he didn't like it, and by the time my turn came, he was often on the move, so more than once I exited in a dive under the fence. He started my aversion to bulls.

One Christmas, I solved this problem by requesting, instead of my usual list of books, an arsenal including a plastic rifle that shot little plastic bullets and a cap pistol with a cylinder that revolved with each shot. I have never liked guns, so my mother wondered at this change of mind, but when I explained I planned to use them to bargain for a better position in the army, she understood.

It worked beautifully. In exchange for getting to use my advanced weapons, the boys were willing to grant high rank and to give up the services of the Red Cross, though sometimes less permanent parts of the group were assigned such chores.

This didn't work so well with the toboggan. My father, so clever with his hands, made it out of a sheet of plywood attached to an old pair of skis, with baling rope running along the edges. The rope helped one to hold on if the toboggan were used properly, with people sitting down, but the boys soon discovered that they could get more bodies on it if everyone stood up. The problem with that was the whiplash effect that inevitably flipped the last rider off into the snow, or more often, onto rocks thinly covered by snow since only rarely do we get deep snow here. Somehow, I was always last on the toboggan. I couldn't think of anything to trade to get a forward position, but it didn't really matter because most of the toboggan runs ended in general disaster anyway, with the boys always wanting to go just a little farther and faster.

During one of our snowstorms in the pretoboggan days, Harry decided he'd like to go down the big hill behind the woodpile. Slipping and sliding, we packed a run and tried it out cautiously with inner tubes. But Harry wanted a greater thrill, so he attacked the run from the top with an old packing crate as a sled. The first couple of passes were okay, but by then the snow was compressed down to an icy glaze over the sand and rocks, so the makeshift sled flew down the hill and dumped Harry flat at the bottom. I think someone else was on the thing with him, maybe even Jamie since snow was a great social equalizer, but only Harry got hurt. He thrust his hands forward as he fell, and they skidded through the rocks and glass at the bottom of the hill. Harry wasn't impressed with his injuries once we could see that no stitches were necessary, but that ended the runs from the top for the day.

One of the better forts was on that hill for a while. It was exactly the kind of ground any army would want to hold, high and hard to attack, with a view of the ranch and the desert clear to the mountains. The boys deepened a natural hollow and added a little scrap wood for walls and to hold up the tarpaulin roof. This fort was supplied with some of our best equipment, including a flashlight and a deck of cards. We would meet under the canvas, plan strategies by flashlight, and creep forward periodically to peer over the brow of the hill. Undetected, we could watch all the ranch activities and the people below.

Inadvertently, that fort came as close to teaching us how to fly as anything ever could. After a heavy rain, we hiked up to see what damage had been caused. The tarpaulin had collected water until it collapsed from the weight. We were lifting it up when Harry yelled. Writhing beneath the canvas was a nest of centipedes.

It was the best example of mass hysteria I've ever witnessed. We shrieked in chorus, and we all flew off that hill as if the centipedes were going to come after us. Gone was all the care we normally took going up and down the trial; we just ran straight down, jumping obstacles—I saw Harry sail over much of the woodpile in Olympic leaps. No one fell or twisted an ankle. It was as if the adrenaline pounding through our veins made us superhuman and kept us from harm.

That was the end of that fort, and even the site was abandoned until years later when David and I as young adults with a different set of friends celebrated summer with bonfire parties on the hill.

One of the most elaborate and best camouflaged efforts was the tunnel fort that Harry and Elsie constructed in the bushes in front of the Main House. It was particularly convenient for Harry because he lived in one of the apartments close by. The fort roof was formed of the bushes themselves and the walls were dirt. There was a concealed entrance in the brush, and to get in, one wiggled through a fairly narrow passageway to the main room hollowed out of the earth. For some reason, we believed that we had built this marvel without being noticed by the adults, but this proved untrue.

One day the bushes caught fire. Like that in other arid regions, the desert foliage here is an arsonist's dream, heavy with oils evolved to protect plants against moisture loss. So the bushes didn't really catch fire; they exploded into a wall of flame so fast-moving and hot that there were fears for the Main House right across the road.

All hands were summoned and garden hoses and shovels put to work until the fire department arrived. As soon as the fire was out, my mother interrogated each of the children. I was able to tell the whole truth as I knew it, which was that I didn't have any idea at all of how the fire started. I suspected a piece of glass might have done it, focusing the sun into flame just as a magnifying glass could do. The other children claimed equal innocence and ignorance.

More than twenty years later when Harry was face to face with my mother for the first time since his family had moved away from the ranch, the first thing he said to her was, "I started that fire. I didn't mean to, but I was fooling around with matches in the bush fort. You checked all my pockets except the one that still had matches in it. I've been worrying about it ever since."

Mother allowed that two decades of guilt were enough punishment. For my part, I was relieved that I had not known of Harry's crime at the time of commission; I would have been torn between loyalty to him and telling the truth to Mom.

Besides the forts, Harry built other things. The box kite was almost too successful. Elsie and others helped Harry build it. It was enormous, constructed of wooden struts and lengths of sheeting. When it was launched, it pulled hard at its string, and that made the boys want to test its power.

At that juncture, the permanent group included another boy whose family also lived in the apartment house where the Crosses resided. Teddy Van Eck was a beautiful child, perfectly formed, but he was also tiny. I never saw him as an adult, so I don't know if he increased his stature. All his clothes were trimly tailored to fit him; he reminded me of a doll. But what he lacked in size, he made up in enthusiasm. He was game for anything, as long as the big kids would let him play.

It was too tempting. One day the boys launched the box kite down on the main road, and when it was aloft, they let Teddy take the line to see if the kite could lift him. It could. I was an eyewitness. He left the ground. How far he would have gone—and he was game to go—is anyone's guess. The boys panicked and reeled him in because it suddenly occurred to them that he might let go at a hundred feet or so, or just continue to rise into the heavens. Teddy thought the whole episode great fun.

That was his reaction to the Brahma bull, too. When we were running cattle on the ranch, the family tested various crosses, needing cattle that would achieve maximum weight while grazing on poor grass, and further, that would be resistant to heat and to ticks. Brahmas, silvery gray and humped, fitted that description well, but the bulls, with the exception of one tame one inexplicably named Judy, were a menace, bearing no resemblance to the part of their blood-

162

line that originated in India and which seems to have been mellowed by living amongst people, the majority of whom don't eat beef. Here, Brahma bulls were huge, but fleet, and able to jump the fences as if they didn't exist.

I don't know how I missed the mad bull episode, but I'm glad I did. I suppose I just wasn't on hand when my father and Uncle Joe went out to feed the cattle, offering to take any children who wanted to go with them. The boys, including Teddy, went.

The cattle to be fed were penned for various reasons out near the silos, and among their number was a particularly evil-tempered Brahma bull. But when the men arrived, they discovered that the bull had broken out of his pen. He eyed the open Jeep with clearly malicious intent, and the men, wanting the children out of harm's way, tossed the boys up on top of the haystack, intending to then lure the bull away with the Jeep. But the bull charged the haystack, hitting it with such force that the top layer and the boys flew up into the air before settling down again. The men were horrified, and all of the boys were terrified except for Teddy. He leaned over the edge and called, "Do it again, Bull, do it again!"

To the men's relief, the bull did not heed Teddy's order, and they were able to drive the animal out of the pen area and take the children home. Word went out that no one was to go walking or riding on the ranch, and the next morning, the best hunters in town gathered to shoot the bull. The result was eight hundred pounds of hamburger and a selling off of the Brahmas.

Harry had his own encounter with a bull, the mean dairy bull who had chased me out of the pasture when I was the Red Cross. He was passing the pens and chutes that led into the dairy barn when he saw that the bull, angered at being denied access to the cows that had gone in for milking, had gotten one of the dairymen down and was preparing to paw him to death. Harry vaulted the fence, ran past

163

the bull, jerked its chain as he passed, and vaulted the far fence, the bull hot on his heels as the dairyman scrambled to safety.

Openmouthed, I watched all of this from the road where I had been riding my bicycle. When I told my grandmother, she hailed Harry as a hero but asked him why in the world he had risked so much.

"Oh, I wasn't worried," he said. "I knew I could run faster than that bull."

His claim was valid. He is still a marathon runner, and even as a young boy, he was built for speed.

Prior to the publication of my first novel I had not heard directly from Harry, though I got occasional reports of him from the older generation who had known him and his family. Among other things, Harry had joined the Peace Corps and served south of the border where he had used his running as a way to make contact with the local children. What a picture that must have been—this so-blond man running with a stream of dark children behind him.

When we finally managed a visit, it was as if all those years apart had never been. We are still friends, lucky to have known each other for long enough and through the right years of childhood to establish enduring common ground.

The last I knew of Elsie, he was a prosperous dairyman celebrating his wedding with a huge party in Chino.

As for Teddy, I know nothing of his life after he left here, but I am sure whatever he has done has been with great spirit and courage.

The only time I ever saw him afraid was when he developed a sudden conviction that Indians were lurking in the bushes beyond the garden wall at the apartment house where he lived. Perhaps one of our games had given him the idea of an imminent attack.

Adults and children were out on the apartment lawn

enjoying the summer evening, except for Teddy who kept saying the Indians were coming.

"There aren't any Indians here," he was told. The words had scarcely drifted away on the evening breeze before an Indian vaulted the garden wall and staggered before an amazed audience.

"See, I told you there are Indians," Teddy muttered.

It was really more sad than funny. The Indian was one of those employed for road work by the railroad. He was very drunk and no trouble to haul away. But Teddy was right; there were Indians.

Friendship in childhood is so intense; oaths are sworn, secrets shared, promises made, but all of it exists on the whim of parents and the companies that employ them. Because of our proximity to George Air Force Base, many of our schoolmates were air force brats. Considering the demands of the career, those families managed very well, but I noticed early on that those children had a way of severing ties almost as soon as they were made. They were always aware they wouldn't be here long, and they protected themselves. They also had their own boogeyman— the commanding officer who might give their fathers bad reports if the children misbehaved.

The guest ranch expanded the number of children we would otherwise have known, but most of the guests' children just passed through our lives for an Easter week or a space of summer, though a few became long-term friends. Within this category was another class, people who came to stay at the ranch and who either became close family friends or who already knew the family from college or other contacts.

Three of these families were interwoven with mine for years, and I have sharp, specific memories of visits to their homes. They are memories of the time when Grandma was taking care of David, five, and me, seven, while our parents were in Europe. Though I didn't realize it then, those three families were really helping Grandma to care for us by taking us, separately, for a week or so at a time.

I also know now that the ranch seemed spectacular to the children of these families, as spectacular as their diverse lives seemed to me.

One family lived in Pasadena in a mansion they had renovated to accommodate their large brood. They were the only people I knew who had their own elevator, goldfish pond, and treehouse furnished with pots, pans, and furniture purchased at the Salvation Army store.

However, even with all this elegance, they lived somewhat like the Swiss Family Robinson. Eating there was more a matter of foraging for the staples—ice cream, cereal, milk, and peanut butter—than of any set routine.

I know I was sent there with the expectation that the two daughters would welcome me like another sister, but the older one was way beyond my touch—I thought her a most elegant young woman and wanted to be just like her, red hair, pale skin, and all—and the other one, who was only a couple of years older than I, greeted my arrival by locking herself in her room. In my defense, she was not any more welcoming to other guests. It fell to the oldest boy, Joel, to entertain me. He had a whole room full of trains. When you opened the door, you ducked down and crawled to the opening in the center of the huge board. When you stood upright, you could command a whole world of tiny mountains, houses, rivers, bridges, towns, and stations.

Joel became my Prince Charming that summer, and I had a terrible crush on him for years. He was tall, dark, and handsome, the stuff of fairy tales, and he was kind and patient with me. He allowed me to play with the trains, and he showed me the ropes in the treehouse. Perhaps he was used to sharing, with four siblings, but when I'm honest with myself, I have to admit it was more a matter of the fact that I was a tall, stringy, shy ranch kid used to playing with

166

boys, a tomboy who probably didn't seem female to him at all.

Years later I went to a theater party that Joel was due to attend. I was dressed in yellow. The dress was from a posh designer for whom our friend Pat O'Brien worked, but the designer made dresses for women who were built like Sophia Loren. It had been cut down and taken in for me, but it was still a disaster. I'm sure I looked like a wrinkled daffodil, particularly since the material was linen. And though I was only in my midteens, I was already at my full height.

I don't remember a thing about the play. I remember hoping that Joel would finally see that I was not only female, but desirable.

Joel arrived with his date, and instantly I knew what I was, a great gawk of a girl in a made-over dress. His date was a model. She was incredibly slender and sophisticated. She was wearing a beige, knit-lace dress (beige had always made me look like a sickly philodendron, even worse than a daffodil) with a burnt-orange scarf draped oh so casually around her neck. Her hair was mahogany with brighter strands, swept into a neat chignon. Her purse and shoes were real leather and matched. She looked right through me. She is forever burned on my brain, and I have seldom worn yellow or linen since. She was the first I knew of what I call the "porcelain" women, those women who never sweat, rumple, or ruffle, but always look as perfect as china figurines.

However, I am happy to report that Joel did not marry the model. He chose instead a lovely, earthy woman who can walk as fast as I can even if she is inches shorter. It is a great relief that I like her as much as I like Joel.

The second family I visited had only two children, but again, the older girl couldn't think of anything worse than having me visit, and the brother, also older than I, took over.

Mark was too much like a brother for me to have any romantic feelings, so time with him was just pure fun. His family lived in a big house on a steep hill in Los Angeles, and he introduced me to Flexible Flyers. The terrain at the ranch was no place for these sidewalk sleds, and I can still feel the bumpy thrill of my first flight down that sidewalk on a hill. There was also the matter of the squirt-gun war against a gang of neighborhood children. Mark and I holed up in the wood-block fort in his backyard and held them off. It was heady stuff.

Though not romantic, I had a special bond with Mark. He had been born after his father had left to fight overseas in World War II, and his father had not met him until Mark was old enough to wonder what the strange man was doing in his home. His father seemed to wonder the same thing about Mark, though he had better information. Mark's father scared me silly; he was even bigger, louder, and angrier than mine. He thought nothing of shoving Mark up against a wall to make his point. Though unspoken at the time, I think it added to the understanding between Mark and me. Fortunately, Mark's father wasn't there much when I was, and when he appeared, I hid if there was time; otherwise, I just looked at my feet and played the polite child, one of my few real skills.

Mark's mother was like most of the mothers of that era: there, but not there, providing amenities for the children almost as if she were a servant in someone else's home. But I did feel obliged to warn her of a grave danger.

"There is something very wrong with your water," I told her. "It's even happening to the ice cubes."

It is the only time I can remember seeing Mark's mother laughing so hard that she cried. She tried to explain the necessity of adding chlorine to city water, but it was incomprehensible to a child who had been raised on artesian-well water so pure that it wouldn't do for a test of a new milking machine because it had too few filtrates.

It took them a long time, but Mark's parents eventually realized what the children had known forever, that they were making each other and everyone else miserable. They divorced, married other people, and became much nicer and more responsible spouses. It sounds like a happy ending, but it frightens me that it took so long for so many of my parents' generation. I still wonder how that could have been, when the children knew.

I would not have been surprised had Mark grown into an abusive, secretive man. But he did not. Physically, he grew to be even taller and broader than his father, but with all of that, he brought a gentleness, a care that those smaller and weaker than he not be hurt and that they also be helped. He chose the opposite from what he had suffered.

The third family I stayed with was unique in my experience. They had a citrus ranch in the Santa Barbara area—that wasn't so odd to me—and the children were wild people—that was unique. Their parents were great believers in the most liberal interpretation of Dr. Spock's theories of child raising. As far as I could judge, the three Cardene offspring had no chores, obligations, or other encumbrances. They did exactly as they pleased all day long. Their dog was more bound by society's rules than they were. (He was a Great Pyrenees, and when he contracted mange and his tail went bald, he was so ashamed, he spent the entire time of his convalescence under the front porch, waiting for his plume to be rehaired.)

Playing with the Cardenes, one boy and two girls, was like running wild in Eden, even to the Serpent in residence. The orange and lemon groves seemed endless and were fragrant and shadowed. But there were also more rattlesnakes there than we ever encounter on the desert. I found this very impressive and watched where I went with extra care.

The parents thought their children were being conditioned for high society. They went to all the "right" activities—tennis and riding clubs, and cotillion. Cotillion was supposed to teach young people how to behave at formal parties and how to dance as if they were from another century. I attended one of the dances. It started with dinner and a vast array of cutlery, which was okay with me since that usage I had learned at home. But as soon as the chaperones disappeared for even a few minutes, all hell broke loose as the boys competed to see who could flip butter pats high enough to stick to the ceiling beams. That night, the boys also had a plug of chewing tobacco that they passed around in macho style. The last boy to take a chaw was unlucky since the chaperones reappeared and he felt obligated to swallow the evidence. He turned some interesting colors before he threw up. The adults thought he was probably violently allergic to the shrimp.

I must not have disgraced myself in general because I was invited to stay a bit longer with the Cardenes so that I could enjoy Fiesta, a grand annual Santa Barbara celebration. Mrs. Cardene found an old black velvet skirt for me, and we appliquéd yellow roses over the moth holes. That was before yellow had betrayed me, so I thought my Fiesta skirt was the most gorgeous thing I'd ever seen.

Most exciting of all, the youngest Cardene, Dee Dee, had a donkey named Dynamite, and the two of them got to be in the parade. The rest of us waved madly from the sidelines and felt that the parade was ours.

Dee Dee could also bite her toenails and used to stick blue fuzz from her security blanket up her nose, so she was a child of many accomplishments.

David and I had some historic battles, but the three Cardenes fought continuously and savagely—shrieking and running were skills one needed around them. Once when they were visiting here, the son went after one of his sisters with a pair of scissors. My grandmother ordered him into the bathroom to cool off, telling him he could come out when he was ready to apologize. He stayed in there for hours, and I don't think he ever apologized.

By all the evidence, the Cardenes should have gone directly from childhood to the penitentiary, but instead, they all grew into nice people who married other nice people. Permissive child raising may be hell on the parents and spectators, but it doesn't always result in delinquents. However, I do wonder how they've raised their own offspring.

Despite all of the companions of my childhood, much of the best time was spent alone. I read, wrote, and dreamed alone without feeling lonely. I made up stories and played the choice roles.

One of my favorite characters was Princess Tonka of the Seven Tribes. She was an American Indian who spoke English and seven Indian languages. She spent most of her time going from tribe to tribe, advising her people to put aside their differences and to unite against the "white-eyes." She warned against believing in the white man's treaties, and she told her people that white men killed everything and would ruin the land. I think this last idea came from the family friends who were allowed to hunt the lakes during duck season. These men talked joyfully about killing things as they swapped hunting stories, and there wasn't an Indian among them. Nor did I think they needed wild meat when they had easy access to grocery stores, something Princess Tonka's people did not have.

Actually, now that I renew her acquaintance, I see that Princess Tonka was quite prophetic.

The only problem with slipping into alter egos was that the guests didn't recognize that I was Princess Tonka or someone else. They knew me as the oldest grandchild and the only girl.

I remember trotting along on a Princess Tonka mission when a couple who had been visiting the ranch for years stopped me. "Oh, Celeste, it's so good to see you again!

171

How is everything? How are you doing in school? How is
. . ." etc., etc.

They are undoubtedly still convinced that I was a
strange child. I simply stared at them for a very long time,
mumbled "hello," and trotted on. For me, it was like being
wrenched out of a time-travel machine in midflight. When
I'm writing and someone interrupts, I get the same feeling.
I know that Princess Tonka would understand even if no
one else does.

When I was a teenager and things were difficult at
home, I trusted the desert night as I trusted nothing else. I
would slip out and wander the earth and feel comfort wrap-
ping all around me. Nothing that cut the sky or scurried or
slithered over the ground was nearly as frightening as what
human beings could do to each other. In all those wander-
ings, I was never harmed.

I am thankful that I knew the land when it was safe for
me, when so few humans lived here. Now the security of a
small, tightly knit community is gone, vanished as it has in
so many parts of California. Even on the ranch, burglar
alarms and locks guard our doors and windows. When the
wind blows, everything disappears in a sea of dust, not the
normal drift, but evidence of countless acres scraped raw
for new housing tracts. Some of the people who come genuinely like the desert, but most migrate only to take advantage of lower housing costs. Many of them still work in
other, more expensive municipalities "down below," in the
urban world beyond Cajon Pass. Many of them leave their
loyalties and their willingness to be part of a community
down there, too. That lack of cohesion seems to bring out
the worst in humans, and the crime rate climbs every year.

I would not go out to walk in the darkness now. When
I was a child, the mouse was prey when the owl swept down.
But even here on the land guarded by the Narrows, the hills,
and the river, we humans have become mice to our own
monsters who are far less merciful and logical than owls.

THE GETTING
OF WISDOM

Chapter 7

DUCK AND COVER

I was seven years old when I knew I would never be able to fly under my own power. Up until that day, I had not noticed any adverse effects from gravity. That was simply a convenience, a way of keeping my feet on the ground without effort. I do not recall making any general assessment of the human race's ability to fly, though I was sure my parents and little brother couldn't do it.

I understood that flight for me was a special attribute that must not be abused by exhibitionism or overuse. It was secret, special, but there, a power that could lift me up to soar with the hawks were I just to raise my arms and wish it. I am glad I conceived of this more in the manner of Peter Pan than Superman, whose mode caused many children to tumble off of barns and buildings with flimsy capes fluttering uselessly as they plummeted to the ground.

I loved Barrie's story when Grandma read it to us and later when I saw the Disney version. I used to tell David that as soon as he fell asleep, I'd be off with Wendy and

Peter. This was a safe brag because no matter what vows David made to stay awake, he never did. However, it did lead to one odd episode.

When our parents were out for the evening, we were allowed to fall asleep in their bedroom, and they would move us when they got home. One morning after this ritual, my mother asked, "Who in the world is Peter?"

When she had led me to my own room, I had protested, "Peter won't be able to find me now." This was shortly after I'd realized I couldn't fly on my own power, couldn't be Peter Pan myself, but would need some magic assistance.

I remember that awful day when I knew flight was not within my own power. Confirmation of my earthbound status was not triggered by any dramatic event or by an attempt to fly. The fact that I couldn't just came to me as if some cosmic calendar of aging decreed that it was time to give up this particular illusion.

For that day and several after, I plodded along, horrified at how leaden my body had become, how difficult even the simple task of walking was since my feet were being drawn deeper into the earth with every step.

I did not discuss this tragedy with anyone. That has led me to believe that I would be a bad choice for angels or aliens to visit. I would be apt to keep their messages to myself, trying to puzzle out exactly what was meant. Far better for such beings, or nonbeings, to visit people who can't wait to share the experience.

As an adult, when I and countless other people were experimenting with Eastern meditation, I did finally fly. I lay in a field until I could soar with a hawk, feeling the rush of air through his/my wings, seeing the earth from a strange, telescopic perspective, flying so fast that my body was growing smaller and smaller, left there in the grass, believing that if I flew out of sight of that body, I would never find it again, and when others found it, it would be dead.

DUCK AND COVER

It was one of the most terrifying experiences of my life.
I was not on drugs: the mind is the strongest drug on earth,
and in those instants of flight, I understood how fragile our
handclasp with life can be, breaking when we least expect it,
holding fast when we would sever it. I also learned that the
loss of flight at seven was not so tragic. I was never intended
to fly, no matter the lure of some archetypal memory.

Another seminal event occurred long before the loss of
wings, so long before that I don't remember what age I was.
It was the realization that everyone else was looking out of
his or her body just as I was. The bodies, mine included,
seemed like boxes with eye holes cut in them, just like the
inevitable Christmas-package costumes for the theatrical
productions most children experience at some point in early
school days.

It was a startling discovery. Suddenly a vast, empty
plane was bustling with other people looking out of their
containers, wanting, thinking, dreaming, living just as I
was. There wasn't any judgment to make. It was just this
way and would never be any other way again. But I confess,
I still find it astonishing that each being in the vast herds of
humans on this earth is peeking out of his or her package,
watching the world, though there seem to be an ever-in-
creasing number who do not realize that others are watchers, too.

I consider both of these events to be important milestones in my education. Unlike the currently popular
theme, I did not learn most of what I needed to know in
kindergarten. In fact, kindergarten was pretty much of a
bust for me. I discovered that I had weak ankles that would
give way in circle games and that boys had much better
toys—hammers, pegs, trucks, etc.—and much more space
to play in than we girls who were relegated to miniature
kitchens and mock ironing board setups in the corners.

Nursery school did a much better job of offering revelations than kindergarten. I learned not to steal or lie in

nursery school, and that adult-size toilets can be dangerous for small people.

Stealing and lying were already clearly marked as forbidden activities by that time, but on one occasion I wore a sombrero home, and when questioned by my mother, I told her that the teacher had been giving them away as special presents. This was so obviously untrue that the hat went back with me the next day. On another excursion into criminality, I told my mother that there was going to be a chicken-and-dumpling dinner at the school and that she was invited to come. Since juice and graham crackers were the extent of nursery school cuisine, this invitation came as a shock to my mother and was easily, as in the case of the hat, proven to be fiction. I had hoped to lure Mother to school where she would have such a good time, she would stay.

The toilet episode concerned the tiniest student in our class. Zelda was so slight, she looked more like an elf than a child. She was even smaller than Teddy Van Eck. One day, instead of coming back from the rest room, she called for help in a reedy voice as frail as the rest of her. In panic, the teacher flew to her with the class trailing behind her. Zelda had fallen through the toilet seat and was stuck there with arms and legs in the air.

Our nursery school was in a converted building, and in those days, there weren't many places that had special facilities for children, the theory being that if children were toilet trained, that was enough, and they must know how to use regular plumbing. I have no idea how Zelda managed at home, but I was so horrified by the public exposure of her embarrassing predicament, I eyed commodes with caution for some time afterwards.

I will always be on the side of compulsory education, and there were many things I did learn in school, particularly how to get along with people of my own age, but the most important things in my life, I learned at home. With

Grandma teaching me to read so early, with books all around, with music and art discussed and enjoyed, and with the steady stream of interesting people, the ranch was the best of all classrooms.

In school, I worked hard to get good grades and to please the teachers, but the whole process seemed just a shade odd and distant to me, and I was always glad when I finished school assignments with enough time left over for "real" learning.

I read Shakespeare's "The Rape of Lucrece" when I was seven or eight. I wasn't at all sure what rape entailed, but I knew it was something hideous and evil, and Shakespeare's works were on the bookshelves, available for reading. I think I can mark the beginning of my feminism with that reading. Some of the language was tough going, but nonetheless, it was clear that the Roman matron had taken the blame for an offense committed against her. It seemed to me that she should have killed her attacker instead of herself.

Formal education, as I knew it, certainly had little to say about the achievements of women. I used to collect such lore wherever I could find it, for reassurance, but the names brought up in school were few. Elizabeth I, Mary Queen of Scots, Sacajawea, Dolly Madison, Florence Nightingale, Clara Barton, Elizabeth Blackwell—that was about the extent of the list, except for a couple of others who were thrown in as examples of historical hysteria—Catherine the Great of Russia for excesses that were never described in detail, and Mary Todd Lincoln, who was usually presented as a sore trial to Honest Abe, specifically because of her extravagantly large glove order while in the White House.

It was a dismal picture not brightened in general by the classics of American literature, which are mainly from the nineteenth century and which, if they bother at all with female characters, too often offer portraits of nagging hindrances to man's spirit of adventure. I liked Hester Prynne

179

in *The Scarlet Letter,* but her case seemed much like Lucrece's. "Lucrece swears he did her wrong." So should Hester.

English and Continental writers did somewhat better by women, but aside from the most sexless of Shakespeare's plays (and thus the safest for teachers to teach), *Julius Caesar* and *Macbeth,* there wasn't much exposure to these authors in the classroom until college. Again, for me, the variety was to be found on the ranch bookshelves.

My formal education and that of my brother and, later on, our cousins was complicated by Catholic school.

In one of the freakish weather changes typical of this high desert, a day that had started out warm and fair suddenly turned cold and snowy. Mother came to public school to bring extra clothing to me and David. She was directed to my third-grade classroom. She found utter chaos. The teacher had given up and was gazing blankly into space while the inmates ran wild on the storm's energy. At first, Mom couldn't locate me, and then she spotted me pressed against a window, staring at the snow, trying to stay out of the stampede. The sight chilled Mother more than the weather had because she thought there was a good chance that I would disappear into myself altogether in such a setting.

"Modern" education, according to the philosophy of A. S. Neill and his Summerhill project in England, had hit the American public school system, and the basic tenet was that children would drift into reading, writing, and arithmetic when they pleased, and that when they did, the learning systems ought to be much simpler than before. In the case of reading, syllabication and an understanding of word roots were deemed unnecessary. Instead, words were to be associated with pictures. This led to a bizarre kind of rote learning that offered little insight into how language works.

Given my tendency to make myself invisible and David's ability to take off on a track entirely unrelated to

The last picture of myself that I've really
liked—at age three.

The Main House. *Courtesy John Saul and Michael Sack.*

View from the front porch of the Main House.

The Main House living room. *Courtesy Bob Paluzzi.*

The Play Barn.

The Red House.

View from the Main House toward the Narrows. You might get the impression that it snows all the time here. It doesn't—one or two good snows a winter are normal, but the land looks so beautiful that snow days always bring out the cameras.

The back garden of the Main House.

Easter, 1988, with Pat O'Brien.

The Hibben
girls in 1965:
Great-Aunt
Lola,
Great-Aunt
Lura,
Grandma.

Grandma, 1965. *Courtesy Herbert Bruce Cross.*

Grandma and Mom on New Year's Eve,
1966. Right before midnight we throw
funny hats from the balcony to the guests
below. Then we wait for the grandfather
clock to chime in the new year.

David, 1968. Taking pictures of David was like trying to capture the wind. He was usually in such vivid motion, many pictures just show a blur.

Mom and David, 1972. After chemotherapy, David was bald; then his hair would grow back; then it would happen all over again.

David and our cousin Craig, on David's 25th birthday in April, 1973. He died in September.

Mom
and Dad—
Christmas,
early 80s.

Christmas, 1985. Back row, left to right: Celeste, Diana and Scott Campbell,
Uncle Joe Campbell, Laura and Craig Campbell, Nicki and Kemper Campbell
with their daughter Alison and their son Brian. Front row: Jean De Blasis,
Great-Aunt Lola Elkins, Aunt Donna Campbell.

the matter at hand, and add to that one freak snowstorm, he and I were off to Catholic school where the "three R's" were taught in traditional ways.

I am still cross about my first week in Catholic school. I spelled every word correctly on the spelling test, but I received a 0 for my efforts because I had printed instead of written in longhand. Public school hadn't yet required me to write in script, but my printing was very tidy. My handwriting was developed in a matter of days and is, unless I go very slowly, execrable to this day, a slide and jolt of printed letters connected by ungraceful cursive strings. Not even the hours spent in class doing penmanship exercises helped. Those were done in pencil, and I always had a large eraser handy to take out the overlaps of my loops and lines, though I had to be careful while doing this since the nuns frowned on such imperfection.

As far as I could tell in the early days at the school, the nuns were perfect, and this fascinated me. They were sisters of the Immaculate Heart, and they wore the traditional black habits with white wimples. They seemed to glide from one place to the other, their hands never fidgeting, their voices always calm. And even the plainest among them achieved beauty within the frame of the wimple. For a time, when I was on the verge of adolescence, converting to the Catholic church and becoming a nun was a very appealing idea, though it appalled my Adventist grandmother. By then, I was one of the favored few who were "privileged" to help with the housework at the convent, and the cool austerity of that place was infinitely soothing in contrast to the cluttered confusion of growing up. However, as soon as I had my first real boyfriend and my body began to accept that being a woman might be interesting, becoming a nun lost all of its appeal.

The Immaculate Heart of Mary order was known for its high level of education, and the sisters were good teachers and intelligent, to the point that some years after I was

181

out of Catholic school, the order got into a battle with the church hierarchy, and many of the nuns I had known left the discipline, quite a few of them leaving so completely that they married and had children.

As far as selecting the school for the rigors of the education offered there, my parents made a good choice, but since neither of them had ever attended a parochial school, they did not consider what effect that would have. And since David and I, and our cousins in their time, were all sent to the school by our families, it did not occur to us that they were unaware of the peculiar slant given to some subjects.

It did not color mathematics much, but the same could not be said for many other subjects. Geography and history were taught from the perspective of where the true God had been worshipped before Christ and of what the popes or Christian kings had controlled once Peter had been chosen by Christ to establish the church.

I remember sitting in class one day and hearing about the "Line of Demarcation." It was based on the 1494 Treaty of Tordesillas and gave Spain and Portugal equal shares in the "known world." The real division was between papal influence (through the domination of Spain and Portugal) and savage darkness, waiting for papal illumination. Suddenly, that didn't seem quite right, though I didn't have the courage to point this out to the nun.

American history did not escape. Though not Catholics, the Puritans were given full credit for risking so much to be able to practice their faith in freedom. No mention was made of the fact that the Puritans were entirely unwilling to allow any other sect such freedom. This was an odd omission since Puritans hated Papists so much. But Catholics in America were given full treatment, too, so that most of what we heard about American Indians was related to the brave, and often martyred, priests who worked so diligently to convert the pagans. And many cities were presented as significant only because of the churches built or because of the priests or nuns who had labored there.

No "primitive" culture was ever presented as having any artistry or virtue before conversion, and most were granted precious little after. Again, I am thankful that so much of what I learned came from home. In the case of the native Americans, the respect and attraction to their history that we children felt was pretty much self-generated, though it was helped along by the family legend of that faint connection to Pocahontas. I think it had more to do with our adventures in the woods and fields, with a closeness to the land that made us feel as if we might be kin to not just one, but to all the Indians who had once roamed the wilds. Added to that were a couple of guests, including Gwen Polkinghorn, who visited periodically and told stories of the great Indian nations that had once existed, tales of the Hurons, Iroquois, Cherokee, Cheyenne, Apache, and others.

There was an artist who lived on the ranch, and besides a huge collection of silver-and-turquoise pawn jewelry made by Indians of the Southwest, she also had walls of African masks. The fine craftsmanship and the power of these articles made it difficult to believe that all of these people were benighted.

No mention was ever made in school of what missionaries and the accompanying armies had done to native peoples, but we certainly heard the lurid details of endless cases of brave priests and nuns who were sliced, diced, roasted, and otherwise martyred for God's greatest glory.

One of the annual visitors to the school fit right in with this. He was a missionary who came to solicit funds for the Society for the Propagation of the Faith. A freckled and rusty-haired man, his underlying pallor was emphasized by the black cassock he always wore. Hair sprouted from his nose and ears and tufted on the backs of his hands. He spit with the fervor of his preaching. I often lost track of what he was saying while I stared at his foaming mouth. He disgusted me so thoroughly that I dreaded his arrival. His particular line was about how hungry the children were in Africa. He was perfectly right about that, of course, but he attacked the subject with such cold fury that it was much easier to picture the size of the rats the children ate if they could catch them and the smallness of the bananas they would kill each other for than to imagine the children themselves. He was also full of gruesome stories of missionaries being hacked to bits while trying to spread the Word. I wanted to tell him that maybe those people didn't want to hear the Word from him any more than I did, but I never spoke to him. How grim and terrifying his black-robed presence must have seemed to those African children. He reeked of unkindness. How unjust that they had to contend with him along with starvation.

Contemporary history had a sectarian slant, too. The godless Russian Communists who had forbidden the celebration of mass behind the Iron Curtain were surely devils come to earth, and the first thing they were going to do when they invaded America was to kill all the Catholic children plus any Protestants who happened to be friends of Catholics. Privately I thought this made me quite brave to keep being friends with Catholics, a chancy business anyway with the comic books that warned Catholics about how Protestants would try to tempt them into sins such as eating meat on Friday or attending non-Catholic church services. But by then, Mother, David, and I plus our aunt, uncle, and cousins were officially Episcopalians, and I could not imagine that the Communists would have any special problem with that. I knew that Episcopalians were the American version of Anglicans, which were the English version of Catholics, but I doubted that the Russians knew that or would care if they did. After all, it was a Catholic prelate, Cardinal Mindszenty, they had trapped in the U.S. Legation in Budapest, Hungary, not an Episcopalian.

My cousin Kemper, five years younger than I, was not so sanguine during his stay at the school. When Khrushchev came to visit California, Kemper had screaming nightmares, having been warned that the archenemy was actually on his way to kill good Catholic children—*and* their Protestant friends. His parents thought this was an outlandish fear and assured him there was no danger; only later did they understand the extent of the propaganda that had made him believe such a thing.

Worst of all was the specter of the godless Communists dropping an atomic bomb on us, utterly destroying the world, making it so unliveable that only scorpions, roaches, and a few specialized rodents, kangaroo rats, for instance, would survive. I don't remember who told me that these were the creatures that would make it, but the image was vivid—a sere landscape with hordes of insects and rodents swarming over it until, presumably, they would eat each other.

People started building bomb shelters in their backyards, and one enthusiastic local citizen proposed that an old mine be equipped for six hundred people. Since even then the town population, without counting outlying areas, was more than double that, I was sure I didn't want to be in that mine with hundreds of people outside pounding to get in. I didn't want to be underground anywhere. My hope was that when the bombs dropped, I'd be on the ranch. I planned to climb part way up on the hill behind our house, dig a little hollow for comfort, and then watch the world explode.

But at school, we regularly practiced "duck and cover" drills, diving beneath our desks, covering our heads, supposedly to protect ourselves from the flying glass and fallout of the initial blast. I and every other child I knew performed these exercises obediently, but I didn't know any child who really believed he or she would be saved this way, especially since we lived so close to the important George

185

Air Force Base, which we thought would be a target. For earthquakes, duck and cover made sense, but not for atomic bombs.

John Hersey's *Hiroshima* was another of my early discoveries among the bookshelves, and from that, I judged it far more likely that we would all be carbon smudges on the school floor than that we would survive.

A friend of mine who lived in the Los Angeles area at the time remembers seeing a public service film that carried all kinds of useful hints, including the suggestion that should a family be trapped out in the open, on a picnic, for example, during a nuclear attack, they should cover themselves with their picnic tablecloth, or failing that, newspaper, in order to avoid being contaminated. My friend didn't believe that any more than I believed in duck and cover.

Living on the California-Nevada desert after World War II was not the safest choice. The government conducted a lot of atomic testing accompanied by institutionalized lying, so that some of the truth is still obscured.

One summer night in the fifties, we, a wagonload of children, were out on a hayride. Suddenly the dark night turned bright red from horizon to horizon and the light limned our bodies and made it seem as if our hands were transparent. We never knew what it was, and the possibilities are horrifying, but worse was how easily and calmly we all, including the adults who were along to supervise and to drive the tractor that pulled the wagon, accepted the flash of blood red light. "They must be testing bombs somewhere," we said, and that was all, but now I wonder when I think of all the people, young and old, I have known who have died of cancer.

But still, despite such acceptance, we children believed in the power of the atom, believed that the bombs would be dropped sooner or later and that they would kill us. I don't think the older generations believed it; I'm not sure they do yet. It's not that they don't know the scientific basis of

186

atomic theory; it's as if the theory came too late to be incorporated into their psyches, so that the idea of complete annihilation has never taken root. The bomb shelter building seemed to me symptomatic of that, believing that if one stayed underground for a day or two, or maybe even a week, it would then be fine to emerge and resume life with only minor adjustments. I think the first crack of the great chasm that eventually opened between my generation and the ones before may well have started here.

The stockpiling of nuclear weapons was another indication to me that the people in power did not give due credit to the forces of destruction. It seemed a matter of pride that there were enough warheads to kill the world many times over, and the count was going up. That never made sense to me or the other children I knew, and it still doesn't.

I am grateful that it finally made less and less sense to more and more people. Bomb shelters were abandoned or turned into wine cellars; Khrushchev's missiles were not set up on Cuba; and we did not "nuke" Vietnam despite the rabid voices that screamed for it. Nuclear disarmament has been on the "big" powers' agenda for decades now, and events in the past year (1990) in Europe are cause for hope. But there are other countries that are not involved in this, countries which are increasing their nuclear capabilities as swiftly as they can. The child who thought duck and cover was an inadequate defense is still alive and well within me.

In addition to the peculiar slant given to many subjects in parochial school, there were also religion classes. Non-Catholics were allowed into the Catholic school for two reasons—they paid higher tuition, revenue the school always needed, and there was the hope that conversion would take place, even though the extra dollars would then be lost.

I attended Catholic school for seven years, from the time I was eight years old until I was fifteen. Those are like dog years in the life of a child, so much happens and changes in such a short span. The days have an exhausting intensity; there is so much to learn, so much to think about. Catholicism was something I thought a lot about. There were the intelligence and serenity of the nuns contrasting with the arrogance of the priests. The nuns seemed to be trying to assure the children that God was indeed love; the priests wanted us to know that we could be in deep trouble if we weren't very, very careful. It was sort of like a good cop–bad cop act.

One of my third-grade schoolmates was worried because her mother had just given birth to twins who had died before they could be baptized. My friend was not only distressed by the deaths, she was frightened that she would not get to meet them in the afterlife because they would have to go to limbo. The priest confirmed this but assured her that the babies would be happy enough in limbo; they just wouldn't have the capacity to be as happy as people in heaven, who would have been equipped by baptism and various other rituals to fully appreciate gazing on the countenance of God, which was the principal activity in heaven.

My friend was heartbroken, but as soon as the priest had left, one of the nuns said, "I refuse to believe that God does not welcome babies into heaven. Limbo is not dogma; it is not a matter of faith and morals; and until it is, you don't have to believe either."

This was intriguing stuff, enough to make me see that the Church wasn't as serene as it wanted to be. The pope and all of the priests were men, and they bossed everyone around, but prayers were usually addressed to the Virgin Mary that she might intercede with her Son, and the nuns ran the school and the first hospital built in the valley, and they did so with little interference from the priests.

And aside from the overall view, limbo seemed to me to be a very silly idea and rather grotesque, particularly because it was original sin, not even sins committed by the babies themselves, that caused the exile from heaven. I pictured it as a puffy-cloud place draped with acres of holy-card, cherublike babies. To be honest, I wasn't that keen on heaven, either, at least not on the version that was presented at school. Animals didn't have souls, so there couldn't be any in heaven; neither could there be trees, grass, flowers, etc. Not even the fact that this meant there wouldn't be any spiders or scorpions made such a place attractive. My private policy was that I didn't want to go anywhere where my dog, horse, birds, and other pets were not welcome. And staring at God did not sound like enough activity to be interesting for eternity. The answer to this doubt was that while we were in our earthly bodies, most of us could not understand (holy people apparently could), but that once we were pure spirit, staring at God was all that we would want to do.

The church had such a complex, complete system, it reminded me of a gigantic board game. There were rules for every eventuality, including what the priest had to do if a fly landed on the consecrated Host—eat the Host anyway and the insect if unavoidable. This was the sort of question students asked during catechism. But the most appealing thing was that you could go to confession and not only be forgiven right there, you could also do penance that would take time off of your stay in purgatory after you died. I used to wonder if you could save up penances, like money in the bank, so that you could use the credit if you sinned and didn't have time to pray right then. I never asked, so I'm still not clear on this. In the Episcopal church, though a general act of contrition was made, sins remained a matter between the sinner and God. This seemed a lot tougher to me than having the priest act as referee—except for the fact that, according to my Catholic friends, there was no guarantee of anonymity as the priest usually knew who they were.

The visuals in the Catholic church were spectacular, making our much plainer Episcopal church (which made no pretense of being "high church" in those days) pale in comparison. I liked the clothes, the vestments embroidered in gold and rainbow silks and the stark black-and-white habits of the teaching sisters, the flowing white of the nursing staff. I liked the smells, too, the incense in the church and the same perfume blended with floor and furniture wax in the convent. Best perhaps were the sounds, the sonorous singing in Latin, the tolling of church bells and the little high-pitched bell rung during the mass, and the click of rosary beads. Even the nuns made a special music with the sweep of their heavy robes through doorways.

All in all, it was stately, hypnotic, a pretty heady business until I looked more closely at the details, particularly those regarding women. Not only did the church say that women had no right to prevent conception by "artificial means" (early on I encountered several children who were known as "rhythm method" members of their families—so much for "natural" means), but it also said that in a desperate situation that threatened the life of both mother and child, the child was to be saved. That conjured up images of legions of children left motherless.

My disenchantment deepened immeasurably after a trip to Mexico. I went with American friends who spent part of every year in Puerto Vallarta, and this was in the days before it had been made into a tourist spot. There were only a few other foreigners in the village. My friends had been visiting every year for so long that they were as much a part of local lives as any outsiders could be, and along with the other things they took south that summer were birth control pills for Maria.

Maria had married at twenty-four, late for her culture, but seven years later, she had seven children, and she was wretched. She, the children, her husband, and her mother all lived in a one-room hut. They had no plumbing but enough electricity to illuminate one lightbulb and an old-fashioned sewing machine. Maria sewed for locals and visitors, and when he felt like it, her husband ran a string of burros that carried goods into the hinterlands. Together they made just enough to keep from starving.

Though only thirty-one, Maria looked like a hill farmer's gaunt wife a decade or so older, and the eyestrain she suffered from the long hours of sewing in such poor light made her terrified of going blind. But she was more terrified of having another child. She knew that one more mouth to feed would be the end of all of them. Yet in her village—indeed, in her country where the church held such sway—there was no access to birth control. And even had she worked out the intricacies of the rhythm method and had her body cooperated, her husband was not the sort of man to deny himself, and he regarded her pregnancies as her problem. Maria had gathered up her courage and her pesos and had gone to a local doctor, but he had been outraged by her request for help. My friends knew it was dangerous to give birth control pills to a woman without medical supervision, but they also understood that Maria was already in danger.

After I had seen Maria's life and those of other women in the village, after I had seen the children's lives, after I had seen the control the church exerted on all, my enchantment with the system faded rapidly, but this is not to say that I didn't keep searching.

I understand why so many saints and martyrs have had their visions and heard their voices while so young. Childhood and adolescence are surely times of enough energy and turmoil to set voices in the wind and faces in the mist. As far as I know, older people do not suffer from poltergeists unless there is a child in the house.

My dog Waif used to present me with small animals as gifts. They were never injured, just wet from being carried in his mouth. Once he brought me an antelope squirrel, the desert version of a chipmunk. I named him Piccolo and raised him with the intention of returning him to the wild. He became very tame, sitting on my arm to be fed, chattering and chirping all the while. It was late spring by the time Piccolo had grown enough to be released, so I started leaving his cage outside where he could become accustomed to the sights and sounds of the outdoors but would still be protected from predators.

The days had been mild, but this one turned suddenly hot, a spasm of summer dropped into the spring. I felt every rise in degree on my own skin. Most desert creatures are very sensitive to heat and cold and use various means of shelter to avoid the extremes. Antelope squirrels hide from the heat of midday in summer. I worried, squirmed, and prayed that three o'clock would come sooner than it usually did, but I could not summon the courage to change the orderly progression of the day by asking the nuns if I could use their phone to call home for the sake of my pet.

The price of my cowardice was immediately apparent when I finally got there. Piccolo lay dead in his cage on the back patio.

I was overwhelmed by grief and guilt, and then I thought of the perfect plan. I asked God to restore Piccolo to life, and I promised I wouldn't mention it if He didn't want me to since it might not be the sort of miracle He wanted discussed. I reminded him that Piccolo was completely innocent and therefore deserving of grace. I held the tiny corpse in my hand, and for a long, luminous time, I fully expected him to open his bright bead eyes and chatter at me.

He remained just as dead as he had been, and the universe expanded until it was far too large for any single living thing to matter. I understood that life in general mattered, that the wholeness of seasons mattered, but I never again fully believed that there was one voice out there to answer mine. The tragedy was that Piccolo was still dead and would never be otherwise, but the comfort was that I also had doubts about the overseer causing misery.

Unfortunately, this did not totally eradicate the heavenly ledger theory which held that God, or more likely, his secretary St. Peter, kept track of all the good and bad one did in a vast account book. I left Catholic school as a fallen away Protestant with Catholic guilt. I also left with a brand new missal, won as the prize for placing highest on the religion test, a result, I think, of having studied the faith from the outside in instead of having inherited it as my Catholic friends had. One of the questions was, "What are the four kinds of spirits?" I don't recall the correct answer, but I do remember that one of the boys offered, "Bourbon, rye, vodka, and gin."

The missal was presented to me during the graduation ceremony at the church, and as the monsignor handed it to me, he whispered, "We hope you will be one of us one day."

Though the monsignor was always kind to me, he was one of the chief reasons I came to believe that priests had too much power. The giving out of report cards was a time of terror. It didn't matter that my marks were good and congratulations from the monsignor were always forthcoming. He was so cruel to the boys who hadn't done well, it spoiled everything. He would scold them verbally in front of everyone, and then he would twist their ears and bang their heads on the desk. It made me feel like throwing up. Looking back, I rather wish I had. The greatest injustice was that many of these boys were doing their best; they simply were not good students. Girls, even those whose marks were not high, were not thus abused. Undoubtedly, the monsignor did not believe it was important that girls were good or bad students, or any kind of student at all, despite the praise dutifully given for high marks.

Monsignor was Belgian. He had come to the United States after World War II, but in his mind, he had never left the old country and old ways. And he was wholly unprepared for the onset of puberty in the pupils of his school. He would have been much more at ease had the school stopped at the fifth or sixth grade, but by the time I spent my final

193

year there, it went through ninth grade, and Monsignor had decided we were headed into the welcoming arms of the devil. His solution to this was to request a harsher nun to be in charge of the school.

Our principal, a nun we had liked and respected, was replaced by a madwoman. She was transferred from a tough inner-city school in Los Angeles and sent to the desert to do her duty despite a phobia about reptiles.

The principal who left might not have liked them much either, but she never made any point of it except for the day she beat a sidewinder to death with a baseball bat when it looped onto the playing field while children were there, an act which seemed quite normal in the context of holy cards that depicted the Virgin Mary as crushing the Serpent beneath her foot. But the new nun suspected that every lizard that wandered in to take advantage of a spot of warmth had been deliberately put there by a student. She accused the older students of a good deal worse than that, too.

While the lizards wanted warmth, we students often needed shade, and the only patch of shade at the upper end of the campus was under a short space of covered walkway. This also happened to be where the rest rooms were. When the weather got hot and drove us to shelter there, the principal accused us of having immoral purposes for gathering. We were intrigued, though ignorant, about what she might mean.

Dan, one of the clumsiest and most socially inept of the boys in our class, was caught trailing after Jean, one of the prettiest of the girls. Dan was bouncing a basketball as Jean walked across the court, and his "sin" was that he was trying to summon the courage to ask Jean to go to the movies with him. The nun accused him of lewd behavior, making obscene motions with the basketball. That's when we knew for certain that, nun or not, she was crazy, though we still would have liked to have known the details of what she assumed was going on.

She could not have been sent to a school of more innocent children. We were, with few exceptions, very naive sexually and socially backward.

One of the few exceptions was Steve. He was an air force brat like many others, but he was also the victim of raging hormones that had turned him into the "Incredible Hulk" at twelve years old. He was big, shambling, hairy, and deep-voiced while the other boys were just approaching those attributes in uneven stages. He was also truculent, and he looked mean-tempered enough so that no one bothered him. I suspect he was simply miserable to be so fully grown in the midst of children. He used some daringly foul language now and then, but I never knew him to hurt anyone.

He was too much male for the new principal. She watched him balefully and sniped at him constantly. Finally he lost his temper. Towering over her with his hands bunched into fists, he just barely restrained himself from flattening her. His tongue was not so guarded. He said things most of us had been thinking—that she was nuts and should never have come to our school—and then he called her "a fucking penguin." Most of us would not have thought of that, certainly not of saying it, but to this day, I am grateful to him for standing up to her, albeit crudely. None of the rest of us ever did; we just puttered along, marking time until we could get out of her range. Steve never came back to the school after that day.

The school did teach basic mathematical, reading, and writing skills, but the curriculum was dreadfully inadequate in subjects that required special equipment or were considered frivolous. In the first category was science, and in the second were art and athletics.

I had the microscope my father had given me, I lived on the ranch, my grandmother could identify most of the living things on the land, and I was fascinated by biology, so I conducted my own experiments, including inspecting the magnified creatures from the horse trough. They could have played lead roles in science fiction movies. These were outside of Grandma's knowledge, and I'm not sure what all of them were, but I can still visualize the wacky splendor of them—those that looked like partially split M&M's with cilia sweeping busily inside; those that were animated tubes; the ones that waved or jetted or oozed; all that busy life.

Science was also aided by the head nun at the hospital. For years, though my first love was writing, I planned to be a doctor. I figured that way I could make a living doing something both kind and valuable, and I would write on the side. Sister Augustine encouraged this interest, allowing me to work in Central Supply while I was still too young to be allowed officially on the floor. Later on, Aunt Donna helped organize the Candy Stripers so that I and other girls could work with the patients. I was fine, even tough, about the sights, smells, and sounds of the hospital until some bizarre hormonal change zapped me in mid-adolescence, inducing a sudden horror of most of what went on under the guise of curing people. My medical career ended so absolutely that I was no longer even able to do minor surgery and patch-up any more on wounded friends and pets.

If I was a reliable source for information on the biological sciences from an early age, I cannot claim the same accuracy involving other scientific fields and technology in general.

Living at the ranch, I never felt any need to join such organizations as the Brownies or Girl Scouts. However, I once attended a Girl Scout meeting. The troop met in the basement of a recreation building at the air force base, and as the guest of a friend, I got to ride a school bus with her. School buses were not a usual part of my existence, so the ride home was an adventure, and the meeting was even more so.

The troop leader was very agitated because water was

dripping off of the electric bulb that hung from the ceiling. She kept wringing her hands and fretting about the safety of the building and of her troop.

Since I knew what was wrong, I was astonished by her behavior, but, thank heavens, I wasn't brash enough to set her straight. I was a visitor, after all, and she was an adult who should have known the score.

When I arrived home, I told my mother what had happened. "The lady was very silly. She was so worried, but there was nothing wrong except that some of the water hadn't been made into electricity yet."

"What are you talking about?" my mother asked.

It was bad enough that the troop leader didn't know, but it was really distressing that my own mother was equally ignorant.

"I told you, some of the water hadn't been made into electricity, so it was coming through the wires and dripping off of the bulb."

It took Mother a little while to gain control of her laughter. "That isn't the way it works! Water power runs engines that make electricity; water itself isn't made into electricity."

Art was another homegrown activity. Jean Turner, a fine commercial and landscape artist, she of the Indian jewelry and African masks, lived in the back apartment of the Main House. My parents arranged for her to give me art lessons and she did so for years. She was exceedingly patient, and I loved my sessions with her. I was intoxicated by the smell of the paints, turpentine, and linseed oil, by the textures of canvas, paper, and brushes.

Mrs. Turner used to show her work in the Main House hall, and sometimes, guests bought from her. She worked in oils and watercolors.

One day, my friend Harry conned me into seeing what would happen when vinegar was added to baking soda. He provided the cigar tube for the experiment. Unfortunately, we were standing by one of Mrs. Turner's big paintings when the cap blew off the tube and the solution ran right down the middle of the watercolor, dragging pigment with it. Chemistry wasn't one of my strong suits, either.

I was sick with grief over what I had done, even though it had been an accident, and I knew that watercolor work could not usually be corrected once it was dry. I was sure that painting was worth more money than I would ever see in my whole life, and I was equally sure that Mrs. Turner would never speak to me again. Sobbing, I went to her to confess my sin. She was incredibly gracious about the incident, and she managed to repair the painting, a near miracle.

Her husband died years before she did, and when she died, her family came to clean out the apartment. Her daughter-in-law called me in. "Jean was so fond of you," she said. "Please take any of the art materials you want."

It was all there. There were sable brushes and the purest pigments. There were palettes and palette knives, easels, paper, canvases, charcoal, and chalks. I looked at everything and felt the greed to possess it all, all the wonderful possibilities contained in those supplies.

I chose a sheaf of tracing paper and two cheap brushes.

Jean's daughter-in-law was puzzled and asked, "Are you sure that is all you want?"

I assured her it was, thanked her, and fled. My family had taught me that greed is one of the least attractive human characteristics.

Years later when I told Grandma this story, she was flabbergasted.

"For goodness' sake! Jean's family didn't have any interest in that stuff. You should have taken it all. It would have saved them the bother of clearing everything out." She shook her head. "There is such a thing as training a child to be too polite."

Virtue is not always its own reward; I still think of those artist's supplies with longing.

Science and art were therefore taken care of by life on the ranch; athletics were surely served as we rode, swam, and ran during our adventures, but most of us at the ranch never cared for formal team sports. At the Catholic school, with its dearth of equipment, softball was one of the big activities because we brought our own gloves, though bats and balls were provided. I hated that game. I played second base because few players could hit that far.

After years of parochial school, of uniforms and limited, strictly supervised social activities, high school was a terrible shock. I never felt comfortable there, though there was a kind of kinship in being with the "eggheads" who were in the accelerated program, headed for college. While we might have been the swans intellectually, socially we were the ugly ducklings.

The social scene in high school was a nightmare. I felt as if I were decades older than the other students, as if any attempt to learn the current passwords and dance steps would not only be graceless, but that the results would be revealed for the shabby copies they were. The students who were the social leaders were, for the most part, totally dedicated to high school, as if it were an end in itself. It seemed odd then and it still seems so that they had no plans beyond graduation. It's no wonder that many of those people still look back at high school as the peak experience of their lives and long for those days to repeat themselves. Now, there's a horrid thought.

The dating scene was as awkward as the rest of it, sometimes so much so that I would think, "I'll look back on this and laugh," even as it was happening. For one prom, the boy I wanted to go with would have asked me, but his best friend wanted to, too, so to avoid bad feelings, they flipped a coin, and the friend won. I liked him well enough, but I certainly didn't have any romantic feelings about him. He showed up wearing elevator shoes because he was noticeably shorter than I.

This was not a problem with the boy I dated for quite a while. R.T. was six feet four inches or so and hardly wide enough to cast a shadow. We weren't romantically involved, but we were good companions. He helped me with my math and chemistry, and I helped him with his English assignments. He owned a battered VW Bug and a beagle named Oglethorpe. Every time I rode in the front seat, Oglethorpe sat in the back, growling. R.T. was on a very tight budget because he'd stayed in the valley to finish high school when his family moved away. Whenever I took him home, my mother fed him. It was amazing what that skinny kid could eat.

One night when he came to visit, the house was full of Italians, relatives and friends, mostly male, and all in dark suits. R.T. responded politely to each as he was introduced, and then as soon as we were out of the room, he said, "Good Lord! Is there a still in the back room? I expect the Untouchables to break down the door at any minute."

It might have been a tad anti-Italian, but it was funny and apt—the men did look like Mafia dons as pictured in popular films.

As in academics, my social salvation also came through the ranch, through three young men I met here. They were a few years older, and they were special in that they liked women with working brains. One of them died in a plane crash while he was still very young, but the other two remain friends.

By the time I went to college, I was growing more and more intolerant of the educational system in general. I attended three colleges in four years and still managed to graduate with honors in English. This was untoward behavior in the family; prior to my rebellion, one chose a college and stuck with it for the duration. I broke ground for my brother and my cousins; they did not feel obligated to stay if they didn't like the institution, though the pressure was still there to get a degree, and David was the only one who so followed his own course that he avoided a diploma.

I figure I was taught by sixty teachers, give or take a few, from nursery school through college. Ten of them, or about 17 percent, were extraordinary. I can't judge whether it is sad that there weren't more or wonderful that there were those ten. I give full credit to them, but they had competition from a peerless source.

In the rounding of the seasons, in the wild and domestic theaters of the land, in the endless profusion of books, music, and conversation, in the blend of people who lived and worked there, the ranch in its entirety offered a wider, deeper education than any formal school could. I know how fortunate I was to be one of its students.

Chapter 8

ODD JOBS

My brother and I were always adequately fed, clothed, and sheltered, and there were windfalls—this parcel of land sold, a good swing in that business—which were turned into journeys and adventures that made us well traveled when we were quite young. But from day to day, cash was in short supply and allowances small. Anything apart from necessities had to be earned.

My first jobs were typical of the era—baby- and house-sitting, gardening, car and window washing, and shoe polishing.

My cousins, Kemper, Craig, and Scott, were born in 1951, 1953, and 1955 respectively. Since I was already five years old when Kemper was born, it was natural that my aunt and uncle would hire me to baby-sit. I think I was nine or ten when I started.

The cousins spoiled me for later clients. They were bright and cooperative most of the time. When there was dissention, it was usually between Kemper and Craig.

Kemper and Scott, the oldest and youngest, are much alike, quiet and even-tempered unless thoroughly provoked. Craig is the most emotional and open of the three, usually on top of the world or down in the pits, seldom on the middle ground.

One night I heard Craig laughing hysterically over Kemper's agitated mumble, and I thought he and Kemper were going at it. Instead, I discovered that Craig was trying to help.

They were in the bathroom where Kemper had given himself a haircut. His hair was pretty short to begin with, but he'd managed to take out a big chunk in the front, right down to the scalp. It was not the effect he'd intended.

"Oh, no! Oh, no! Mom's gonna kill me!" Kemper was moaning, while Craig was trying to help him stick the hairs from the sink back on to his scalp with Butch Wax, that thick hair dressing boys used for grooming short haircuts.

"Your mother is not going to kill you," I assured him. "The worst thing that's going to happen to you is that you're going to have to go to school like this until your hair grows back."

Perhaps it had something to do with being the last of the grandchildren, the youngest of the five raised on the ranch, but Scott as a child was the most self-contained person of any age I've ever known, even more than his brother Kemper. With quiet insistence, he did everything at his own pace, in his own way.

He had a series of alter egos, indicated by specific accessories. Engineer Bill, of television fame, had a railroad cap. Office Man appeared when Scott was dressed up in his best. But Mac was his favorite. Mac was modeled after a heavy–construction equipment operator who was a particular idol of Scott's.

Woe betide any of us if we missed the clues and greeted Scott as Scott. He would get a look of patient disappointment, and then he would protest, "I'm not Scott, I'm

Mac"—or Office Man or Engineer Bill or Chef Boyardee, or one of the others I have probably forgotten.

Office Man had his own little desk in the main office of the ranch, and Scott would spend long stretches there scribbling on paper and stapling and taping while his mother and mine carried on the work of the guest ranch.

When birthdays came around, and we were asked what we'd like, most of us tended to think in fairly liberal terms—books, a new saddle or bridle, new boots, specific toys—but Scott was not so greedy. One year when Grandma asked him what he wanted, he inquired, "How long until my birthday?"

"Your birthday is in three weeks."

"Oh, by then I will be out of Scotch tape," he told her after considering the matter.

Scott was very enterprising. When new gardens were going in, he hauled manure for a penny a load in his red wagon. Like my brother, Scott could drive the tractor, Jeep, and other farm equipment just as soon as he could reach the pedals, but the little wagon served well enough for its time.

As a small child, Scott was prone to frightening bouts with bronchitis. After one of these, he emerged looking big-eyed and waifish.

I greeted him with, "Hi, Mac," guessing that I knew who he was that day, though there was no specific article of apparel to tell me.

He shook his head and announced, "I am Scott Ballenger Campbell."

I was stunned and asked where Mac was.

"He's dead. I killed him. I killed them all. They were hanging on hooks in the closet, and they got into a fight, so I stomped on 'em all."

The story became even more bizarre when Donna related what Scott had babbled while delirious with fever. He had said that Mac and his wife had been in an accident, and Mac's wife had died, but nobody would tell Mac. He kept pleading with invisible beings to please tell Mac what had happened.

Scott was only five or six, so this adult concern was frightening at the time, but in retrospect, it makes sense. Scott was a sensitive, aware child, and even the most secure children fear the loss of people they love.

As for the violent end to the alter egos, that, too, turns out to be quite natural. Years later, I read that a majority of personas are dispatched violently because when children are old enough to dispense with such imaginings, they need to do it in such a way that a clear line is drawn and the invisible companions are forever banished. I did not do this to my own Princess Tonka of the Seven Tribes, but she was not the same. I was older than Scott when I conjured her; she was a deliberate piece of theater.

Something Scott and I had in common was sometimes receiving too much attention from the guests. I was the first grandchild, he the last, so the guests took a lot of notice.

One day, Donna found Scott in the main living room, trying to push guests toward the door and saying, "Go home now. I don't want you here."

Since the first lesson ranch children learned was to be polite to the paying guests, and since Scott was by nature polite, this was startling behavior, not excused by the fact that the guests were amused.

"These people have the right to be here," Donna told her son. "If you can't be nice, you'll have to go home."

Scott thought this over. "I can't be nice," he said, and home he went to the Campbells' house toward the other end of the ranch. He stayed there all day, unrepentant.

In a way, I am guilty of the same sin as the guests. Scott is nine years younger than I, and I cared for him while he was still in diapers, a service I do not recall performing for his brothers. Years later, Donna told me that it was always intriguing to see how I'd put the diaper on since I seldom followed standard procedure. The problem was the diaper pins. In those days, they were lethal weapons, and I had a phobia about puncturing the baby. It took a lot less than my vivid imagination to picture Scott with multiple stab wounds, so everything I did with the diapers was designed to provide extra padding against the pins.

I didn't mind when Kemper grew up and married Nicki, when Craig grew up and married Laura, but it has always been difficult to watch Scott pass the milestones. Seeing him graduate from law school and later marry (though his wife Diana is every bit as wonderful as Nicki and Laura) were rites of passage that made me feel much older than any of my birthdays ever had. I know my rather indulgent attitude drives him nuts, but I can't seem to help it. Even though he's over six feet now and looks very professional in his suits, it is still easy to see the little boy who was.

After practicing on my cousins, I took other babysitting assignments and continued doing the odd jobs available on the ranch, to the extent that to this day, I hate washing cars and polishing shoes, though gardening is still a pleasure.

Later came more dependable and time-consuming labor, official work. My first town job was at a local drugstore. Mr. and Mrs. Graves, the proprietors, had known me and my family for years, but only a long time after the fact did I realize what a compliment it was to trust me enough to hire me as their youngest clerk.

I approached the job with a good measure of trepidation. The store carried a wide variety of general merchandise in addition to the pharmaceutical items, and I was intimidated by the Graveses, who were both a bit gruff and sharp. They seemed to have more faith than I in my ability to learn the job quickly. But Mrs. Graves, while judging me quite sophisticated for a fifteen year old, also knew I was very innocent in some ways, and she was determined that I not be embarrassed. She took me aside and explained that it was only a matter of time before some young man would ask me for condoms, perhaps because he genuinely wanted to buy them, but more likely because he would want to see how flustered I might become. This possibility was heightened by the fact that as junior clerk, I worked the off-hours such as evenings and weekends.

Mrs. Graves showed me the products, reading off the various brand names the drugstore stocked as well as telling me the slang terms for condoms. "If anyone asks you for them, just send him back to the druggist, and you won't have to bother any further about it."

The instructions made sense since those were the days when condoms were kept out of sight, and thus out of reach of anyone who wasn't very bold, very desperate, or very matter of fact—further reason to believe that any man who asked me about the product was probably more concerned about my reaction than in protected sex. Women simply did not buy condoms in those days, so that possibility wasn't discussed.

I practiced my reaction innumerable times, hoping I would be able to react with calm authority and without blushing.

It was near closing time one night when my moment of truth arrived.

He was short and swarthy, with stubble heavy on his cheeks. His clothes were shabby, and a knit cap was pulled low on his brow. He sidled up to me and muttered his request, his eyes never meeting mine. "I want a Tonette," he said, and my brain raced over all the brand names in the special drawer. I was sure a Tonette was a cheaper brand trying to capitalize on the popularity of Trojans.

The blush swept up my face, red hot in spite of my efforts to stop it by will. "You'll have to go back and ask the pharmacist," I muttered.

The little man looked utterly baffled and even more uneasy than before, but he said, "Yes, ma'am," and went obediently to the counter in the rear of the store where I heard him say, "I don't know why I'm back here; all I want is a Tonette, a permanent wave for my little girl." I am sure by then he was ready to murder his wife for sending him on such an unmanly errand.

The pharmacist knew instantly what had happened, but he restrained his mirth until the man had made his purchase and left the store.

"Sold any Tonettes today?" remained a cause of inside laughter at the store for a long time. And when I was actually asked for condoms, I couldn't help the customer fast enough. Stocky, rumpled, exhausted looking, with thick-lensed glasses, he was pushing a pram with twins in it. It was all I could do not to ask him if he didn't want to buy more than a dozen.

Despite the Tonette disaster, working for the Graveses was a good experience for me. They paid three-sixty an hour, a princely sum for the time, and they trusted me and treated me as an adult. And for Christmas they gave me a pair of black gloves with gathers to midarm and a long, flame-colored chiffon scarf—perfect, wondrous gifts.

I know Mrs. Graves chose those gifts, and that is much of the wonder. I have no idea what she was like in her youth, but by the time I knew her, she was a woman of angles—blunt cut hair, square hands, and rectangular body. Her skin was weathered by years on the desert. There seemed to be little that was soft about her. But there was appeal in her straightforwardness, her no-nonsense approach to everything, and her sardonic humor. And somewhere behind that stolid exterior was a woman who could choose long black gloves and a chiffon scarf for a teenager who needed, more than anything else, to be assured that being tall and dark and dramatically foreign looking in a state renowned for its cuddly blondes was all right after all.

By the time she died, I knew Mrs. Graves well enough to call her, at her insistence, by her first name, albeit I always felt a twinge of unease. "Vivian" was always "Mrs. Graves" in my mind.

I did not weep at her funeral. The service was conducted by a minister who obviously knew nothing at all about the deceased. I'm sure that young man meant well, but the words he spoke were generic, suitable for many of the blurred, cosseted wives of the era, but not in a single syllable fitting for Mrs. Graves.

"Are we at the right funeral?" I asked my aunt, and she whispered back, "Well, all of Vivian's friends and family are here so it must be, but you certainly can't tell from what the minister is saying."

It was all we could do not to burst into laughter. It hit us at the same moment, how silly Vivian would have judged that service to be. It was no stretch at all to hear her muttering and swearing at the display.

All these years later I still have the gloves and the scarf.

Another venture into retail sales was at a local gift shop, The Pirate's Chest. It was one of the first of such establishments in the valley, a store that catered not only to tourists passing through but also to the locals who wanted fine towels, table linen, cookware, dishes, and the like for themselves or for others, particularly as wedding gifts.

On my first day, I slipped money *into* the till. There was a towel sale in progress, and the mathematics involved was complicated, with various percentages to be taken off at the register for different styles, sizes, and prices. In those days, cash registers did only the simplest tasks, and I was so nervous, I made a ten-dollar mistake in the customer's favor. I was sure my employer would fire me if he found out, so I made up the loss. I remember it so clearly because, obviously, I hadn't been paid yet, and having to shell out ten dollars from my meager resources was awful.

Long after that first day, I told my boss, Mr. Keel,

what I had done. He was appalled that I'd thought it necessary to make up the difference. "I make mistakes myself during those sales," he confessed. "You should have just told me."

Mr. Keel was a nice man, but I still wonder what he would have thought of an employee who fumbled on the first day, so I don't regret my action.

Mr. Keel's one weakness was gift shows. He should have sent an agent rather than going himself. The vast displays dazzled an otherwise-temperate man, and when the cartons arrived at the store, I and my co-worker, Helen, would unpack them warily. Most of the merchandise was quite nice, but there was always something that was, to Helen and me at least, so ugly that we couldn't imagine why anyone would want it. We called the style Neo-Grotesque, and the pieces were usually in the knickknack category, things such as reproduction carnival glass in garish colors, cutesy figurines, and my all-time favorite, plates and bowls made from specially processed cow manure. I think these last items might have been a local product, though I know the basic material was not purchased from the ranch.

Helen and I developed a game. The rules were simple. We picked out the things we thought most typical of Neo-Grotesque, and then we raced to see who could sell them faster. We picked our victims carefully. People in loud polyester prints were usually good marks. With some shame, I confess that we were usually successful and had a lot of fun. The game seems mean in retrospect, but then, those who can be talked into buying cow-poop plates probably deserve to have them in their houses.

One summer when I came home from college, I took the job of "game warden" on the ranch. As defined here, it meant organizing the guests' children and keeping them out of their parents' way. I hadn't ridden horseback for nearly six months, and my first week on the job, I had twenty-six children who wanted to ride, most of them daily. The mathematics were even more difficult than those connected with the towel sale. The children ranged in age from six to seventeen, and some were beginner riders while others were fairly skilled. There were only ten horses in the string, and three of them needed firm, preferably adult, riders, while the others varied from docile to capable of a nice lope. The schedule worked out to a minimum of three two-hour rides a day, beginning at 7 A.M., and that was in addition to dodgeball, pool games, and other activities. For the first time in my life, I knew what dudes were suffering from when they complained of being saddle sore. I was walking very, very gingerly by the end of the week.

But that summer was, for all the hard work, a great deal of fun. I was fortunate in the children I had in my charge. They were mostly well behaved and wanted to learn everything they could about ranch life.

The only kid I had trouble with was a teenage boy who wasn't happy about taking instructions from a female. He was fifteen or so, and short, which undoubtedly made matters worse.

I had iron rules on the rides. No one was to abuse a horse or another rider, and no one was to pass me; I set the pace according to the terrain and the group in order to prevent accidents. The children had fair warning that if they disobeyed, they would walk home on their own two feet.

The boy hated this routine. Though he bounced all over the saddle, he was convinced he was a terrific cowboy, and given the chance, he would have run his mount until the horse dropped dead. On this day, he was riding Major, the half-Arabian, half-Welsh pony. Major was tart-tempered but dependable.

The boy complained all the way that we weren't running enough. I explained that we weren't running at all, that a canter was as fast as we were going to go. We had just loped through a stretch of forest and desert when I signaled for everyone to slow to a walk.

211

"Why can't we go fast up there?" the boy whined.

"Because there is soft, deep sand up there," I explained patiently, though by then I wanted to yank him out of the saddle and dump him in the brush.

He just couldn't stand it. He kicked Major hard and shot past me. It happened so fast, there wasn't anything I could do except watch in horror as Major lost his footing in the soft sand and did a complete flip. I saw Major's hooves in the air and then nothing but a huge cloud of dust. I was sure the poor beast had broken his legs and that the boy was crushed beneath him.

"Stop your horses and hold them here," I ordered the other children before we reached the crash site, and they obeyed as neatly as a cavalry troop. They were as horrified as I about what we were going to find.

First Major emerged from the dust, shaking himself off, but standing firmly on all four legs. Then the boy came out of the cloud, finely powdered head to toe and paler under that but intact, with nothing more serious than a few bruises.

I have to give him credit. He had a certain panache. He looked up at me and said, "You were right. This is a bad place to go fast. Next time I'll do what you say." He did, too.

My favorite children of that entire summer were the six-year-old twins, Susie and Sheri. Their parents had, when they had made reservations, checked to make sure other children would be here for the week of their stay. The twins were dependent on each other and shy with everyone else, and their parents wanted them to be able to play more easily with others.

I didn't perform a miracle that week; the other children did. I explained the situation to them and asked their help in making the twins feel welcome, and every one of them took it on as a special project.

The first day or so, the twins clung to each other and

scarcely said a word, but they were defenseless against the onslaught of friendliness. If a dodgeball game was starting, they were pulled into the circle gently but inexorably, and no one said a word about lack of skill in the youngest players.

Once it was proved that they could swim, they were offered prime seats on the rafts and inner tubes.

At mealtimes, it was deemed a privilege if the twins were at one's table.

They blossomed visibly. How could they not with so much attention being showered upon them? By midweek, they no longer cared where their parents were for most of the day, and they were no longer clinging to each other. Even the early silence was gone, though they both still spoke shyly.

One day Susie came up to me and said, "I bet you can't tell us apart, cuz' nobody can 'cept Mommie and Daddy."

"Well, I can. You're Susie."

She was dazzled by this display. "How do you know that?"

I couldn't tell her the truth, that she was slightly cross-eyed and her sister wasn't, so instead I said, "You're just a tiny bit taller than Sheri." She liked that explanation, and she stood so straight afterwards, she added substance to the imaginary measure.

The twins gave me hugs and tears on the Sunday afternoon of their departure, and their parents gave thanks. I accepted all on behalf of the other children who had dealt so kindly with Susie and Sheri. I wish I could say that I saw the twins again and watched them grow up. But that wasn't to be. Many families did return year after year, but for some, even our low rates were a once-in-a-lifetime indulgence, and for others, going to a guest ranch was just one thing on a long list of vacation plans.

There are some advantages to not knowing. I can imagine that the girls grew to be fine women who never forgot what it is to be shy and who taught their own children to extend a hand in friendship to the shy ones.

Sometimes jobs offer surprising advantages. I started wearing glasses when I was twelve. The world had become an Impressionist painting, full of swirling color, rather nice, but not clearly defined. The first day of wearing glasses was a voyage of rediscovery. I had forgotten that leaves and flowers had precise edges, that birds were sharply cut against the sky, that every living thing was delineated from every other.

But in those days, there was little choice of frames. I ended up with the same ones my grandmother had: ugly, black cat frames that were too small for my face. I didn't mind what Nature thought of me in glasses, but I used to take them off whenever possible when I was around people, particularly those of my age, even though it meant greeting posts and shadows in a cordial manner while unintentionally ignoring friends. The scruffy-surfer episode was a direct result of those hideous glasses.

By the time I was sixteen, I was getting stronger glasses about every six months. The ophthalmologist didn't really approve of the new-fangled contact lenses, but she had to concede that they sometimes arrested the progress of myopia. In my case, they did just that for decades, for which I am still thankful. But the ophthalmologist dealt with an optometrist I didn't care for, so eventually I went to Dr. Nassif. It was a serendipitous move. I worked in his office as a receptionist for a while, and he and his wife became very close friends of mine, which they are to this day. And they still give me a professional discount on eyeware. For someone like me who is very hard on contacts and glasses both, the value of this discount far exceeds any benefit I brought to their office while I worked there.

My other office experience was in the law. I worked for my uncle as a secretary/receptionist and later on for the man who bought the practice when Uncle Joe became a judge. Much of the work was very precise and tedious, such as the filing of updates in various volumes of legal codes— hundreds of pages that flooded in periodically—and the typing of standard contracts. The latter task was simplified when the office got a machine that could, once the model was typed, repeat it over and over again, pausing only for specifics to be added. Despite the work it saved, I hated that system. When the machine paused for a date or for a company's name to be inserted, it would hum impatiently, and when it was causing the typewriter to reproduce the text, it had no sense of where a page began or ended. One day I got so hypnotized by the automatic typing that I allowed it to go on long after it had reached the end of the page and tossed the paper out. The machine tapped on, unconcerned by the absurdity of invisible words.

That was not the only machine that terrorized me. There were others, including a big copier that sometimes ate original documents. Corky was the office manager, the probate department, the chief secretary, and the head mechanic. It's a good thing she was so patient with me and the machines; otherwise, the whole operation might have ground to a halt.

Legalese is a painful language at best, twisting around on itself like a snake trying to bite off its own head. But Uncle Joe was one of the most eloquent of its practitioners, insisting on clear, concise English wherever possible. And while many of the office tasks were dull and repetitive, his practice was not. He took all kinds of cases, and had a reputation for being willing to listen to almost anyone with a problem. He was a lot like a country doctor. It was more important to him to help the clients than to collect the fees. This might have made money scarce sometimes, but the trust and gratitude he received for his services were immeasurable. Even the hill people came to him. These were hermit types, male and female, who lived far off in the foothills or out on the desert, having as little contact with civilization as possible, but forced to come in when problems arose concerning mining claims, property-line disputes, etc. Many of them were quite odd, dressed in motley and more comfortable talking to themselves than to someone else. But Uncle Joe always treated them as if they were as important as any CEO. To him, they were.

Some cases were very sad. In one bitterly fought custody battle, the mother prevailed. There was a lot of evidence that she wasn't a fit parent, but in those days, it was nearly unthinkable to deny maternal rights. Joe's client, the father, was heartbroken, but there was nothing he could do when the mother took their son and moved to Texas. Some months later, Texas authorities called the father to come get his son. The boy, then about twelve, had waited patiently, alone in a rented house, for three days after his mother had deserted him. Neighbors had reported his predicament to the authorities. When his father arrived to take him home, the child flew at him, cursing and attacking him with his fists.

The mother's sole object in gaining custody had been to turn the boy into a weapon against the ex-husband she despised. She never tried to see her son again, and it took a long time for him to learn to trust his father as he had before the custody case. And there isn't really any way to tally the ultimate damage. I wonder what kind of man he grew to be. Did he ever fully trust anyone again? As an adult, how did he feel about women, about children, about other people in general?

I tried to be very professional when I worked for Uncle Joe. I didn't want him to be sorry he had hired a relative. But sometimes even the best intentions go awry in the face of greater need.

During the time I was working in Joe's office, my dog, Waif, brought me a baby sparrow, which I named Smidgen. He needed to be fed very, very often. By then, I had raised

216

enough baby birds to be pretty good at mixing various human baby foods—I was not willing to chew and regurgitate worms, insects, or even seeds. There was no one else to care for Smidgen, so I took him to the office. I kept him in the utility room, where there was a small refrigerator, the Xerox machine, and office supplies, and where Joe seldom ventured.

I managed to keep up with the telephone, billing, typing, filing, receptionist duties, etc., as well as tending to Smidgen for three days before he betrayed us. I was feeding him when the phone rang. There was an extension in the utility room. I answered it in my best secretary voice. It was a major client. I put him on hold and buzzed Uncle Joe. But in the course of my telling Joe who was on the phone, Smidgen got impatient. He was perched on my finger, and he was hungry. He was very small, but the sound he made was not. It sounded like a ten-ton turkey vulture demanding unlimited road kills.

"What in the . . . never mind . . . I'll find out later. Put the call through."

Uncle Joe knew me too well. The minute the call was completed, he stalked down the hall, took one look at me and Smidgen, sighed and said, "I should have known," and went back to his office.

At the end of the summer, Joe took my aunt and my cousins to Hawaii. I "manned" the office while everyone else was on vacation and I prepared a special welcome for Joe and the staff for when they would return on Monday. I cut out huge construction-paper bird feet and put them in a trail leading from the back door, down the hall, through the door into Joe's office, over his desk, and back out again until they reached the utility room. I left dyed ostrich feathers here and there, as well as a bill for five hundred pounds of birdseed on Joe's desk. The trail of prints and feathers led to the little refrigerator and inside was perched a little fake bird.

I'm not sure Uncle Joe has ever fully forgiven me because I rained on his parade. He arrived via the back door in complete Hawaiian tourist mufti—floral shirt, lei, straw hat, and toy ukulele—only to discover that his staff was already in hysterics over the bird joke. To his credit, he laughed as hard as anyone.

At this point, I want to state that I never, ever answered the phone with, "Uncle Joe's office," though that is the legend. At least, I don't think I ever did.

The lawyer who purchased my uncle's practice was as kind to me as Joe had been. But his prose was very different. He entered law in middle age, and he had lived a rough and ready life before that. When he gave me briefs to type, the grammar often made me nervous. Finally, I went to him and asked if he wished me to correct it.

"What in the hell do you think I hired you for?" he asked, and that made my job much easier.

My last "regular" job was with that lawyer. After that, it was a matter of piecework with most of my time devoted to trying to become a full-time, self-supporting writer. I made macramé accessories—necklaces, headbands, and belts, one belt pattern taking an average of seven hours to knot, though I sold the belts for only ten to twelve dollars a piece. It was the same with the copper necklaces made of yards of wire twisted and coiled into intricate, interconnecting spirals. I hand-painted notecards and embroidered shirts. I was never sure whether getting a large order from a store was a good or a bad thing. Lord knows, I needed the money, but an order for a dozen of one item meant seemingly endless hours of repetition. I have great respect for those special craftspeople and artists in various media who stuck it out and who are doing well today. I would have starved to death had I not been living in my parents' house.

Another of my stints seems to be a classic writer's desperation job. I hand-addressed, stuffed, sealed, and stamped the ranch's Christmas cards. That included folding the cards and enclosing a separate recipe card in each one. The list was thirty-five hundred names long. The movements became so automatic in the sealing phase, sometimes I would run my fingers along the flaps until, having worn the skin off, I would notice smears of blood. I hasten to add that I did not lick the stamps or the envelope flaps but used a brush or sponge. I suspected that anyone who licked that amount of stamps and envelopes might die of glue ingestion, though I have no scientific proof for this. The first year I did the job, I got three cents per card, then it moved up to five cents, and finally, for the last year, it was seven cents, which was $245 total for the job. I was thankful for the money, but it was awful work. To this day, I feel as if an enormous weight has been lifted each year when my own much-less-numerous Christmas cards have gone off with the mail carrier.

Whenever I talk to young, would-be writers, there is always some point at which they ask about work experience, and they want to be assured that all the jobs were somehow useful to the process of becoming a writer. Usually I tell them that the most useful thing is never to have to do any of those jobs again. But in a way, their wish is half right. Most tasks have something to teach the doer, even if it is only patience. But there is a point where the task has been done so often, whether it be going to someone else's office every day or twisting copper wire for jewelry, that it has nothing left to teach and becomes a vampire, sucking time and energy away. There seems to be a general belief that writers, particularly writers of fiction, always ought to be doing something besides writing, as if the writing itself should never be a full-time job. No one expects the same of doctors or lawyers or the like. I don't know anyone who would like to find out that his or her surgeon is moonlighting as a bartender on weekends, or that the bank manager is waiting tables or selling handicrafts.

This imbalance in society's judgment teaches its own lesson, a measure of defiance that boosts the persistence needed to do a job that is only listed as "other" on the check-the-box questionnaires about where one fits in the scheme of things.

I tell would-be writers that if they have doubts, they ought to consider becoming brain surgeons or corporate lawyers instead; either course would take much less time and would pay far more and more regularly than the wages earned by the vast majority of writers. But I acknowledge what would-be writers with dedication, determination, and talent already know, that nothing I or anyone else can say will make any difference. That is the curse and the blessing of the job. Dream spinning, taking all the tangled webs in the brain and weaving them into a pattern that will imprint itself on the minds of others—there is power in that; there should be responsibility, too. And there is despair when the words won't move. But always, always there is the lure of that fierce joy that comes when the blank pages fill with the shape of tales told around the first fire and ever after. It is a job I plan to keep.

CROPS AND CREATURES

Chapter 9
BUY HIGH, SELL LOW

When people talk about chucking the stress of urban life in order to take up the peaceful life of farming, I become an instant Cassandra, foretelling doom at every turn of the harrow. The best tool a farmer can have is an independent income large enough to support the addiction of trying to make the land produce. Even my small garden is so demanding that I sometimes think I ought to plow money into the dirt instead of going through the intermediate steps of buying seed, plants, soil amenders, fertilizer, stakes, ties, etc.

The ranch is beautiful in its wild state, deadly for farming. It is marginal land that has been scoured clean by cyclical floods of the river, rather than enhanced as land is along the Nile. In some ways this land is like that in the tropical rain forests, so fragile that though it will give generously for one or two crops, it then takes back the hope of balanced accounts and demands that more and more be sacrificed to the acres before they will yield.

People who are not farmers often wonder how people who are can get into such dire financial straits, borrowing and borrowing until not even the bank wants the land.

It is the passion that cannot be quantified and cannot be quenched even by years of failed crops.

Spring is always glorious. The first green shoots burst free of the soil. Calves and foals are born. Birds fill the woods with song, and the swamps hum. Everywhere the earth is rich, fragrant, new, and ripe with promise. Every spring is the beginning of a love affair, and it is impossible then to think that the mistress is treacherous, the promises empty, disaster inevitable.

My family was not composed of "simple farmers." There probably is no such thing as a simple farmer. To farm at all, one has to be cunning and determined, the land has to be at least willing, if not enthusiastic, and outside pressures must be taken into account as well. If the crop you raise isn't what the market wants that year or is part of a general abundance that drives down prices, all the work can be for naught.

Given the prices they fetch these days, Arabian horses would seem a good investment. However, while my family was raising them, as well as palomino-Arab crosses, the preference shifted from the trim desert breed, such as those raised on the ranch, to what some call Polish Arabs because of the influence of animals raised in Eastern Europe. The desert breed are finely sculpted animals that look like chess pieces. The Polish Arabs are just as purebred, but the breeding has selected much larger and bigger muscled animals. Actually, they are more suitable for taller, bigger riders, but I don't find them nearly as appealing as the desert breed, which look as if they are ready at any moment to sweep off across the sand dunes.

The market in general declined in the late forties and early fifties, so Arabian horses, even large ones, didn't sell well any more. But there were always the beef cattle. Admittedly, the grazing here is too poor to support many head to an acre, but this was in the days before anyone suggested that eating meat might not be the greatest thing for one's heart. And in any case, these cattle were range fed, so they carried less fat anyway. Then beef prices dropped so that it cost more to raise the animals than could be earned back in the sales, and both my father and Uncle Joe had come to the realization that farming was not for them. Uncle Joe went to law school, and Dad began to study various professions, though he continued to do a lot on the ranch because he was skilled with tools and machines. The cattle were sold off as the horses had been. Though a few horses had been kept, all of the cattle went. This was a tragedy because of Twinkie.

Twinkie was a maverick, deserted by her mother at birth. Uncle Joe found the heifer right after the birth and cleaned off the birth sack and brought her home. Joe was the first living thing the calf saw or smelled, so it naturally assumed that Joe was its mother. Named Twinkle, nicknamed Twinkie, for the star pattern on her forehead, the brown-and-white animal followed Joe around like a puppy the minute the gate was opened. Even when she started getting quite large, she thought she should still be able to curl up on Joe's lap. She never thought of herself as a cow. When she was put out with the others, she kept her distance and would trot right over to the fence the minute any humans came by.

In the upheaval of selling off the herd, Twinkie was forgotten and loaded with the others. Down at the stockyards, Uncle Joe was crossing on a catwalk when he heard her bawling below him. There she stood, looking up at him as if to ask what in the world she was doing in that dreadful place.

To his enduring shame, Joe did not save Twinkie. The count had already been done, the deal made, and the stockyard was crawling with hard-bitten cattlemen who would not have understood the idea of a pet cow. My uncle is neither unkind nor cowardly, quite the opposite, so the Twinkie episode remains an unhappy aberration, made sadder by the old movies my mother has of Twinkie bouncing along, playing tag with Uncle Joe.

When I think back to the cattle-raising days, I marvel at how natural it all seemed, herding the cattle in for branding, castrating, dehorning, and inoculating—procedures I now find so repulsive, I know I couldn't stand to watch, let alone smell, the scene. Everything was covered in a fine pall of dust, and the constant lowing of the cattle was loud enough to make shouting necessary for any communication. And the odors were the worst. The scents of dust, of manure, of hot leather, and hot horseflesh—these were the ingredients of fine ranch perfume. But it is the other smells, the burned hide, the copper tang of blood, and the general stench of panicked animals that I hope I will never smell again.

Back then, we did not consider such things, and in any case, I witnessed only the last few years of our cattle business. I was an inept hand at best, which makes me wonder why, several years later, I went along to help with cattle belonging to someone else. The man was renting pasture space out on the ranch and needed some extra hands.

I took my pinto, Scout, the first day. He was young, fast, willing, and totally unused to cattle. A cow broke loose, and the foreman pointed at me and snapped, "Get 'im!"

Off Scout and I went, streaking down the field until Scout realized that we were actually chasing that beast in front of us. Scout reared in midrun, spun around, and raced back to the company of the other horses, all without noticing that I was hauling on the reins and giving him hell for disgracing both of us.

The next day I took Teresa, the palomino-Arab mare. She had worked cattle in her youth. But the foreman, not too fond of female help anyway, had had it with my lack of

226

skill. He assigned me and another girl, a friend who was visiting, to scour a dense stretch of woods for strays. He clearly did not believe any animals were there, but it was a good way to get us out of his way. To our delight, we found a pocket of yearlings hiding out in the willows like the lost boys, and with great pride we herded them in. But it was my last roundup; I did not volunteer again.

Once again a rancher is renting pasture space, from us and from the park across the tracks. I enjoy watching him and his family move the animals with their perfectly trained cutting horses and their herd dogs, but I feel no envy and have not offered my services.

There were various field crops raised at different times, and they were not always failures. Alfalfa, ryegrass, and such were cut and baled for hay, some of it sold, some of it used to feed livestock on the ranch. But the more sophisticated plantings weren't so successful.

Sugar beets raised for seed for a specific company sounded like a wonderful idea because the buyer assured payment by contract before the crop was in. And the first year, the crop was fine. Then, as usual, reality set in. The seed from subsequent plantings was smaller, not to the company's liking, and there were other problems. The crop required expensive spraying against insects. This was accomplished by crop-dusting planes piloted by lunatics who flew under electric and telephone wires and skimmed the tops of trees before dropping down to the fields. The task had to be done early in the morning with no wind. We shudder now when we think about how we would all troop out to watch the aerobatics, never considering the hazards of being enveloped in a cloud of insecticide.

There were also the horned larks. They are one of my favorite birds, small, but so distinctly marked with a black breast band, a facial design of yellow and black, and little black "horns." No one had thought of them as a problem.

227

They were the good news–bad news birds of sugar beet–seed raising. The good news was that they ate insects. The bad was how they got to some of these insects. They would walk down the rows of seedlings, carefully pulling up the plants and setting them aside in order to devour the lively goodies that lived in the soil around the roots. Alas, they did not replant the crop as they strutted along.

The potatoes were a memorable failure. Aunt Donna, who grew up on a potato farm in northern Maine, turned green at the thought of being involved in the potato business again. But she is too gentle a woman to accuse her husband and in-laws of madness, so the potatoes were planted.

The water didn't get to them at a crucial time and moths did. The result was weird-looking gnome tubers totally unsuitable for commercial sale. They had no standard size or shape; they were a collection of knobs. But as if in apology, they tasted divine, just as potatoes ought to but so seldom do anymore.

In order to clear the fields, we ran a "come dig your own" ad in the local paper. I think the charge was one dollar for a pickup load. At best, we figured a few hardy souls would come.

That weekend, my parents happened to be gone, so Aunt Donna ended up in charge of the great potato-digging rush. People came in droves. Donna spent most of the day down at the gate, collecting money, and dwelling on the irony of having moved three thousand miles away from Maine only to be pursued by the potato demons.

Another scheme was the gravel pit. By the time I was really aware of it, there were just a couple of tall cement structures to remind us that it had ever been. I was sorry that plan hadn't worked. As a child, the idea of selling dirt seemed splendid, and the gravel pit was far enough out in the desert so that it didn't detract from the rest of the land. In later years, adolescents from town discovered the possibilities of the place as a necking spot. The two buildings were open at ground level, but ladders led to the upper stories, platforms with low walls but no roofs, very private. The intruders left graffiti, including some pretty graphic stuff and words we were not allowed to say, let alone illustrate. Sometimes if we thought certain children staying at the guest ranch were worthy of the honor, we would take them out to show them the gravel-pit art.

The ski lake seemed like the perfect match of some swampland and the rising popularity of waterskiing. The marshy area had a firm island in the center, but the tules surrounding it had to be dug out. A huge piece of dredging equipment was brought in by rail. Unloading the thing took longer than expected and the boom was swung across the tracks on which trains came from the opposite direction. A train was en route and there was no way to radio the engineer to stop. However, a railroad man became an instant hero by running for miles to warn the train, which was able to stop before it smashed into the dredger.

Rent on that dredger was by the day and terribly high, and, of course, the digging took much longer than anyone had expected, but finally, the lake was formed. Water-skiers had an oval of more than a mile in a beautiful setting, with farmland spreading out on the east side and desert on the west.

Nature presented some problems, mainly rapid weed growth in the summer that turned the lake into plant soup. Expensive chemicals were one answer, and the Rube Goldberg weed cutter was another. It was a bizarre contraption built by the men to putt around the lake and chop up the foliage.

But the worst miscalculation of the whole project was regarding the stupidity of people. Never, ever underestimate how mindless humans can be. No amount of sign posting or buoy lines could keep the skiers from doing suicidal things. One woman ignored the signs marking off a wading beach and tried to ski to shore. She caught the skeg of her ski on the shallow bottom, flipped over, and broke her dentures. She sued. People ran over each other's tow ropes or caused rope burns, and they sued.

One man decided to try a ski kite, but when he lifted off, he was near a high-tension wire. He was lucky to get off with no more than burned hands. He could easily have been electrocuted. He sued.

It was impossible to anticipate all of the idiotic things people were capable of doing, and the insurance rates went higher and higher. No matter what happened or whose fault it was, we, as operators of the lake, were sued.

I can't say that I was sorry when the ski lake was no more. Each summer I would ski around to prove I could do it, but I never liked it. Speed sports have never been my favorite, and I didn't care for sharing the lake with catfish the size of the Loch Ness Monster when I fell off my skis.

The dairy was one of the better routines because it had evolved into a rental operation wherein, as noted before, a succession of Portuguese families paid to use the fields, barns, and pens and did all the work. Dairy farming is one of the most all-consuming types of farming because milk cows cannot be neglected; they must be milked two times a day no matter what.

But eventually even this closed down when mechanized milking machines made it possible and more profitable for the dairy families to have more cows than could be accommodated here. They moved away with their cows, leaving behind a vast amount of manure.

The best business the ranch ever engaged in was the selling of this manure. With a dairy in place for decades, a lot of free poop had piled up. Many people think cow manure, properly cured, is the best thing that can happen to lawns and gardens.

The fertilizer grinder the men built was as eccentric looking as the weed chopper. It still stands in the high weeds of the north pasture. My cousin Scott dubbed it the "nure chine," because he was too young to say "manure machine," and that became its affectionate title.

People who wanted the product had to come get it themselves. It was one dollar for a sack or four dollars and fifty cents for a pickup load. And while this enterprise was flourishing, we discovered an interesting fact. People do not steal cow manure; at least they never stole it from us. The buyers would knock on every door of the ranch, seeking to make payment rather than drive off with a free load.

Customers came in a variety of shapes, sizes, colors, and ages, though most of them were men, due to the lifting involved. My favorites were the old men. They seemed so much the same, brothers in the earth. They were broad, their skin weathered, their hands blunt, calloused, capable. Age had marked most of them with arthritis so that backs were a bit stooped, joints enlarged, gaits not quite what they must have been in younger days. But they moved with steady purpose and surprising strength. Most of them wore overalls and billed caps. They were from different states and backgrounds, but they were all bound together by a passion for making things grow. They had flower beds or vegetable gardens or orchards or lawns or a combination thereof. They had visions of new growth, plans of how to encourage it. No wonder they seemed so undiminished by their years.

We used to put on a New Year's Eve show at the guest ranch, and one year my grandmother's contribution was a song of tribute to the "nure chine." She sang it to the tune of an old hymn:

> Every little cow chip has a meaning all its own.
> Every little dung heap wears a shiny crown.
> And every skip load of cow manure
> Makes our future the more secure
> And the odor we must endure
> Until the grinder pays the loan.

Another venture that provided clear profit was leasing land to television and movie companies. And because the action was taking place on our land, we got to watch.

The first one I remember was a Western with Andy Devine in it. Since he usually played someone's sidekick, I presume there was at least one principal and maybe more, but to David and me, Andy was the big draw because we knew him from a kiddy show on television.

We dressed for the occasion, I in a "squaw" dress, a bright cotton with rickrack, and moccasins, and my brother in his cowboy outfit, complete from hat to holster to boots. The film company was working on the mesa across the river, a setting perfect for the genre, with the tumbled rocks of the Narrows in the background and brushy desert spreading out from the low cliffs near the river.

Mom drove us out in the station wagon. We saw one brief stagecoach chase, and then cast and crew broke for lunch. David and I were so shy, we hung back, just watching, trying to summon the courage to meet Mr. Devine.

He was a very large man, and they ate lunch off of a flimsy card table set up on the dirt. Either he or someone else bumped the table, and Mr. Devine's peaches in syrup slipped out of their bowl and down his buckskins. Some of the juice made it into the pocket that held his lighter. With that, he sprang up, and he said words he never, ever said on television.

David and I watched and listened in awe, but we did end up with a picture of the two of us standing with our slightly tarnished (and damp) hero.

Observing the process of movie making tends to erode the illusions of the final product. Once I rode out in the star's car because I was going to ride the horse (faithful Teresa again) that the production company was borrowing back to the stable. They'd trailered the mare out earlier, but it was easier all around if I brought her back. I was honored. I was a teenager by then and had a crush on the

232

handsome, tanned leading man who was popular in Westerns and adventure movies. He was very nice, but the glove compartment fell open, and there was a bottle of Man Tan. He didn't seem so ruggedly outdoorsy after that.

The pilot episode for another Western series was filmed out at the ski lake, and unlike many of the other projects, the pilot did lead to a regular slot on television. To this day, I wonder how it was managed. The star of this one could not remember more than a few words at a time. The dialogue went something like this:

"Well, hello there . . . damn! What's the next part?"

"Well, hello there, stranger."

"Oh, yeah. Well, there, stranger . . . hell, how does that go again?"

And so on. It was amazing that the series was ever made at all and more amazing that that actor is well-known and respected to this day. Maybe he had had a bad night before filming began.

That day, there was the added attraction of a very buxom young actress whose chief job was to be repeatedly dunked in the water so that her blouse would remain transparent. Uncle Joe stayed out so long watching and taking pictures that he got quite chilled. Aunt Donna told him it would serve him right if he got pneumonia.

One particularly exciting movie-making incident happened before my time. The scene involved the burning of a building, a specially built facade that really would burn, so the shot had to be done correctly the first time. The movie people had rented a car from Homer, the handyman. The car was to remain parked against the backdrop of the burning building until the hero and the heroine rushed out to get away. The car was old and rattletrap, but it was Homer's, and it was too much for him when he saw the leaping flames. He jumped in his car and drove it to safety before the actors could reach it.

The production company couldn't afford to build and

burn again, so they had to do the best they could with the footage they'd gotten.

It's no wonder that a lot of film is shot on sound stages where things can be controlled; filming on location means running the risk that the real world will intrude on the fantasy.

One television outfit was doing the pilot for a series about the early days of the railroads in the West. To them, this seemed like a perfect place for filming. It was winter, and while they might have to contend with the cold, they were confident that weather would not be an important factor. They built a scale railroad spur through a clearing that is just west of the river. The set was complete with all of the paraphernalia and rugged living quarters that would have characterized an early railroad construction camp. It was laudably authentic, and the film people were patient with visitors, even with the group of guests from the ranch who, in their attempt to avoid disrupting the work, sneaked through a swampy area and came up right in the middle of a scene.

Then it started to rain, and it kept on raining. The film company was nearing the end of their shoot, and they gamely declared that they would just work the storm into the story. But things were moving beyond easy adaptability. The rain plus overflow from other sources feeding into Pelican Lake broke through the earthen work dam (since replaced by concrete), and the water swirled down through the system, making its way to the river through the film set in the middle of the night. A few men had been left on duty to guard the equipment and the horses—very small horses to make medium-sized actors look large, but nonetheless valuable animals. The men were huddled in a tent, playing poker, when one of them noticed that his coffee cup was floating away. He and the others managed to swim the horses out of the flood, but the railroad set was a mess.

Considering the circumstances, the film people were

still fairly sanguine. They said they'd use the wrecked look as a dramatic detail. But in the end, they had a far greater foe than the flood. Another group was making a pilot based on a similar story line at the same time, but this other group was using a known star for the lead rather than a collection of unknowns. The series with the known star went on the air; the one filmed here didn't make it.

Lightning Strikes Twice, featuring Richard Todd and Ruth Roman among others, is one of the old movies that has shots of the ranch, namely the front of the Main House, though the interior shots were created elsewhere. Ranch residents pass the word when the movie is to be shown on late-night television.

Unfortunately, though the profit from leasing the land to film companies was welcome, it was rare because it was random, and the fees we charged were always minimal.

Despite the success of selling ground cow manure and of renting picturesque settings to film companies, the usual result of our commercial ventures dictated the family motto: "Buy high, sell low." When I was old enough to understand what was happening, I suggested we ask the government what commodity it would like to see decrease in price. Then we could raise that, the price would fall, and the government could pay us directly for our efforts. I still think that might have worked.

Chapter 10

THE CHICKEN TRAIN

The main Chicago–Los Angeles rail line runs through the ranch, and the local depot used to be a regular stop. The line here is owned by the Atchison, Topeka, and Santa Fe, shared by lease with the Union Pacific. Atchison, Topeka, and Santa Fe, spoken staccato, is rail music. Chicago to Los Angeles is generally east to west, but obviously there are adjustments to be made, and the rails run more north to south through the ranch.

    The earliest trains in my memory were pulled by black behemoths, steam locomotives with cow catchers on the front. My brother and I called them puffa-bellies, words from a children's song, because of the plumes of smoke and the wonderful gut-level pulse of their efforts as they gathered energy for the pull over the Cajon Pass or strained to slow down their cars coming off of the pass. I was still very young when the steam engines were supplanted by sleek diesels. Now they also have the status of icons, shaped as they were with a view to a future that never quite arrived.

THE CHICKEN TRAIN

Grandma embraced many twentieth-century advances, but flight was not among them. She admired her nephew by marriage, Dick Campbell, a Pan Am pilot, but given a choice, she always chose the train. And because of this, my brother, I, and our cousins had more train experiences than did most of our generation.

In the nineteenth century, time in America was standardized because of the railroads. As the rails proliferated, it was impossible to schedule the shipment of passengers and freight by the idiocyncracies of town clocks set to individual ideas of time.

This rail dominion over time was sufficient for Grandma. She was never very fussy about bedtimes for her children or grandchildren. She believed that children, after a few trial runs with staying up too late, would find a sensible hour to retire. But the summer when she took care of David and me while our parents were away, she decided there had to be some sanity about bedtime since we tended to stay up too late even by her easy measure. The problem was that the guests and Grandma would sit out on the front lawn and talk for hours after dinner, and David and I didn't want to miss any of it. Therefore, Grandma designated the "bednight train" as the signal that we were to retire. The bednight train was a passenger train that put on its brakes as it came through the ranch, thus throwing showers of sparks from its wheels. These fireworks were clearly visible from the lawn and were accompanied by the screech of metal on metal.

Train schedules were good enough for the nineteenth century, for Grandma, and for my brother and me. Our easy obedience brought an unexpected reward. To this day I don't know quite what happened, probably some strange alchemy from the combination of firm railroad time and daylight savings, or perhaps it was just the railroad's inability to keep the run on schedule. For whatever reason, the bednight train began to run later and later until David and

237

I drowsed as we sat on the lawn with the conversation swirling around us. Having met our part of the bargain, we did not feel obliged to point out the change.

Finally the sparks of the bednight train were especially glorious against the deep black of the night, and they burned their way into Grandma's brain. "Oh, Children!" she cried. "It's so late! How long has this been going on?"

We confessed that it had been going on for some time, but there was no censure from her since she had set the standard. However, a new bedtime was established, this time having to do with the transition from summer dusk to true darkness. Just as well: the mosquitoes were fierce on the lawn after sundown.

We didn't just watch the trains go through; we rode them. Every year for Grandma's birthday, she and we grandchildren would board the train in Victorville and travel to Los Angeles where our great-uncle Louis Elkins would pick us up and take us to the Griffith Park Zoo before the rest of the family, having driven down from the desert, gathered for the birthday dinner prepared by our great-aunt Lola at the Elkins's house in Glendale.

Moments after the train pulled out of the depot, it would pass through the Narrows and through the ranch. None of us needed any reminder of where we were, but Grandma would always exclaim, "Oh, look, Children, we're on *our* ranch!" as if this were a great surprise. She wanted other passengers to know exactly who owned the green land they were traveling through.

The trip became more difficult as we all grew older: schedules of other activities began to intrude for adults and children alike, and the zoo wasn't so appealing anymore. The last birthday train was memorable for macabre humor. We rode the train as usual, but instead of going to the zoo, Grandma and Great-Uncle Louis took us to Forest Lawn, a huge cemetery that not only has all the services generally associated with mortuaries, but also prides itself on its art collection, mostly copies of old masters.

We spent quite a bit of time driving around the old section, looking for a distant relative who had reportedly been buried with some victims of the San Francisco earthquake of 1906 who had been sent south for burial. We never did locate him/her, but we saw quite a few examples of old-fashioned, elaborate tombstones before we went on to the area that looked like Astroturf tightly tacked down with metal markers. I can still hear the conversation between David and Cousin Kemper.

"Dave, how come those are so close together? Is everybody buried here real short?"

"No," David replied. "They're regular sized, but they're buried standing up. Most of them are businessmen, so they're buried with their hats on and newspapers under their arms."

The day degenerated from there. While viewing the copy of Michelangelo's *David,* my brother remarked with innocent snobbery, "It doesn't look like the real one. It's too thick in the waist. Michelangelo had to make his David narrower there because of a flaw in the marble."

I'm not certain that story is true, but it is one of the legends we heard in Florence regarding the *David,* and I'm sure my brother's casual recounting of it plus the refusal of any of the rest of us to be impressed with Forest Lawn convinced Grandma that we'd grown too sophisticated for such simple pleasures as visits to zoos and cemeteries. We continued to celebrate her birthday in Glendale for years after that, but the routine was simplified to driving down by car for dinner only.

By the time we ended the birthday train trips, the transcontinental crossings were over, too, but they were never to be forgotten. That was the era of starched tablecloths, flowers, heavy cutlery, and wood paneling in the dining rooms, of observation cars that put one high above the landscape, of compartments that were perfect for children because everything was done in miniature, from the tiny wash basins to the fold-out beds. And in my memory, all of the porters were black men in pristine white coats. Now I realize that there must have been many cases of discrimination, that the job itself, that of glorified waiter, might have been discriminatory, but then, in my child's eyes, those porters were lords over their moving cities. There was nothing they could not provide or fix. There was nothing along the route they did not know. They were friendly yet aloof to the adult passengers. But to the children, they responded without reserve, with pride and enthusiasm for the sights along the way. Thinking back, I hope they felt that way; I hope that narrow corridor really did make them feel whole, proud, and delighted in a country that had so little room for them on wider roads.

Like the characteristic drawl of the astronauts, those porters all seemed to speak the same language, no matter where they were from. Their voices were never raised, always soft and soothing. And in those days, the trains made music, too, a steady clacking rhythm as the wheels passed over the rail joinings. Now, in the days of much longer rails, the sound is different, hesitant and discordant to my ears, though logic tells me it is a song no less regular, just different.

Of all the memories of those long crossings, the one etched most deeply is of a fox on a vast snowy landscape, everything, even his red coat, softly blue under a full moon. The fox stood with one foot raised and his ears pricked, waiting for the train to pass. I think I know what he was doing. Not long ago, I was walking on the ranch near the tracks, and I saw a coyote in the distance. Very deliberately he put his paw on the tracks, and then he backed away and sat down, waiting. I had neither felt nor heard the train, but the coyote was right. Before long, a freight came roaring through, and the coyote crossed after it had passed.

Foxes and coyotes are not the only animals I associate with trains. Circuses used to stop regularly to set up their tents at the fairgrounds, and watching the arrival was, to my mind, better than attending the performance. They would unload down by the depot and parade through town, the elephants and teams of horses pulling the wagons that contained everything from equipment to the big cats. The equestrians, in the full splendor of their spangles, rode their trick horses, keeping time to the music of the steam calliope.

I never aspired to be in a cage with lions or to wire walk high above the ground, but oh, to be one of those riders! That I could imagine. A simple exchange of jeans and shirt for finer fabric and glitter in white, red, yellow, silver, and gold—the circus colors of light—and a change of mounts as well, my western ride for one of those big-haunched horses that seemed to know exactly what to do without much effort from the rider.

Unfortunately, the clowns came too, and they were one part of the circus I could have done without, the reason I didn't like the actual performances as much as the arrival of the troop. The clowns played far too large a role in the shows for my taste. I found them horrifying rather than amusing with their painted smiles and fake tears hiding their real expressions. Most of all, I hated the casual malevolence of their routines that consisted of slapping, pinching, punching, tripping, and tricking each other—grown-ups behaving like the worst schoolyard bullies. I suspect there were a lot of children who felt just as I did but never said anything about it because adults seemed to think we should love the clowns.

The last circuses that came to town arrived by truck. There were no parades, and performers and animals alike had a sad, mangy appearance, as if their glory had whistled

241

away into the night when their union with the railroads ended.

As the trains brought delight, so did they bring destruction. More than one person has died at the crossing. The trains' size makes them appear to be going slower than they are, and living so close to the rail line, it is easy to grow so accustomed to the rattle and thunder that danger is forgotten. But the most common mistake is to cross after one train has passed only to be hit by another coming from the opposite direction, as Freida's father was.

Horses and cattle have fallen victim, too, wandering onto the tracks and then dying there because of trying to outrun instead of sidestepping the train. All the engineer can do is to sound a warning, an angry blasting of the whistle that further terrifies the animal. Once the family heard the whistle screaming and watched in horror from the Main House as Monarck, a prize palomino-Arab stallion ran in front of the train until it crushed him.

Derailments have thrown freight cars into the pastures and sometimes just the cargo is enough to chill the soul. During the Vietnam era, a seemingly endless number of freight trains rumbled through carrying tanks, big guns, Jeeps, trucks, and the multitude of other things needed for war, the loaded trains heading for the West Coast, shipping point for Southeast Asia.

The trains brought death in various guises, but they also transported life in myriad forms, and beyond the birthday trips, the transcontinental crossings, and the circuses, my favorite was the Chicken Train that stopped once every spring. It didn't matter to me that it paused only briefly or that it carried cars and cars of other freight; to me its sole purpose was the safe delivery of baby chickens.

On that night, my brother and I were allowed to stay up for hours past our normal bedtime in order to meet the train. And because nights are cold until late spring on the high desert, we went to the station bundled up in our winter coats, but our concern was all for the chicks that must not be allowed to catch a chill. The train would wheeze into the station, panting as it waited for the cargo to be off-loaded, before it trundled off.

The cardboard boxes were large, though scarcely more than chick high; they had ventilating holes and were tied with string. The chicks peeped sleepily as the boxes were loaded into the ranch station wagon. The mission then was to transport the chicks as swiftly as possible to the warmth of the brooding shed. The sawdust there smelled of cedar and was encircled by a funny little fence that must have seemed very high to such small creatures. Low-hanging lights with metal shades kept the area warm.

One by one we lifted the chicks out and put them down in the sawdust. Then we showed them, with pecking motions of our fingers, where food and water were. It didn't matter that they would soon become scrawny, smelly, and stupid chickens destined for Sunday dinners at the guest ranch. For this brief time, they were everything life is—soft, fragile, and yet so determined in the palpable beat of their diminutive hearts.

In those days, with the night sky inky black and cast wide with brilliant stars, there was a vast and visible universe over our tiny patch of life. I don't know why that contrast comforted me so, but it did.

Raised for Sunday dinners, the chickens were butchered at a facility in Phelan, a little community about thirty miles from here. This necessitated an annual chicken roundup. When the birds had reached the proper size, we, meaning the kids, would do the work under the supervision of whoever was the handyman at the time. We would wait until sundown, when the chickens had gone to roost, and then we would go into the henhouse, grab the birds by their legs, and stuff them into wood cages that went into the back of the station wagon. This work was accompanied by a chorus of squawking, a cloud of feathers and poultry dander, and the smell of warm chickens. But the chickens' resistance was an example of "sound and fury signifying nothing." Chickens are rigorously obedient to light and the absence of it, so that once the sun had vanished, they were ready to settle, whether or not they were being carted off to the slaughterhouse.

Freida's father, Fred, was in charge of my last chicken roundup. I got through all the catching and loading just fine, but as we were driving off of the ranch, I asked Fred to stop the car. "I've had enough," I announced. "I'm going home now." And I did. It was like those other watershed events: at one moment I was able to do the task or believe in the impossible, but in the next, I wasn't. In this case, the smell of the whole process so overwhelmed me that it was years before I could eat chicken again, and even now, I find poached chicken revolting because it is somehow closer to the original than other versions.

Having presented chickens as being so mentally inferior, I feel it only fair to acknowledge two chickens of great individuality and enterprise. The first was Henny Penny. She left the coop and came to live with us, all on her own initiative. She would have preferred to live in the house, but my parents didn't think that was suitable, so she nested under the evergreens close by. However, she spent the day peering in windows and waiting for a chance to scoot in through any door, and eventually she had to have her own dish on the porch because she intimidated our dog, Sniffer the Beagle, to the point that he would let her eat all of his food. Taking her back to the chicken coop was useless; she would get out and come right back to the house. But despite her independence, roosting orders dominated her brain when darkness came, and one night, an opossum killed her as she slept on her nest. We felt silly to miss a chicken, but we did miss her.

The other standout was Glenn. He was a white rooster.

Someone dumped him on the ranch, and it didn't take us long to understand why. He staked his claim to the Main House patio and by some inner calculation decided who would and would not be allowed in the patio. He was not subtle in ousting the unwanted. He went after them with his spurs. Those who engage in the nasty "sport" of cockfighting enhance the natural spurs of roosters with metal as an exaggeration of the natural defensive/offensive weapons that roosters have, but the natural projections do very well outside of the pit, and Glenn's spurs were exceedingly effective against unprotected human legs as he jumped and stabbed at them.

We admired that rooster—to the point that he had been given his name, though I don't remember who chose it—but we couldn't live with a fowl who terrorized guests according to some hidden agenda. There were quiet discussions in progress regarding ridding ourselves of him when rescue came in the form of a guest couple who had poultry at home. They were charmed by Glenn's bravado and were sure they could handle him. I think they saw him as a super stud for their hens, though we did tell them that he, like Henny Penny, detested other chickens of either sex. The funny thing is that Glenn liked these people as much as they liked him. The last I saw of him, he was sitting, like a sultan with a chauffeur, in the back of their station wagon as they drove away.

Trains don't stop here anymore, not the Chicken Train nor any other, and the abandoned station burned down a few years ago. Amtrak passenger service from other stations is nothing like what used to be. And I know I am not the only one who is nostalgic for past glories. When the old diesel service was to cease, the Santa Fe Chief came through on its final run. All the chrome was polished, little flags flew from the engines, a sign reading ADIOS hung from the back, and white-jacketed porters waved from the door windows and from the back at the crowds of people who turned out in tribute. We had our own gathering down at the ranch crossing, and it was as sad as saying good-bye to a friend.

One May morning last year, we waited at the crossing again because the railroad, for public relations, had brought a steam locomotive out of storage, and the black Number 8444 came through the ranch. We heard it long before we could see it, and we remembered why we had loved the old trains so well. Steam whistles had their own music, a long, full-throated wail that seemed to hang on the air as the smoke from the stacks used to hang over the river pastures after the trains had passed.

When the steam locomotive met another train for a race through Cajon Pass, ten thousand people were there to watch, their cars blocking all traffic. The highway patrol soon stopped giving tickets and trying to make the cars move on; the officers undoubtedly watched the race with everyone else.

The accusation is often made that Americans have no sense of history. That is not always true, at least out here.

Chapter 11

THE YEAR OF THE SKUNK

For me, the drawbacks of living in the country are far outweighed by the advantages, but I admit there can be problems with some of the wild things that periodically take up residence in the ranch buildings.

Elsewhere I mentioned the skunk who stole eggs from the kitchen, but he was only a fraction of the cast that performed during what we came to call "the year of the skunk."

My great-aunt Lura was minding the ranch desk one evening when the first intruder appeared, but the next morning there was some confusion because the note on the door of the hall bathroom seemed to read: "Be Careful. Shark in the bathtub." There was a towel tucked neatly against the bottom of the door. Great-Aunt Lura wasn't there to clarify, but the rest of us decided that a shark in the bathtub wasn't too likely on the desert.

The towel was drawn away, the door opened very slowly, but the tub was empty and so was the bathroom. By then, "skunk" was the guess, but it seemed to have vanished.

Indeed, it had tried hard to do just that. The hall connected the office with my grandmother's apartment. Grandma had a little solarium where she kept her plants. It looked as if a highly selective vandal had been in the solarium. The pots were still up on the ledge, but the soil and the plants were scattered over it and the floor. Apparently, the skunk had climbed up and had tried to dig his way out through the pots.

The solarium is right off the living room, and in the living room is an open staircase leading up to a loft, a loft that has its own little hall connecting it to the attic of the Main House.

Finally, the skunk was found. He was asleep in the bottom drawer of a built-in storage unit in the loft hall. The potential for the spread of skunk stench via the attic was appalling, like dropping a stink bomb into the central heating unit of a very large house.

No one wanted to awaken the skunk, but everyone wanted him out of the house. My mother called the animal-control people because it seemed to her that they would be just the ones to remove a wild animal from one's attic. They did not see it that way; they said they couldn't do anything unless the skunk bit someone, in which case the danger of rabies would have to be considered and the animal taken care of. The animal-control attitude made us wonder how they would have responded had Mom reported a lion in the attic—probably the same way.

She called them back, but this time she said, "Pretend the skunk has bitten someone, what would you do then?"

This time they suggested anesthetizing the animal, though they weren't sure of how this should be accomplished. It wasn't an easy problem, after all, since the object was to remove the skunk without angering it.

Ether was sent for, and Mom waited downstairs while

the men went upstairs to drug the animal. However, it was soon apparent that things were not going as planned. The skunk had awakened. He wasn't aggressive, but he wasn't moving either. He was curled up in his drawer, blinking at the men. Meanwhile, the men were in other jeopardy.

Mom kept calling to them, asking them if they were all right, and though they kept assuring her they were, she could hear by their slurring voices that while the ether might not be doing anything to the skunk, it was putting the men to sleep. She ordered them downstairs for another strategy session.

We never did understand the physiology or the chemistry involved, but chloroform worked where ether had failed, and the skunk was carried out of the house.

That was only the beginning of the invasion. Next came the skunk in the kitchen, and then there was the one in the linen closet. Freida discovered his depredations, and she was so amused, she had a difficult time explaining coherently. The best evidence of the skunk's presence was a feather duster. Skunks love poultry, and the feathers were genuine, but they were also bright orange, a fact that hadn't impressed the color-blind skunk. He had plucked every feather out of that duster until all he had left was a plastic stick. Freida said he must have been disappointed to have caught such a skinny chicken.

The thresholds of the doorways in the Main House are worn, and that spring and summer we discovered that skunks can get in anywhere once they've squeezed their wedge-shaped heads through, particularly the spotted skunks, which are smaller than the striped ones. On a couple of occasions, skunks, heading for the pleasures of the kitchen, trotted right through the living room, past guests who were playing cards or otherwise enjoying themselves. The guests remained still and quiet. And we learned a bit more, that skunks are quite patient and don't spray unless they are startled or threatened. Even then, they will do their furious little dance of warning, tail in the air, feet pattering, before they let fly. But they are also exceedingly stubborn and expect everything and everyone to get out of the way.

We blocked up any opening we could find in the Main House with steel wool, fixed the thresholds, and gradually persuaded the skunks that they did not belong inside the house. But the hazard remains acute outside during skunk season.

I once brought a night-ride home hours late because skunks blocked one trail after another. On a morning ride, we weren't so lucky. Some dogs were after a skunk, ignoring the spray in their frenzy, and the group went right through the noxious cloud. I brought ten reeking youngsters back to their parents just in time for breakfast.

It is advisable to walk carefully at night and to listen for rustling. And taking the garbage out requires care. I dropped a sack right on top of a skunk who had fallen into the garbage can. I saw him just as I let go of the sack, and I was so surprised, I stared for a long moment before stepping back. Lucky for me, he was surprised, too, and just stared back.

Most of our dogs learned very quickly to avoid skunks. Folly, a Border collie, having met one of the animals out in the back of the house and having been sprayed, took responsibility ever after, slinking around and looking guilty whenever a skunk let go, even though she hadn't anything to do with it. Cinca, a Border collie also but of different temperament, was the exception. She chased them as she chased everything else, and she didn't seem to mind being doused. She even ate a dead one and burped skunk for days afterwards. I tried to think of it as the dog equivalent of a garlic-sausage pizza.

A fairly recent skunk episode might have proven profitable had it been properly recorded on film. One of the tenants in the apartments south of the Main House heard a dreadful clatter on his outside balcony. It was late at night in the summer, and Bert went out to see what was happening. He found a skunk staggering about with a Yoplait yogurt cup on its head. Bert was tempted to take a photograph, but he didn't know if the skunk would spray when the carton was illuminated. In truth, it would have been a better picture, or at least a more interesting one, had someone else taken the photo since Bert was nude at the time, so the yogurt could have been advertised like one of those sinister perfumes.

In any case, the last Bert saw of the skunk was when it tumbled, yogurt hat and all, down the stairs and into the garden. But the story didn't end there. The next day, Michael was visiting me, and I was telling him the story, which Bert had already told to me, when Alice, another of the apartment inhabitants, stopped by.

"I know this is stupid," Alice said, "but could you come help? There's a poor little skunk in my garden. He has a yogurt carton on his head, and I think he's fainted."

We all trooped down to Alice's garden, and despite the fact that skunks are pests, Michael carefully removed the carton. After taking several deep breaths, the animal staggered off. I could imagine him saying to his mate, "You won't believe what happened to me last night!"

Raccoons are a recent addition to the ranch, though one of the old-time hunters used to insist that the animals existed along the riverbed in the early days. Perhaps they did, but we never saw them, and they certainly didn't reside close enough to visit our homes. The legend about these particular animals is that they started with a few that an animal-control officer could not bear to destroy after he had picked them up from people who could no longer manage them as pets. Most wild animals do not make good pets. No matter how cute they are when they're young, they don't have centuries of domestication in their genes as do cats and dogs.

However the raccoons got here, they have found the

place much to their liking. They steal fruit, plunder garbage pails, and get into other mischief. I concede they can be a nuisance, but I think they're charming. I am free to think this because I do not have a cat or a cat door. The ranch residents who have both have discovered that raccoons learn to use cat doors as quickly as do cats, and more than one resident has been startled to find a raccoon in the house in the middle of the night.

The classic example of this happened to Alice and Eric. They have two cats, and the cat bowls are on a lazy Susan. One night, Alice and Eric heard a terrible racket downstairs, and when they went to investigate, they found two raccoons riding around on the lazy Susan. Fortunately for all concerned, the raccoons remembered how they had entered the apartment and exited the same way. They have formidable teeth and claws and will use them if cornered, so it could have been a messy battle.

While skunks in the house may be unpleasant and raccoons hazardous, they generally do not raise primitive fears. But there are other visitors that do.

Bats are very useful, especially in a place like this that has swampland which produces vast squadrons of mosquitoes. I heard somewhere that our little bats can eat four hundred mosquitoes a night, but there are estimates that put the number much higher than that. It may be true. The Western Pipistrelle, which I believe is our most common bat, probably weighs one-fourth of an ounce when it's fat. Edmund C. Jaeger, a great authority on desert wildlife, estimated that bats will eat from one-third to one-half of their body weight a night; others say the bats will eat enough insects to equal their own body weight, if they can catch them. These studies were done in captivity, so it's hard to know if the wild ones ever eat that well or want to. Maybe the captive ones eat out of boredom. In any case, I haven't the patience to kill and weigh four hundred mosquitoes to determine how they would figure in the equation.

None of the good news about bats makes me want a colony in my apartment. And it was certainly not enough to make the guests who stayed in Room 3 forgive the bats who ventured in. The animals found a way via the chimney close to the eaves where they roosted, and once in a while, a bat would slip into the room, usually at about 2 A.M., and squeak around, apparently disoriented enough by the echoes to forget the way out. When the guests turned on the light, they'd see the bat flying around frantically. Once a bat was even found in the bed.

The last bat battle that took place in Room 3 was between a very small bat and a very large man, my father, but during the early rounds, it seemed as if the bat might win. Dad had a broom, and his initial plan was to use it to urge the bat out of the room, but the bat was confused by the weapon and everything else and so kept swooping everywhere, including toward my father. Dad gave up the Marquis of Queensberry rules and whacked the bat out of the air. The fact that bats can carry rabies is enough to dictate care in handling them, but Dad's violent reaction went beyond that.

He was sickly gray when he walked out of the room. He handed the broom to my mother and said, "Don't ever ask me to do that again. I hate bats! Goddamn flying rats!" Until that day, rats were the only creatures I knew Dad to be phobic about. When I had a mini-zoo in my room, I had a hamster rather than a white rat in the rodent department because Dad wouldn't have a rat, even a domestic one, in the house. Once he had identified bats as being kin in his mind to rats, it made perfect sense that he should hate them. Dad had a theory that everyone is afraid of some creature even if the person doesn't know what the creature is until, if ever, he comes face to face with it. Given the speculations about atavistic imprints, maybe he wasn't far off the mark. Dad was usually impatient with people's foibles, but in the case of phobias concerning living things, he was quite kind.

My grandmother used to quote, "In whose heart there lurks no dread, there lurks a serpent's nature instead." She favored this because she insisted it bore out her belief that there is something evil, or at least peculiar, about people who do not loathe reptiles.

When I was young, I would pick up lizards and snakes without a qualm, easily done because poisonous varieties are limited to various rattlesnakes here and are thus easy to identify. I could never convince Grandma that snakes are beautiful and interesting, but her own prejudice did not extend to lizards. She allowed a lizard or two to live in her quarters as natural insect controls.

It seems that more people share her view of snakes than mine. I no longer pick them up, but I'm not afraid of them either, though they can startle one with their sudden, silent appearance. As a child, my cousin Kemper claimed he didn't like snakes because "they don't have any footsteps."

As an adult, I have found there are limits to my tolerance. A snake in the house is a very uneasy thing. The snake senses big mammals and a strange environment and so tries to hide under various pieces of furniture, while the big mammals, namely humans, try to keep the serpent from slithering out of reach.

Kingsnakes are useful beasts. They feed on other reptiles, including rattlesnakes. And they are handsome with their black-and-white bands. David and I were fond of one that occasionally came to the Saturday night concerts. He would slip in under the screen door on summer nights; for two restive children, it was a delight to watch the adults, one by one, catch sight of the snake and try to remain quiet and attentive when the general impulse was to jump up and flee. That snake knew the route well and would cross the big room and exit via the opposite door. Not being too certain about the quality of snakes' hearing, I've wondered if the vibrations of the music attracted him, or if maybe he just liked the music itself.

Years later, at my twenty-fifth birthday party, a king-snake, perhaps a descendant of the music lover, attended. We were having dinner in the dining room of the Main House, and there were a lot of us crowded around the long table. People kept turning to each other, looking puzzled, and asking, "Did you want something?" No one knew what was going on until we got up to leave and discovered that a kingsnake had been trapped beneath the table, hemmed in by all the legs and feet. The shy nudges had been the snake trying to find a way out.

One day the sparrows in the eaves of the Addition were screeching frantically. The guest who discovered the cause was admirably calmer but no less distressed. A garter snake had swallowed one of the fledglings and was curled up on the threshold of the guest's room, apparently content to stay there until the large bulge of the bird was digested.

I was past my reptile pick-up days by then, so I got the garden hose and sprayed the snake. The bird was still lodged up close to his head, so he couldn't move with any speed. He unhinged his jaw and left his prey on the side-walk. As he slid toward the road, a friend of ours drove up. This fellow is well over six feet tall and is widely known as a "man's man," but when Mom asked him to take care of the snake, he paled, and the best he could offer was a frenzied attempt to run over the beast with his truck as the snake crossed the road. I was glad he missed, and when things had quieted down a little, I took the dead bird to the snake. It seemed the sensible thing to do as the prey was already dead, and if the snake had it, he was hardly likely to come back in search of a replacement.

My tolerance for the wild kingdom stops at spiders, scorpions, and anything that looks like either. I have been terrified of them for as long as I can remember, an odd circumstance since no one else in my family has this phobia. It's a family joke that while I can't see diddly without my contacts or glasses, if there is a spider in the room I'll know it. Other arachnophobes admit to the same feeling of unease that inevitably leads to locating a spider somewhere too close by. Sometimes I have the sense that spiders are like some dogs that always head for the people who can't abide them.

There isn't really any good defense for this degree of revulsion, but I would point out that spiders bite, and some of them, particularly black widows here, deliver nasty bites indeed. Checking one's shoes or boots before putting them on is standard ranch procedure to make sure no spiders or scorpions are lurking, but I find myself doing it even when I'm staying in a high-rise hotel.

Since the episode of the pantyhose, I check most articles of clothing pretty thoroughly. David and I were getting ready to go to church. Pantyhose were relatively new in my life and came out of a limited clothing budget, so I was trying to get them on without running them. I had one leg all the way on and the other halfway up when I felt a wiggling against the finished foot. It took half a second to discover that there was a large spider in the pantyhose with me. The thought of bringing my foot down hard, pantyhose, spider, and all was too much for me to face, so instead, I ran out of the bathroom like a madwoman, shrieking for my brother to help. But instead of rendering aid, he was rendered helpless by the sight of me hopping around, and he fell to the floor laughing. I never quite forgave him for that. As for the spider, it was substantially damaged by the time I got the pantyhose off, and I finished it by dropping a book on it and then dumping the whole mess in the trash. It was worth the loss in order to avoid having to deal with residual spider legs that might remain stuck to the nylon.

While the kingsnake who came to the concerts amused me, the tarantula did not. He appeared one evening, creeping down the wall from the high rafters when the music was soft, scurrying back up into the shadows when the notes grew louder and faster. No concert had ever seemed as long to me as that one did.

Wolf spiders have one up on creepiness over tarantulas because the females carry their young live on their backs, so that, while you might summon the courage to smack at the adult, you're hardly better off as the myriad young abandon ship. And wolf spiders are hideous to behold—big, fat bodied, hairy, fanged, with bulging eyes.

When I rented the back unit and had it connected to the rest of my apartment by reopening an old doorway, Freida came to help me settle in. She was in the front part of the place when she heard my shriek of terror and knew it had to be a spider. I met her in the new/old entryway.

"What kind is it?" she asked. "And what do I need to kill it?"

"It's the biggest wolf spider I've ever seen. You need a machine gun."

She settled for a shoe, a fly swatter, and a can of insect spray. I explained where the spider was and added that if it weren't dispatched, I was going to have to move out of the place entirely.

The sounds of battle were ferocious, lots of *Oh, my!*'s, shoe banging, and spraying. Then I heard the back door open.

When Freida came back in, she looked shaken, though it is reptiles she dislikes, not spiders. "Well, I took that ol' body outside." She shook her head. "What does something that big eat anyway?"

"Renters, small children, household pets," I told her.

Scorpions are no more welcome in my house, and the first one I found met its end under a facsimile of the Jerusalem Bible as illustrated by Salvador Dali. I did manage to wrap the book in newspaper before I dropped it on the beast. Then I jumped on top of it to make sure the scorpion was truly dead. Despite the need for self-defense, the possible sacrilege of the operation did trouble me, so I offered apologies, just in case.

I didn't pick up the book myself; I waited until my friend arrived for dinner and asked him to do it, "to make sure the scorpion was dead."

"Dead, hell! You squashed him flatter than the paper," he reported, and then, because I'd missed it in my well-spent youth, he proceeded to show me how flammable scorpions are by torching the paper and the corpse in the fireplace. He was right—the scorpion acted like an incendiary device.

Although I am still hopeless about scorpions, I have gotten better about spiders. There was a time when I couldn't kill one no matter where or what size it was, but now if it is small and on the floor where it can't drop on me, I can exterminate it if I move quickly. Otherwise, it is like standing on a high platform for too long and losing the courage to dive into the water.

There are many who want to convince me that having spiders in one's house is good luck and a means of controlling destructive bugs. In their houses, maybe, but not in mine. I am far happier in the company of friends such as Susan. Susan Wells is an entomologist, and included in the fascinating decor of her house are spectacular displays of butterflies, moths, and beetles, but no spiders. Entomology is the study of insects. Spiders are not insects; they belong to the class Arachnida, along with mites, ticks, scorpions, and their kin. Susan is intelligent, sophisticated, and dignified; she is also, despite her scientific background, as terrified of spiders as I am. Aside from that fear, she shows no signs of being a madwoman, and that gives me hope. When we get together, we exchange our latest survival-on-the-planet-of-the-spiders stories.

I thought it was bad enough when I found out years ago that there are spiders that live underwater, but recently

I learned that they are also found at the farthest edges of our atmosphere, carried there on wind currents. I will have to tell Susan that the next time I see her, just in case she doesn't know.

Chapter 12

PAW OVER PAW

I hope the old saw about people being like their dogs is true, at least some of the time. We have had wonderful dogs—gentle, funny, intelligent beasts with just enough of the peculiar to make them interesting.

Sausage was white with black patches and looked like the dog in the "His Master's Voice" Victrola ad. He was one of the assets my mother brought to her marriage. He attended the wedding with a bow designating him an honored guest.

My father mentioned that the "damn dog" growled when he discovered my mother had invited a husband to share the bedroom. However, Sausage treated my brother and me as extensions of our mother. He was endlessly patient with us. I can remember him padding along behind me with his slightly bowlegged gait. But by the time my cousins began to appear, Sausage was ancient and not inclined to be patient with eye-poking, ear-pulling rug rats who were not, as far as he was concerned, close relatives. Over one Easter vacation, my cousin Kemper pulled Sausage's ears in a clumsy attempt to kiss him. Sausage nipped him on the cheek and thus signed his own death warrant. The dog was taken to the vet's and put to sleep.

For years, David and I thought that Sausage had bitten one of the guest children, a piece of misinformation designed to prevent us from loathing our cousin. We understood that the safety of paying guests was of the utmost importance; we might not have been so understanding had the truth been revealed then. I was in my thirties before I learned that Kemper was responsible for Sausage's demise. By then I was quite fond of Kemper, so I was able to forgive him.

Our next dog was a beagle, Sniffer, the runt of the litter. The cousins got Prince. Maybe that was punishment for the Sausage affair. Sniffer was smart, playful, and sweet-tempered; Prince was obese, lazy, and dim (I hasten to add that this was not a case wherein the dog reflects the owners).

The sound of beagles baying in the night ranks right up there with coyotes singing and wolves howling. Tragically, that instinct to hunt was Sniffer's undoing. Apparently he cornered a bobcat, and the bobcat retaliated by clawing his throat. Sniffer was trying to make his way home when a kindly stranger, who was out on the ranch looking for her own missing dog, spotted him. She loaded him into her car and raced him to the vet. At that point, Prince performed the only heroic deed of his life. He became the blood donor for his brother. But Sniffer was too badly hurt and died.

Prince went on for years, becoming a living legend. He was such a glutton that he had to be penned up and put on a special diet because of a thyroid condition. He had slimmed down some when he escaped. He was found at the dump, sound asleep with a stale dinner roll in his mouth, the empty package beside him. The only other time he lost weight was when he was missing for three days. He had gotten himself wedged in a rabbit burrow. We finally found him when he was able to back out enough so that the sound of his baying could be heard faintly in the hills.

Prince was narcoleptic; he slept anywhere, any time. But someone always found him and brought him back from his slumber. On one occasion guests found him sound asleep on the railroad tracks, and on another my aunt received a call from a town dweller who had read the address information on Prince's tag and had called so that the dead dog could be removed from his lawn. My aunt asked Bill, the handyman of that period, to go pick up the corpse. Bill complied, loading the body into a box and the box into the truck, thinking all the while that though he himself didn't like the dog much, it was going to be hard on the boys to be told about their pet. While Bill and my aunt were discussing where Prince should be buried, Prince sat up, appearing to be pleased to have gotten a ride home.

That was not Prince's last trip to town. He went courting but found, after inviting himself into the house where the bitch lived, that he liked sleeping on the couch there better than making love. The wife half of the couple who owned the bitch and the couch called my aunt and explained that Prince had appropriated her husband's favorite TV-watching spot and woke up enough to growl every time her husband tried to move him. My aunt was terribly embarrassed.

Prince was around for a long time, but I don't believe he died of natural causes; it's a subject I haven't raised with my aunt and uncle.

"Prince" was one of the few normal pet names my cousins used. More typical names were Ernie, for a dog, and Stanley, for a horse. Ernie was a town prowler, and early one morning Donna found herself driving up and down alleys calling, "Ernie, Ernie, where are you?" On the way she encountered the unfriendly stares of various housewives as they peered from their yards. Donna was sure they thought she was looking for an errant husband. When she got home, she warned the boys that they were to give their pets less human names in the future. The warning made little difference; Kemper and Nicki have a dog named Homer, Scott and Diana have Taylor, and lord knows what Craig and Laura will call the dog they are planning to acquire.

One of the dogs who followed Sniffer in our household was Mischief, another hunting dog, a black Labrador–springer spaniel cross. He acquired his name within hours of his arrival. He had been delivered to the tack room, and my brother and I weren't to disturb him, but he was howling so pitifully, we disobeyed and then hadn't the heart to lock him up again. Though only just weaned, he was already an amazingly powerful and quick beast, and he spent that first afternoon breaking things, chewing things, and piddling on everything.

Mischief was my father's last attempt to envision himself as a countryman, preferably an English country squire stalking the grouse on the moor with his trusty gun dogs accompanying him. Unfortunately, there are neither moors nor grouse here; my father was at that time working as an aeronautical engineer in Los Angeles, coming home only on the weekends because he'd finally faced the fact that he truly hated farming and had not yet found other work locally; and Mischief didn't like hunting anyway. The first time Dad took Mischief out to show him the routine for bagging ducks, Mischief showed his true colors.

Dad was operating under the assumption that the dog's impeccable breeding would make most of the process instinctive. It was a cold morning during duck-hunting season, so Dad took his car instead of the ranch Jeep. Luckily, he left the window on the dog's side open. Dad and Mischief were standing on the dam at the marina; Dad fired at a flight of ducks; Mischief was gone. At the sound of the gunshot, he had leaped off of the dam, sailed through the open window, and was sitting in the car, staring out at Dad as if to say, "Didn't you hear that dreadful explosion? Better get in the car where it's safe."

Dad abandoned the idea of making this dog hunt, but Mischief later took it up on his own as a hobby. He would go out to Pony Pond and paddle after the mud-hens; he even caught a few.

Mischief was ever anxious to please and usually got it wrong, even to the basics of toilet training. One day when he was out on the ranch with my father, Mischief ran all the way back to the Jeep to do his business in the vehicle rather than on the thousands of acres surrounding it. On another occasion, he made a special detour to lift his leg over a guest's knitting basket. The guest was sitting on the patio, enjoying the country air, but I doubt she had planned on such an organic scene.

Waif and Mischief grew up together and were good companions, but they were utterly different in personality. Mischief was fiercely territorial, aggressive with male dogs other than Waif, and not above threatening humans he didn't like. Waif wasn't fierce about anything.

Mom saw him first and hoped we wouldn't see him at all. Her plan was to come back for the puppy and take him to proper authorities, but the carload of children she was transporting spotted him on the side of the ranch road where he'd been dumped, and nothing would do but stopping immediately.

Mom let me get out of the car, warning, "Now, don't touch him if he seems too wild or scared. We don't know anything about him."

The minute I touched him, I knew everything I would ever need to know about Waif. He was so glad and grateful to be rescued, when I sat down with him in my lap, he nuzzled close and held on with his front paws.

Mom's last hope was the vet. The puppy was obviously in very bad condition, so starved he was little more than fur and bones, so Mom trusted that the vet would pronounce the animal unfit for adoption. Instead, the doctor became Waif's instant fan. "Of course he needs good care and feeding, but he's a perfect dog for the children, and he's not going to grow too large."

Well, he was right about most of it, but not about the size. Somehow he neglected to look at Waif's feet, which would have told him that either this was going to be a small dog with monstrous paws or the animal was going to grow a great deal before it reached maturity.

Waif was a collie-shepherd mix with the tricolor markings of the former and the broader muzzle of the latter. But due to the deprivations of his youth, he was always skinny and ramshackle with hind and fore quarters that were never quite in agreement about the principles of locomotion.

Waif hated dissension of any kind. It was impossible to fight if he was in the room. At the first raised voice, he would begin to cry, and then he would go from one combatant to the other, his mouth stretched in a wide, goofy grin, his whole body shivering in supplication that the anger stop.

He had an enormous heart but no courage whatsoever. With no provocation, the backyard cat, a gray harpy named Sheba, jumped off the roof onto his back and rode him down the sidewalk. He was terrified of cats from that day forward. Shaking with terror, he accompanied me into the ducks' pen until the day the drake, Mallard Fillmore, walked up to him and tweaked his nose. Even insects had the power to scare him. Once, in a rare burst of bravado, he put his paw on one of the long, disgustingly roachlike beetles that haunt summer nights. He flipped it over, but then the bug started to click angrily, and Waif slunk away, despite cheers of encouragement from the crowd of children who were watching.

Mischief seemed to know that this companion needed special care. He and Waif used to play a chase game that had very strict rules. The lawn in front of my parents' house was for hard play, but the porch was sanctuary as was the world outside of the picket fence, and it was always Waif who claimed time-out. He would skid up on to the porch, and Mischief would wait patiently on the lawn, or Waif would jump over the fence and run around the back of the house while Mischief trotted to the other end of the lawn to wait for his reappearance.

Waif used to bring me gifts, babies from the wild—a kitten, a rabbit, an antelope squirrel (Piccolo), and birds. None of these creatures was ever damaged; they were just very wet and stunned at having been captured and transported by a huge dog. It gives me an odd turn to think about it now because during that period of my life, my playmates constantly brought me wild things that needed care before repatriation, and I have to wonder if Waif observed my interest in these offerings and acted accordingly.

We came to grief over the English sparrow. Waif presented it to me as usual, and I thanked him, but things went downhill from there. This was Smidgen of law office fame, and because he was so small and unfledged, he needed constant attention. That was a part of the bargain Waif had not anticipated. Waif's normal place at night was beside my bed, and I was accustomed to the touch of his nose on my hand at two or three in the morning when he checked to make sure I was still there. But the first night of Smidgen's stay changed that pattern. Just as Waif settled down to sleep, the bird peeped. Smidgen's shoe box was resting on the steam radiator (turned to pilot only!). In the light from the hall, I watched as Waif stood up and looked at the box and then at me.

"It's all right," I assured him, but it wasn't. He left my room and did not sleep there again for as long as Smidgen lived. And the next day and on, whenever I fed Smidgen in the kitchen, Waif would sit in the middle of the floor with his back turned to me, up to then the ultimate sign of disapproval from that gentle soul. But Smidgen changed

266

Waif's personality. The bird required continued attention, and Waif's resentment grew as the days passed.

Finally it was time to teach Smidgen to fly, no easy task since even my belief that I could fly had long since vanished, let alone any practical application of it. During the practice sessions, I left Waif in the house and worked with Smidgen on the front lawn. Smidgen was perfectly happy to run after me on his tiny legs; flight seemed to hold no appeal for him. Short glides were as far as we'd gotten when tragedy struck.

I had a quick errand to run in town, so I left Smidgen on the lawn and Waif in the house with instructions to "stay!"

It was the only time Waif ever deliberately disobeyed me. When I got back from town, Smidgen did not run to meet me, and Waif was outside, trying to conceal his scrawny length under a rose bush. He looked up once through the bush and then ducked his head again.

I found Smidgen's body not far away on the lawn. I expect Waif stepped or sat on him, but he hadn't had the sense to eat the evidence.

It was the only time I ever spanked Waif. But if I was heartbroken, so was he. To the end of his life, the mere mention of the word *bird* in any context was enough to send him into hiding under the piano or any handy shelter. Waif's idea of hell was to displease someone he loved, and the sparrow killing surely did that.

Waif's noble disposition was not without cost to himself. He once nearly starved to death out of politeness. While the family was away, he was left in the care of Freida's parents, Fred and Alma, who dutifully fed him but reported that he "jus' didn't seem right and had fallen off some," while we were gone. He had, in fact, grown so thin and glassy eyed, he looked like a wild dog. After a frenzied reunion, I checked his dog run and discovered that he had dug a pit and had hidden most of the food he'd been given. He was always a picky eater, and though he hadn't wanted to eat, he hadn't wanted to displease Fred and Alma either, so he'd buried the food to avoid conflict. As soon as I was home, he started eating again.

Waif never really needed dog obedience school, but Mischief did, so we hauled them in the station wagon to classes out in the desert. They, and we, were taught by a short, square woman with cropped hair, cropped nails, leather skin, and a standard uniform of Levis, man's shirt, and boots. She would have made a good marine drill sergeant, and she reduced Waif to a quivering mess with as little as a look, let alone a verbal command.

One day the command was "heel and sit." Waif and I knew how to do that, but the session had gone badly, and both of us were falling apart. Instead of saying, "Waif, heel and sit," I said, "Waif, shit," and Waif, who had been made too nervous by the trainer and all the dogs, and who had been unable to make me understand what he needed, lifted his leg and peed on mine. He then hung his head in complete shame while I blushed scarlet.

I didn't appreciate it much at the time, but that was the only occasion when I saw the trainer's face take on a human cast, and her voice was kind when she said, "Miss De Blasis, you and your dog are excused. The rest of you, watch your dogs!" Her mouth kept twitching; it took all of her considerable discipline not to laugh outright.

Waif and I had a miserably long trip back to the ranch, and we did not return to obedience school. David and Mischief quit, too, though not for the same reasons. Mischief wasn't impressed by the trainer as much as he was by a boxer that seized every opportunity to growl and threaten. Mischief could be a savage defender on his own turf, but he was not aggressive on foreign ground. I think he was puzzled as to why the boxer was not abiding by this rule.

The boxer belonged to a slight woman who could hardly hold him, and finally the boxer strained so hard, he broke his choke chain and lunged for Mischief. Thank

268

heavens, David had the sense to drop Mischief's leash and back up.

The boxer had chosen the wrong victim. In seconds, Mischief had him by the scruff of the neck and was shaking him like a rat. Mischief didn't have a mark on him, but the boxer had a torn ear and a ravaged ego. He cowered in submission, and formal training became a thing of the past for our animals.

There is a great risk in having a dog who is attached to only one person. Waif loved everyone in the family, but I was his particular human. He survived the first semester that I was away at college, but he showed his displeasure by refusing to greet me when I arrived home. He sat in the middle of the floor with his back to me as he had when I had been feeding Smidgen. "Oh, Waif!" I said. "Aren't you going to talk to me at all?"

He couldn't resist. He jumped up, spun around, and planted his paws on my shoulders, offering squeaks of joy and sloppy kisses. He followed me around the entire Christmas vacation, even on the long horseback rides across the ranch. But when the suitcases came out again, the idyll ended. He tried sitting on the suitcases or huddling so close to them that he must have believed it would be impossible for me to leave without him. We were both miserable. I detested the college I was attending and dreaded going back to the drab life there, and Waif was beside himself.

The day I left was the last time I saw him. Within a few weeks, he had started to die in the same gentle manner he had lived; his spirit and his body just gave up, and the decline was aided by the hard conditions he had endured before we had rescued him from the roadside.

My grandmother, who didn't even like dogs, offered to buy a plane ticket so that I could fly back from the East Coast for a weekend, but the vet said it wouldn't do any good because I would just leave again.

The first I knew of any of it was when I made a regular

269

Sunday call home. My mother said the words very fast, her voice high-pitched with the strain of trying not to cry. "Waif is gone. He died this week. If you want to know any more about it now, you'll have to speak to your father because I can't talk about it."

When I came home for summer vacation, my mother thought it was time to add a new dog to the household. Mischief had been gone for some years, a victim of bad veterinary care. Living on a ranch seems to require a dog, and being dogless for any length of time was lonesome.

David, Mom, and I went to the animal shelter, an agonizing experience. The dogs were barking and pushing each other out of the way, as if they knew only one of them would be chosen.

"Kids, choose one now, or we'll have to go home." Mother had visions of taking thirty or so animals with us in the back of the car.

David and I saw the puppy at the same time. It was huddled against the mesh with its nose poking through, and while the others barked, it just cried softly.

David was surprised to discover it was a bitch. "Cats are female and dogs are male," he observed. "At least, at our house they are."

Dad said it was "Jean's folly," to get another pet after the trauma of losing Waif, and thus the dog was named Folly. She was black with a white ruff, a white tip on her tail, and white markings on her face, feet, and belly. She was, in fact, a beautiful example of a Border collie, but at that time we weren't familiar with the breed since they were not as popular then as they are today and were very rare in this area. We didn't know what she was until a guest asked to see her papers. "Papers?" we asked. "She's a beautiful Border blue," the guest replied. "Surely you have papers."

Border collies are working dogs, so they are still bred for intelligence and temperament rather than the exaggerated showy appearance that has ruined so many breeds.

Until the advent of Folly in our lives, I had not understood the passionate commitment to a specific breed that so many people have, but Folly began our enchantment with Border collies, and now, twenty-five years later, it would seem strange to have any other kind of dog.

Folly was a delight from the beginning, gentle except in defense of the family, and exceptionally easy to train except in the matter of the cattle. Teaching her not to herd livestock was a trial.

One day the ranch foreman came to Mother and asked, "What would you do with a dog who herded all of the cattle into a corner and then waited for someone to come and get them?"

"Folly?" Mother said, and the foreman nodded.

The foreman wasn't a noticeably tender man, but he had a sneaking sympathy for Folly. "It's the damndest thing. She looks so proud of herself."

The problem was that we didn't want the cattle, which belonged to someone else, taken anywhere, and it wasn't good for them to have weight run off of them.

For a month, Folly was forbidden to go past the front gate. She complied with this edict so well that when Mom suggested I take the dog out on the ranch to see if she'd learned her lesson, it took me an hour to convince her that it was allowed. We'd get as far as the gate and then Folly would cry and run home. When I finally persuaded her that it was all right, she went out with me and ignored the cattle as if she'd never seen them before. She never herded them again.

Guests adored her and courted her favor, often letting her join them in their rooms. This infuriated my mother because she didn't want subsequent boarders to find dog hair in their rooms, especially if they were not themselves dog lovers. Besides, Mother judged that extending such privileges to Folly was little different from entertaining a child while the parents searched frantically for her. Repeat

271

guests soon learned that Jean would not look kindly on them if they were guilty of spoiling the dog.

Folly's good manners faltered only a bit as she grew older. Once completely trustworthy when food was left on the coffee table, she came to regard it as her private buffet. It started with the hazelnuts, about two pounds of them. One of the guests at a Christmas party cracked one for Folly and gave her the nutmeat. When the party was over, the guests gone, Folly was left with the nuts. In the morning, every nut had been eaten, the shells left in four neat piles on the rug. I think she must have moved from one spot to the next as the shells piled up and became uncomfortable to sit on. The nut bowl had not been tipped over; Folly had carefully removed the contents, probably one by one.

But her greatest coup was the cake. It was left on the coffee table while we went out to celebrate a friend's birthday. When we returned to the house, Maggie started to cut her cake but then stopped in puzzlement. "Oh, I think someone already cut it, but in such an odd way."

It was more of a tunnel than a slice, a tunnel that exactly matched Folly's muzzle. She was trying to look innocent, but there was a ridge of frosting under her eyes.

After the guest ranch had been closed and my grandmother had moved into the rooms above the big living room of the Main House, she missed the crowds of people that had once filled her days even though the ghosts of memory comforted her. Folly was lonesome, too, for the guests who had spoiled her. My mother thought she had a brilliant plan when she suggested that Grandma court Folly as company. When Grandma agreed, despite a lifelong aversion to dogs, Mother supplied a box of dog biscuits as bribery tokens.

Folly would have none of it. She knew Grandma wasn't a dog lover, and when Grandma offered her biscuits, Folly kept right on walking, her head averted.

Far from being insulted, Grandma said, "I admire that animal. She has integrity."

We had Folly for thirteen years, but then she failed rapidly, suffering a series of small strokes that left her gait impaired with a sideways sway made worse by arthritis. Though not the same man who had mishandled Mischief's illness, the vet wasn't much help; he was fond of Folly and didn't want to put her down. Instead, he'd give her vitamin and cortisone shots. The second to the last time we took her in, he confessed, "I just can't do it. It's been a bad week, and I don't want to lose Folly, too. She's weakening, but she's not suffering. She should be all right for a little while longer."

A few days later, Folly was missing. The boys found her lying helpless in one of the abandoned calf pens where she had apparently gone to die.

When Mother asked Grandma if she wanted to go with us to the vet's, Grandma declined. "I'm afraid you'll leave me there to be put to sleep and bring her home instead," she said. "I've loved you as well as I could, but no human being could ever love you with the devotion that dog has shown."

Mom and I were with Folly when she went to sleep for the last time. She deserved no less than to be with friends after all the years of companionship and loyalty she had given us. It was doubly hard to lose her because by then my brother was gone, and, because he and I had chosen her together, she was a reminder of younger, happier days.

It was months before a new dog was discussed, but then there was no doubt that it would be another Border collie. I wanted to purchase it as a Mother's Day gift, but this turned out to be a very difficult task. I followed leads in various states in the Southwest only to discover that there were waiting lists for the puppies, particularly for the females, and the prices being asked were very high, at least for an impoverished writer. Nonetheless, I put my name on a list—twentieth place was as close as I could get to the privilege of buying a bitch.

Then one of the ranch tenants heard about my search. He was connected with the local county fair board and had rancher relatives in the northern part of the state who raised Border collies for herd work. He was fond of my parents and pleased to present them with a female puppy.

Mother called me to come see the new puppy, and her voice sounded so hesitant, I asked, "It is a Border collie, isn't it?"

"Well, yes," Mom said, "but she's different. You'll have to see for yourself."

Our first meeting was not auspicious. I was wearing a scruffy fake suede with fake fur jacket, and when I walked in the door, the puppy backed up, barking hysterically, though she stopped as soon as I took the coat off. I, on the other hand, couldn't stop laughing.

She was black and white, but she didn't look like Folly. Her fur was short and wiry, her ears sharp-peaked and upstanding, and she had no white plume on her tail—she had no tail to speak of, just a little stub. With amber eyes, sharp teeth, and a little pot belly, she looked like a cross between a small Doberman pinscher and a well-fed vampire bat. Her temperament wasn't like Folly's in every particular either. Cinca, as I named her for a variation on the day of her arrival, Cinco de Mayo, was above all else independent and stubborn. Her idea of obedience was to do what she wanted and then trot back for punishment, and what she wanted was nearly always to herd something. Taking her out on the ranch was risky because if she didn't herd the cattle she found something else to go after.

When she was quite young, Cinca disappeared for a day and a night. We imagined all kinds of terrible fates until Mother received a call the following morning from one of the park custodians. We drove out and found Cinca covered with dried mud and tied to a tree. She had been on a

274

ducks- and geese-herding binge until the park people had caught her. She was glad to see us and jumped into the car to sit between us.

Though relieved that Cinca was unhurt, my mother was mortified by the whole affair and scolded as she drove. "I may never speak to you again. You know you are not allowed out here alone, and now all the rangers know how disobedient you are."

Cinca's response was to lean up against her and bat her eyelashes. It was such an obvious con job, I had to look the other way.

For the first year, Cinca wasn't too sure about how she felt toward adult humans outside of her immediate family, but there was never any doubt about her feelings toward children. She adored them. A little investigation into her early days revealed that she had been raised under the working dog rule that some ranchers and breeders favor, meaning that she had been left outside with her mother and not encouraged to be a house pet. However, there had been a number of children on the place, and they had been allowed to play with the dogs.

Cinca hated the sound of gunfire, and one day when shots were fired in the air to scare off some stray dogs, Cinca ran away. The problem was we didn't know she was gone. By then she had the freedom of the ranch and her own routine of visiting favored tenants, so we assumed she'd gone down to see Michael or someone else.

The phone call was a shock. The man explained that he had seen the dog cowering in terror on one of the town's busiest streets. Worried that she'd be run over, he'd opened the door of his car, and she'd gotten right in. He tried my mother's number first from the name and number on the identification tag, but receiving no answer there, he'd found my number in the phone book.

I went to pick up Cinca and found her at a little house with a young airman, his wife, and three small children. Far from being traumatized and eager to go home, Cinca was in heaven with the children petting her and hanging on to prevent her leaving.

Cinca regarded me as if I were some vague memory of the past, and in the end, it was like removing a protestor from the sidewalk as I pushed, pulled, and finally loaded her suddenly heavy body into my car. The family stood on their front stoop as I drove away, their shared expression saying plainly that it was very sad that mean people had such nice dogs.

In truth, Cinca was the most feral dog we have ever had. She ran with astonishing speed, and she not only hunted rabbits and ground squirrels but also killed and ate them. If we had offered Folly a dead rabbit, she would have given it back with the unspoken but plain request that it be skinned and cooked for her.

A white German shepherd, Thor, lived on the ranch for a while and became Cinca's companion, and I have a very clear image of one snowy day when Thor and Cinca hunted together, or rather, Thor drove the rabbits for Cinca to catch. When the final chase was done, there they sat side by side on the front lawn, Thor's light hair making him seem sculpted of snow while Cinca's mostly black coat stood out sharply, and brighter still was the blood splattered over the snow from the rabbit Cinca was devouring. Thor didn't take a bite of it but gazed off into the distance as if ignoring an unfortunate vice in a dear friend.

In retrospect, I think it was a good thing that Cinca, even if peculiar, was so different from Folly. Cinca made her own place from the beginning and was mourned for her own sake when she was killed on the main ranch road. She had been visiting Michael, dozing in the sun, when a heavy, double-axled county truck roared by. She jumped from sleep into the chase and did not see the double wheels.

Cinca's death was hard on my mother. My father had died not long before, and Cinca had been Mom's company during that time when widowhood made the house seem much too large for one person.

Some months after Cinca's death, I started, with Mom's permission, to look for another Border collie. This time the search was easier since the breed was rapidly gaining popularity, though most puppies, especially females, were spoken for before birth. Through referrals, I located a young breeder with the euphonious name of Daryll O'Dell. He had two puppies left unsold from the current litter. The puppies were male, and one was the runt of the litter, but he had all the markings we wanted—the white ruff and white tip on the tail, the white on the face and feet.

Mom and I drove out to the foothill desert where the purple sage blooms and found O'Dell's little farm to be as lyrical as his name. The dogs are raised as part of the family, not confined to outside sheds but allowed in and out of the house, the puppies lolloping around the bitch and sire. Daryll believes that dogs who are going to live with and work for humans need to be with them from the very beginning.

The dog and bitch greeted us with friendly tail wagging and let us handle the puppies, and from the first look at the runt, there was no doubt that we wanted him. Though Daryll had already named him to indicate the sire, we renamed him Piper because his lineage is Scottish.

Daryll first trains his dogs to herd ducks and geese, then sheep and cattle, and he takes them to field trials all over the Southwest, but he doesn't believe that every Border collie must be employed to be content. He has found, as we have, that they make excellent pets as long as they have adequate exercise to run off their enormous energy.

Piper responded from the beginning to vocal and hand commands as well as to a whistle, and with very few lapses, he was easy to train. But one of his lapses put quite a crimp in my mother's social life. Mom had gone out on her first date since my father had died, and afterwards, she invited the man in for a cup of coffee.

277

(In his earliest days with her, Piper would sit beside Mom when she answered the phone. Once when I was on the other end of the line, Piper's ears went up as he recognized my voice, so Mom told me to talk to him, and she held the receiver to his ear. From that time on, Piper has regarded the phone as his special charge and always runs to get Mom when it rings. She says she finds this comforting since she will know when the phone is ringing even as the acuteness of her hearing decreases. However, it was not comforting on the night of The Date.)

Piper skidded into the room at the sound of the phone, discovered a strange man there, and pooped on the rug, clear proof that he was not accustomed to Mother bringing home gentlemen friends. By Mom's description, what had been tense enough without outside interference degenerated into a farce with her trying to get off of the phone while the man dragged the rug out onto the front lawn and Piper cowered in dismay at what he had done. Luckily, Mom's friend had a kind heart, liked dogs, and thought the whole thing hilarious.

Piper's indoor training program was entirely in Mother's hands, but his outside behavior came under my influence as soon as he was old enough to go on morning walks with me.

He learned even faster than Folly had that he was not to herd the cattle out on the ranch, though this still does not stop him from going into his herding crawl and fixing the cattle with his eyes as he passes. Herding dogs are usually either "headers" or "heelers." Cinca was a heeler, herding from behind by barking and nipping at the cattle's heels. Piper is definitely a header. He barks only when he is startled or scared, and his instinct is to hold the gaze of the animal he wants to move and to urge movement by feints and dashes. Collies can be yappy dogs, so it is wonderful to have one who is nearly silent.

Piper is a gift altogether. He makes me laugh, and he

278

keeps me from being lazy. Every morning, he waits at the back door of my mother's house for me to come and take him out. On those mornings when I'd just as soon not get up with the dawn to walk for four or five miles, I know that Piper is waiting for me. Nancy, one of the tenants and a friend who walks with us, calls Piper our personal trainer, though I don't know what the Beverly Hills exercise fanatics would make of him.

In compensation for denying him the pleasure of herding livestock, I allow Piper to attempt to corral the turkey vultures, ravens, and wild ducks because he has such a good time without doing any damage.

Collies are not water dogs; they possess neither the feet nor the ears that make swimming relatively easy for some breeds. While he was still a youngster, Piper danced along the rim of one swampy area for weeks, trying to herd the ducks without going beyond the little ledge that runs just beneath the water along the shore. However, the evidence under his feet made him believe that the water was shallow all the way out, and one day he took off across the swamp, leaping from one grassy hillock to the next until his luck ran out, and he tumbled into the water. His head came up out of the water, he looked scared to death, and he stared straight at me, expecting me to come rescue him. But the mud was so soft and deep, there wasn't any way I could get to him.

"Piper, jump up!" I called and made the same signal I use to tell him to go over a fence wire rather than under it. He obeyed and pulled himself out on to one of the tiny mounds of grass. "Now come to me."

He made an attempt to obey, but he was too frightened to remember how he had crossed that space in the journey out, and he blundered into deep water again, again without a clue of how to swim.

It seemed perfectly reasonable at the time. I stood on the shore and taught him how to swim by miming a dog

279

paddle with my hands and saying, "Piper, paw over paw, Piper, paw over paw."

Nancy was with us, and, converted from a cat-only person to a dog lover by Piper, she added her own motions and voice. It made perfect sense that Piper, who responded so well to hand signals in other situations, would follow these as well, and he did, watching us and pulling himself across the swamp. Only when he had landed, shaken and covered with black mud, but safe, did it occur to us how funny we must have looked.

Piper behaves in different ways, according to whom he is with. If he goes out with me alone, or with my mother, or with Nancy, who takes him out when I'm gone, he stays very close. If two of us go out with him, he feels the protection can be eased, and he wanders a bit farther afield, though never out of sight. But if he is with Michael and Michael's dog, Becker, he becomes a puppy again, playing with Becker and riding around with him in the back of the truck, leaving the protection of Michael to Becker. Michael is kind to take him out so often because he never intended to have another dog in addition to Becker, but he cannot resist the delirious joy that Piper shows in their company.

When I was in high school, a classmate and her mother rented one of the apartments on the ranch. Mary wanted to get a puppy or a kitten, but her mother forbade it. As the woman explained to my grandmother, "Pets always end in sadness; I don't want my daughter to go through that."

How wrong I think she was. There are lessons to be learned from caring for a pet, from having another living creature so dependent on you for its well-being. And with dogs, there is the sharing of emotions, the response the creature gives to the owner's joys and sorrows, the enduring companionship. And there is the lesson of mortality, often learned by children for the first time through the loss of a pet. Not an easy lesson, ever, but an important one, part of coming to the acceptance that life is precious because it can be lost, and because it is always lost in the end.

Sausage and Sniffer were the playmates of childhood; Waif saw me through adolescence; Folly, Cinca, and Piper have all been part of the journey through adulthood. They have measured the passage of days and years with good company, with humor, with love. Perhaps most important of all, they have provided proof that we humans are not alone, that we are connected to other creatures on the planet, sometimes in very complex ways, sometimes in a way as direct as one creature's care for another.

Chapter 14

CHAMPION THE WONDER HORSE

I am not one who claims that horses are merit scholars. I think they are smarter than cats, but every dog I've had has been much more intelligent than any horse I've met. With eyes set on the sides of their heads, horses view the world through a strange perspective that makes a normal-sized human advancing face on look nine feet tall. No wonder they often react with terror to the most benign of approaches.

In the overall scheme of things, horses are a prey animal and are strictly vegetarian. This is a distinct disadvantage for them. People do not ride lions. If horses dumped their riders and then ate them, horses' burdens would undoubtedly have been considerably lighter through the ages. But as it is, these enormous beasts allow puny humans to sit on their backs and to guide their paces. When the arrangement fails, it is usually, though not always, the horse that loses in the final tally. The cowboys were fond of saying, "Never a horse that couldn't be rode; never a man that couldn't be throwed." But those same cowboys were always quick to punish a misbehaving animal, sometimes cruelly.

My mother tells me that my first saddle experiences were riding with her or Dad, held in front of one or the other to get the feeling of riding without being in danger of falling off. But my first memory of riding is of being on a horse by myself with Mother close by on hers.

The first formal advice about riding form I received was "sit like a sack of flour and grip with your knees." This was from an old cowboy, and as unattractive as it sounds, it is the perfect explanation for why the Marlboro Man looks so at home on his horse. Western riding is for sitting in the saddle all day, trailing stock. The best horses do not have a fast trot. The gait after a slow trot is a slow lope. Every aspect is designed for comfort rather than style. From this perspective, riding English style looks like a lot of work. Eventually, I learned to keep the back slouch to a minimum and to drop my heels down so that only the toe of my boot showed beyond my knee when I looked down. This not only looks better and prevents the legs from flapping about and startling the horse, it also helps, along with the heels of the boots, to keep the feet from going forward through the stirrups, which can be very hazardous. If you fall off while your foot is too far through the stirrup, you stand a good chance of being dragged. That was what the family worried about most. It was much more dangerous than just falling off a horse. We were allowed to ride by ourselves once we were big enough and competent enough to handle our horses, but we were not allowed to use a saddle by ourselves until we reached age fifteen. Up till then, bareback was required. After that, the risk was our own.

There was a rating system for the horses. The beginner's mount was Snort. He was a dark brown plodder who considered a trot adventurous. His main concern on rides was to eat as much as he could on his way. This was annoying but harmless. Small arms were not strong enough to get his head up out of the grass, so riding him meant patiently waiting until he was ready to amble on to the next bite. Only once did I see Snort approach wildness. My brother was riding him and dropped the reins. Snort decided that was permission to go back to the barn, and he wheeled around. Mother told me to stay put on my horse, and she took off on hers to catch Snort. Snort thought this was better sport than he'd seen in a while, so he dodged this way and that; I could almost see him smiling. David bounced along on top but didn't fall off, but a short interval of this exercise was enough for Snort. He stopped and allowed Mom to approach him and to return his reins to his rider. David was told to pay attention and not to let go of the reins again.

I was riding Sundae that day. Sundae was the next step up from Snort. For years, the obvious escaped me, and I believed her name was Sunday, and I thought it would be nice to have horses named for the other days of the week. Actually, Sundae was a pinto, black and white, named for the dessert of the same configuration.

She was a barrel-backed mare, who, unlike the best-gaited horses, preferred a rough trot over all else. If you could learn to sit well on Sundae, you could sit well on anything. It took great persuasion to make her break into a lope. Finally, she would heave herself into it with a protesting grunt. By the time I rode her, a gallop or a run was no longer part of her gear box, which was just as well for a child's mount.

After Sundae came Buck, also obviously named since he was a buckskin. He was a gelding with slightly more speed and spirit than Snort and Sundae, but he was also amiable and willing, so it was possible to appear to be quite a rider with little effort.

After Buck was potluck, a succession of horses that were nominally ours but were also used, as were Snort, Sundae, and Buck, as string horses for the guest ranch. It is impossible to overestimate how damaging string duty is to a horse's manners. Ninety percent or more of "dudes" ride exactly as portrayed in comic movies—butts bouncing, arms flapping, legs akimbo. They give so many mixed signals that the horses soon learn to go their own way at their own pace, which usually means stopping to eat, trotting roughly instead of loping, following each other rather than any command from the rider, and heading back to the corral at the slightest chance.

My brother had a palomino named Champion, for the Wonder Horse of television fame. David had long since abandoned him in favor of his own Arabian horse, but he took Champion out again when he was told about the old horse's new trick. There was a caution sign out by the tracks, and Champion had learned to head directly for it. When the rider jerked the reins to guide him away from the sign, Champion would execute a hundred and eighty degree turn and head for home. Most of the time it worked, and at the very least, it caused a lot of trouble, making the other riders wait while Champion's passenger struggled to make the horse go out again.

When Champion tried the routine on David, David allowed him to walk right into the sign, which startled Champion considerably. Then David made him skirt the sign and walk on. A few more times, and Champion gave up, ceasing to misbehave even when dudes rode him.

A couple of my personal/string horses were also named for heroic horses. Fury was an unprepossessing brown horse, but in my imagination, he was the fiery steed of countless books and movies. Stormy was another in the progression, but he should have been called Ugly because he was, inside and out.

We children didn't have much to do with the choosing and purchase of these horses. The cowboys located them and decided whether they were suitable or not, and suitability included the question of cost. The cowboys wanted the best bargains they could get. Even though it was not their money, it was a point of honor that the horse be as cheap as possible and still have the use of four legs.

Stormy was a mottled brown-black with black mane and tail. He had hooves the size of dinner plates and the gait of a camel. His head looked like a shoe box with rounded edges, like those that children draw to depict horses before the artists become more skilled with a pencil. He was mean from his first days at the ranch and got steadily meaner during his stay.

If I wasn't quick when I was getting on, he would try to bite whatever part of my anatomy he could reach. Once I had to walk back leading him from way out on the ranch. He had gotten in a fight with another horse, through a fence, and I had dismounted to drag him back. Then he wouldn't let me remount. He was so big and powerful, my strength was no match for his, and I wasn't tough enough to really hurt him to get his attention.

At the time that Stormy was my riding horse, I was visiting an Arabian mare out in the pasture because her foal would be mine. Stormy often took exception to this. The wrangler told me to carry a two-by-four and bash Stormy when he charged. So I rowed across Pony Pond to the swampy patch where the horses were, and I got out of the boat armed with my weapon.

When I returned to the stable, the wrangler asked me how it had gone.

"I found out how hard it is to run carrying a two-by-four," I told him. When Stormy had charged, I'd turned tail, so terrified that I'd forgotten to drop the plank.

Stormy had other favorite games, including balking at the top of hills and then racing down them full speed, heedless of obstacles so that a couple of times he stumbled over bushes and came close to flipping onto his back.

Finally, I announced that I wasn't going to ride him any more, ever. I had stuck with it too long as it was; he had much to do with diminishing my pleasure in the sport and making me see the myriad opportunities for maiming or death.

Stormy stayed in the string because the general opinion was that I simply was too timid to deal with him, and that if he were given to adult riders, he'd be all right. He wasn't. He started sneaking up on people while they sat on the fence. He'd grab them with his teeth and pitch them onto the ground. You couldn't turn your back on him. He dumped a couple of riders, not accidentally. And then during Easter week when the ranch was full of children and their families, Stormy, who was even worse tempered with other horses than with humans, kicked Buck, breaking Buck's left foreleg.

It was a tragedy. Many of the children had ridden Buck over the years and were fond of him. He stood there in the pasture with his broken leg held at an awkward angle, and there was no choice but to destroy him. All the children were kept inside, and my father and Uncle Joe shot Buck and, with the help of the ranch hands, hauled the body away. My father and uncle were pale when they returned. They said someone else would have to be called if this ever happened again; shooting a pet horse was just too hard.

The decision was made to sell Stormy, but I insisted the purchasers ought to know about his temperament, though the wrangler and foreman, longtime cowboys both, would have preferred to keep his bad habits as secret as possible.

Stormy was sold to a family who had a daughter who was a good rider, but the key was that they had no other horses. Stormy behaved like an angel until they took him somewhere where there were others.

Out of curiosity, we did a little backtracking and discovered that Stormy's record had also been good with his previous owners, who had no other horses. As it turned out, Stormy's problem was an extreme case of equine jealousy. He had not been raised with others of his kind, and he apparently considered all of them to be a threat to his food supply, the attention he craved, and his general well-being. As long as he was not forced to share, he was perfectly happy and perfectly behaved.

The horse I had after Stormy was named Coke. At the time, I thought that meant Coca-Cola or a by-product of steel smelting, but I now wonder if it was an early joke about cocaine. Coke certainly behaved as if he were on some illegal substance, though my adult guess would be sleeping pills rather than cocaine. He was Stormy's opposite. Coke never attacked anything or anyone and never charged anywhere. He ambled along, head drooping lower and lower until sometimes he fell asleep, waking with a mild start when he realized he was expected to keep moving. He stumbled so frequently in his semicomatose state that he was outfitted with special shoes that made him lift his feet a little instead of dragging them. It was exhausting work to urge him to anything faster than his slow walk. If I took him on a long ride, I did as much work as he did, and it was worse for inexperienced riders who ended up so far behind the others, they felt utterly abandoned. So, as docile as he was, Coke was of no use to me or to the dude string.

My last string horse was Scout, named for Tonto's horse in "The Lone Ranger." He was the best of the lot. He was a black-and-white pinto like the mare Sundae, but the similarity ended with the color. Scout had been bred to a few mares before his owners decided he was too small and so were his progeny to make him a good stud, though I saw two of his get, and they were beautiful. He was gelded after he'd acquired the thick, arched neck of a stallion and right before I got him. He still had stallion memories, though he was lacking full equipment. The first day he was turned out in the pasture, he herded all the mares into a corner and held off the geldings, but eventually he lost the urge to dominate and settled in with the rest of the horses.

Scout was like a little tank. What he lacked in height,

he made up in the stocky strength of his build, and he was tireless, plowing ahead no matter what the terrain, except when it involved water. He'd been raised in an arid region where crossing streams and rivers was not part of the curriculum. He regarded water as something to avoid, but when that was impossible, he would bunch his muscles like a nervous high diver and then launch himself. Sometimes he made it to the other side in one leap, but more often he landed in midstream, which in deep mud could make for an exciting time. More than once, I came home with boots, stirrups, and jeans coated in mud.

Scout also disliked cattle. He had been raised as a pleasure horse, not a working animal. Earlier I described how he shamed both of us on his one and only roundup, but it was not only formal dealings with cattle that upset him. He didn't like being close to them under any circumstances.

The stories always sound apocryphal, but it is possible to lose one's virginity while riding, at least on a western saddle. I know this firsthand. I was out on Scout for a night ride with a fairly large group. I had let Scout dawdle because it was such a lovely evening, so he was bringing up the rear. Scout practiced the art of shying with consummate skill. When something startled him—a piece of paper blowing in the wind, a sudden sound, a rabbit darting from cover—he could flinch and sidle so quickly, if the rider wasn't firmly anchored in the saddle, there wasn't much hope of staying on. I had gotten used to his dancing, but this night a cow moved and mooed in the trees right beside us, and Scout was so frightened, I guess shying didn't seem like an adequate response, so he added a new step, putting his head down and kicking his hindquarters up. I went right over the saddle horn, hitting it on the way, and landed on his neck. He had more excitement in mind, but I let out a shriek, and he froze in his tracks. He was not accustomed to that kind of sound from me. I climbed back into the saddle and got home mostly intact. Since I could have broken my neck, the sacrifice of my maidenhead didn't seem like that big a deal, but it did make me believe that excuse when I encountered it later in various romantic novels.

Scout lived out his life on the ranch. Even after the guest ranch closed and the dude string was sold, he remained because one of the tenants purchased him. Alice hadn't grown up with horses but had always wanted one, and she was fond of Scout. He did dump her once, during a shying episode, but generally their association was a good one. Scout was close to thirty years old before he failed so much that it was a kindness to have the vet come and put him down. Alice had not ridden him for several years, but she had thought he deserved the easy years in the pasture. He had even become fond of cattle by then and refused to be separated from the boarding herd when it was moved from one pasture to another.

Scout had ceased to be my horse when I moved up to the final stage of ranch riding. By the time I, my brother, and our cousins came along, the glory days of raising Arabian horses here had passed, but my mother's mare, Madaha, "Mahdi," remained, and she was to provide a foal for each of us. She was bred to stallions that were descended from the Kellogg Arabians.

The first foal was mine, and while Mahdi was carrying, I visited her every day (and Stormy chased me when the visits were out in the pasture), so that she would let me near her baby when it arrived.

When there are no complications, mares, like cows, give birth with dispatch, and foals get up, wobble, and then mince along in short order. It is an evolutionary adaptation that allows an animal that is safest in the herd to finish the business of delivery quickly and get back to that herd where both she and her offspring are safer than they are alone. However, Mahdi was up and down over and over again. She was clearly distressed, so Uncle Joe was summoned to help. Large animal vets were in short supply at the time, but we would have found one had it been necessary. It wasn't. Uncle Joe determined that the problem was that the foal had one foot back instead of both forward over the nose as in a normal birth. Once he'd maneuvered the backward foot forward, the foal slipped out.

Despite the problems of the birth, the filly was healthy and beautiful. Her color was chestnut because that is a recessive trait, and a chestnut mare bred to a chestnut stallion produces only chestnut foals. It is a splendid color, rich and red, shooting fire in the sunlight.

And Arabians are splendid horses. They are the archetypes from which all modern breeds have descended. At their best, they are nearly impossible to believe—no horse should be so horse! Their dark eyes are wide set; there is a dish in the nose, a concave curve that keeps their heads from looking like a shoe box, as in the case of Stormy. Their nostrils flare, and their ears are neat and sharp-peaked, never mulish as in many horses. They are short coupled, so that from stem to stern there isn't the distance one finds in a thoroughbred, nor is there the long, ground-eating gait. In a short race, a quarter horse, with its powerful haunches for fast starts, or a thoroughbred, with its long stretch, will win, but in an endurance race, an Arabian will go on and on long after the other horses have fallen behind or fallen dead. The best of Arabians have fine, clean limbs, but their hooves are still just a shade outsize, better for covering miles of desert terrain, better for the lives for which they were initially bred.

Muhammad is quoted as saying, "Blest be ye, oh Daughters of the Wind." This was in reference to the mares who were ridden into battle—mares being preferred for their courage and steadfastness. And a filly was exactly what I had wanted. I named her Elleb Attil. All of the Arabians from the ranch had traditionally been given Arabic names, and all of them were registered with the Arabian

291

Horse Club Registry of America. But you cannot duplicate the name of a living horse. I can't remember what it was I originally wanted to call my filly, but it was taken. I chose Elleb Attil knowing that no one would have used it yet because, though it sounds Middle Eastern to western ears, it is *Litta Belle,* my grandmother's name, spelled backwards.

From the day she was born, I spent hours with the foal, getting her used to being handled by a human. And because I had worked with Madaha for months before the delivery, the mare was perfectly willing that I be with her and her baby. I taught her about halters and being formally led by a rope attached to the halter, but Elleb Attil was so tame, she would follow me around when she was let out of the pen whether or not she was guided by a lead line.

I turned twelve in 1958, and Elleb Atill was a yearling. I had been to the county fair every year and had always loved the horse show part of it, but I had never competed. However, Elleb Attil was so beautiful and obedient, she seemed like a perfect entry. For the first time, I had fancy cowgirl clothes—tailored riding pants in a soft turquoise with a matching tie, a white shirt, a black hat, and black boots. I had never been so splendidly attired in my life. And to top it off, my seventh-grade teacher, Sister Mary Paul, arranged for the whole class to go to the fair to see me show the horse. In a school not known for field trips, this generated a lot of excitement.

But there was one problem. At least I thought it was a problem. Madaha, for all her gentleness, had always been a bad loader. Try to put her in a trailer, and all hell broke loose. It seemed perfectly logical to me that her daughter would probably have the same trouble. The ranch didn't own a trailer, but the foreman did, and what I wanted to do was to feed her in that trailer for some time before the fair in order that Elleb Attil would go into the trailer willingly. The foreman and wrangler thought I was crazy. Their reasoning, if it can be called that, was that horses went into trailers when they were bidden to do so, and if not, they were made to go in, a process they thought would be easy in the filly's case because she was young and daintily built.

Elleb Attil was to be at the fairgrounds a couple of days before her event so that the judges could get a look at her along with the other entries. The foreman and the wrangler were going to load her and take her over. They didn't want anyone interfering with their work; after all, they were used to managing horses.

I knew something horrible had happened the minute Mother showed up at school midday to take me home. Elleb Attil was dead. She had reared up when the men had tried to get her to go up the ramp into the trailer. The wrangler let go of the rope because it was burning his hands and because he didn't want to dislocate the filly's neck. But Elleb Attil was pulling against force, and when it was suddenly removed, she lost her balance. She went over backwards and hit the soft spot on her skull.

I was heartbroken. I had spent so much time with her, it was as if I'd lost a friend as well as a pet, and all the days of riding and companionship I'd envisioned for the years ahead when she would be big enough were over before they began. I made little plaster impressions of the hoof prints she had left near the stables, and my great-aunt Lura gave me an amethyst ring with a horse's head carved in it, a piece of jewelry from the family's past when English smugglers had come to the United States to make their living legitimately by raising fine horses. But nothing could ease the pain of the loss. The stall she was to have occupied at the fair was left empty with a little wreath on the door and a poem I'd written. Sister Mary Paul and the class didn't go on the field trip to the fair.

Mahdi was in foal again, to Abu Farwa, the same stallion that had sired Elleb Attil, but it was my brother's turn to get an Arabian. He was very generous about it. He

293

really wanted a colt, not a filly, so he said if the new baby was female, I could have it.

Sister Mary Paul took a keen interest in this, as did some of the other nuns, and I gave them regular reports on Mahdi's progress. The foal arrived the following spring. Mahdi delivered, without help, during the night, so that when I went to check on her before school, I found the new baby nervously calling to her mother from outside the pen. She must have fallen asleep near the fence and had then rolled under, waking up on the wrong side. She was quickly reunited with her mother, and the mare and foal were in fine shape. Mom called the convent to tell Sister Mary Paul that a filly had been born.

"Oh, that's wonderful news!" Sister said, and then after a pause, she asked, "Is a filly a girl?"

I had hoped I would feel the same joy in the new foal that I had in Elleb Attil, but I never did. Part of it was that I was just that much older, and my life was getting more complicated with adolescence. But it was more than that. I had invested so much time and love before, perhaps I wasn't willing to do it again. And finally, Nejma was nothing like Elleb Attil. She was an example of the reason some people don't like Arabians, considering them too erratic and in-bred to be good mounts. Though her bloodlines were the same as Elleb Attil's, her personality was from another planet.

Nejma was trained with patience and kindness, just as the other Arabians were, but it never made the slightest difference. I worked her on a lunge line; I petted and conditioned her gradually to blanket and saddle; I gentled her until she should have been able to come into my tent and sleep on the carpet without disaster. Other more skilled trainers offered their talents, too, but Nejma remained the same: dependable one moment, utterly crazy the next. There was no pattern to these outbursts. Riding her was like sitting on lighted dynamite. One day we were at a full canter

when something startled her—nothing visible, mind you—
and she fell to her knees. Suddenly my feet were on the
ground. My brain said, "If you don't get off very quickly,
she may roll over and crush you." I got off, got her up, and
then got on again. On another occasion, though she had
been raised with cattle, she took fright and smashed both of
us up against a barbed-wire fence. Since I was between her
and the wire, she wasn't injured, and since I was wearing
heavy jeans and boots, I got off with nothing more than a
few scratches. She had also been raised right beside the train
tracks, yet one day she heard a train whistle as if for the first
time and bolted as if the hounds of hell were on her heels.
I grabbed one rein and made her circle. Any sane horse
would have given up long before Nejma did, but she went
frantically around and around until I was ready to throw up
and she was ready to fall over. Horses cannot throw up;
maybe she would have stopped circling earlier had she been
able to.

One accident the two of us avoided still has the power
to make me tremble. She and I had had a good ride, but as
I was unsaddling her, a black widow spider crawled out
from between the back housing and the skirt of the saddle.
My whole life and hers passed before my eyes as I pictured
what would have happened had the spider bitten her during
the ride.

My mistake was to keep riding her; for years and years
I rode her because it was a point of honor. In the horse
progression, the ultimate step was the raising and riding of
the Arabian.

The result of this determination was that riding grew to
be less and less of a pleasure. I could never just get on
Nejma and enjoy a ride; there was always the question of
whether or not she was going to behave. Finally, I admitted
defeat. It was one of the best decisions I've ever made. The
relief of knowing I wasn't going to have to climb back on
and risk my neck again was instantaneous.

Graveyard Peaches

While I had been trying to interest Nejma in sanity, my brother and cousins had been acquiring their own Arabians, and one of them, Darusha, a full sister to Nejma, looked very much like her. Suddenly there were reports of Darusha behaving in strange ways and dumping her riders, including an English friend who reported that he had been riding along on Darusha, and the next thing he knew, he was walking on the road, and the horse was a faint dust trail in the distance. The horse made it home long before the rider.

On hearing this, the pieces finally fit. "Are you sure it was Darusha?" I asked. "That sounds more like Nejma."

As it turned out, Darusha was in a pen out by the silos, taken there by the foreman for some reason I've forgotten; the boys had been riding Nejma. Even my brother, who was the best rider of all of us, had taken her out once and said it was enough. I confess to a good deal of amusement and satisfaction over this episode because though I stepped off a few times, Nejma never threw me.

Nejma did serve a useful function as a brood mare a couple of times. Her first foal was a gray colt. He was mine, and he was born in March of 1968. In a further departure from tradition, I named him J. C. Killy, after the great French skier who had just swept the Olympics. Killy was never anything like his mother, thank heavens! Though he was a handful as a youngster, it was nothing out of the ordinary, and even as a stud colt, before he was gelded, there wasn't anything mean or crazy about him. On one ride when he still had stallion impulses, there was a mare in season sharing the trail with us. When the mare drew ahead, Killy jumped into the air and tried to bolt after her. I yipped his name, and he stopped, then looked back at me with as close to an apologetic expression as a horse's face can manage.

Killy's sire was Asil Zenith, a gray, and Killy was

registered as a gray from birth, although he really was a most hideous color, a blotchy strawberry roan. But as he matured, his color softened to silver gray and then white. David's Arabian was Walad Biasnan—"he with many teeth"; it sounds better in Arabic. Wali also had the same bloodlines as Nejma and was born a year after she was. He shared some of her temperament, too. Both he and Nejma were apt to hurt themselves in their passion, a characteristic I deem the most dangerous of all in a horse, because if a horse is willing to hurt himself, what chance does the rider have? But there was a huge difference between my relationship with Nejma and David's with Wali. Though David considered Nejma a nut case and one ride on her enough, his patience with Wali was endless, and he loved riding him. He did get dumped now and then, but he considered that simply part of the routine. He rode as if he were sculpted with the horse. Watching the two of them, you could understand whence came the legend of centaurs.

My cousins were not so successful with their Arabians. For one thing, they are all large men, and the ranch breed of Arabians was just too small for them, particularly for Kemper, who was six foot five by his early teens.

In Craig's case, there was another tragedy, like mine with Elleb Attil. Craig's first Arabian was a gray colt, Aasifah, in whom Craig took great interest. But during our era, there was no reason to keep a stallion here. They take special handling, and none of our stud colts displayed the promise one wants for a breeding animal. The cowboys (the foreman and the wrangler) were in charge of the horses all along, and as in the case of my filly, they made a dreadfully bad decision. Though they were not going to pay for it themselves, they decided to save money on the castration. Rather than calling the vet, they summoned a man who, though he had no formal veterinary training, had cut some of their own horses and those of other cowboys they knew.

Graveyard Peaches

The deed was done, and done badly before my mother, who was running the ranch, or anyone else knew the plan. Aasifah died of internal hemorrhaging.

It was a stupid, needless death, but it wasn't that unusual. Many cowboys mistrust anyone with more education than they have, and they particularly hate having to pay, however indirectly, for that education. In more cases than I can count, cowboys have let their injured or ill livestock suffer until near death before calling the vet, and then when the vet points out that it is too late to do anything, the cowboys use that as added proof that vets aren't any damn good. It's a vicious circle.

And regarding the Arabians, I think there was something else at work, the cowboys' basic dislike and disdain for the high-strung, delicate breed. I have seen female barrel racers ride Arabians, and some modern gentlemen cowboys, too, but I've never encountered one of the old-time cowboys on one. It's as if they think that would be like having a poodle instead of a herd dog or a mongrel in their pickups.

Our cowboys didn't like having to handle one breed of horse differently. They didn't want to make changes in their regular ways of doing things for the sake of pedigree stock, and because of that, two purebred horses died. That's a high price for preserving the "old ways."

One by one, most of the Arabians were sold. Nejma was the first, and I didn't want anyone to buy her on one of her good days and be killed when her mood changed. It was not, after all, a problem. Not only was she listed as half-broken, she also managed to dump the excellent horsewoman who was showing her to potential buyers, leaving no doubt that this was not a trustworthy horse. But her bloodlines were good, so she fetched a good price in a market that bore no resemblance whatsoever to the inflated prices of today.

The cousins were off to school and to various pursuits,

and their horses didn't fit them anyway, so those went, too. But Wali and Killy remained.

It sounds ridiculous, but Wali mourned my brother for a long, long time after David died. David had ridden him right up to the end, spending time with the horse whenever he felt well enough. Wali had no way of understanding why his master came no more to take him for chases through the woods and across the fields.

Wali did have Killy; they had been companions since Killy's birth, and they were a sight to see as they raced in tandem across the pasture, one deep chestnut, the other the color of smoke.

Killy is still here, but I have long since given up my rights to him. After David's death, my cousin Scott began to ride Wali, and I gave Killy to my cousin Craig.

Nothing in this family happens without attendant drama. As Kemper and Nicki were married here in 1973, so were Craig and Laura in 1985, and in the late afternoon before Craig's bachelor party, Scott was riding Wali when Wali stepped in a gopher hole and broke his leg. Wali had to be destroyed, and he was, quickly and kindly. This wasn't just the death of a horse, but the end of an era, the end of part of David's legend, which no one held more dear than his cousins.

It was undoubtedly a good thing that the traditional bachelor party had evolved through the unity of the Tribe. Bachelor party now meant that the men and women celebrated together. As one of the men put it, "My God, we've been together through so much, why in the hell would I or any of the other men want to be without the women? We're all too old for that."

So that night we celebrated the coming wedding and mourned the loss of Wali, the loss of David, all at the same time. And the next day the wedding was perfect. Craig and Laura were married just as the sun went down. The guests were seated in the patio so that the couple were silhouetted against the pastures, the forest, and the desert beyond. The judge, Craig's father, my uncle Joe, performed the ceremony, and all of us toasted the joy to come and remembered all the joy and all the sorrow that had been.

In the actual count of things, Craig never officially gave up riding, but it had long since ceased to be a priority for him by the time I gave Killy to him. And once Wali was gone, it was natural that Killy should become Scott's. Scott is the only true horseman left among us, though my mother would ride if her bones allowed it. She was a superb rider, but her body has long since betrayed her. After her bout with severe arthritis before she was forty, every doctor she went to told her that riding was a foolish risk. She continued to ride occasionally long after that, but now the risk is so great to her brittle bones, no amount of pleasure could justify it.

My decision not to ride any more was caused in the physical sense by a tennis injury, no fault of the horses at all. It was stupid. I pinched my sciatic nerve going two directions at once to hit a ball, and afterwards, strange things caused nasty twinges, namely wearing wedge shoes or straddling a saddle. Half an hour of riding, and I was more than ready to walk on my own two feet rather than suffer the saddle a moment more. But the truth was, it was harder to give up the wedge shoes than the riding.

My entire riding career can be summed up by the "Peter Principle." I probably would have been a happy rider forever had I continued with horses like Sundae and Buck, but in my family, moving up horse-wise was just as expected as going from kindergarten through college at least. The educational tract was fairly workable for me, but with the horses, I actually hit the wall with Stormy. After that, my level of incompetence was always in place, even when I managed well enough.

The wild chases through the forest finished any lingering affection I had for riding, despite Killy's efforts to go gently. My brother and the other boys had no reservations about risking their necks and every other part of their anatomies, but I did.

The day I decided I didn't have to ride horses was one of the best of my life, a thousand times better than giving up on Stormy and Nejma. It was as if I had just heard that World War III was never going to happen. I came as close to flying as I had since the time before I realized flight was beyond my powers.

There are beasts of which I am particularly fond. Otters, elephants, cougars, wolves, foxes, raccoons, beavers, and badgers are among them. Horses were on the list earlier but fell off when I had to master them. When I quit riding, I was able to admire them again purely for their aesthetics.

The best of them are splendid animals, wild or domestic. Because I no longer ride them, it makes no difference to me whether or not I could make their intelligence, or lack of it, and their strange vision conform to my needs.

Though Wali is gone, Killy is not alone. Three ancient riding horses were given to the ranch by friends who no longer needed them but didn't want to sell them, and often the horses share their pasture with cattle boarded there by a local rancher.

Killy is twenty-two years old now, and his coat is snowy white. When I call to him, he comes to visit along the fence. But best of all is to watch him when he is running free, playing with the wind, enjoying his power just as he did as a colt. His neck is arched, his tail curved as he flows over the earth. I feel it then, savor it, know his essence better than I ever did when I bade him follow my course rather than his own.

EPILOGUE
LIVING BACKWARDS

"It's very good jam," said the Queen.

"Well, I don't want any today, at any rate."

"You couldn't have it if you did want it," the Queen said. "The rule is, jam tomorrow and jam yesterday—but never jam today."

"It must come sometimes to 'jam today,'" Alice objected.

"No, it can't," said the Queen. "It's jam every other day; today isn't any other day, you know."

"I don't understand you," said Alice. "It's dreadfully confusing!"

"That's the effect of living backward," the Queen said kindly, "it always makes one a little giddy at first—"

"Living backward!" Alice repeated in great astonishment. "I never heard of such a thing!"

"—but there's one great advantage in it, that one's memory works both ways."

—from *Through the Looking Glass*
by Lewis Carroll

The ranch as I have known it has always been about living backwards.

One day, after the guest ranch had closed, my grandmother found a man wandering along the front sidewalk, lost in his own reverie, stopping now and then to gaze out over the ranch.

"Are you looking for someone?" Grandma asked.

"Yes, I'm looking for the young man I was when I first came here. I'm looking for my youth. If it is any place at all, it is here."

He was one of my mother's suitors, someone who had dated her before she met my father and married him in their quick, wartime courtship. This man had not asked her to marry him in those uncertain times, but when he heard she was to marry another man, he raced to the ranch just in time to stand on the outside balcony of the main living room as the ceremony was beginning. Mother came out of the little complex of rooms upstairs and was walking toward the inner staircase. As she made the turn to go down the stairs, she saw him standing outside. The only thing separating them was a glass-paneled door. They did not exchange a word. It was a pantomime. He cocked his head and shrugged his shoulders, asking if she was sure. She nodded, turned from him, and made her way down the stairs, across the living room to where my father waited for her in front of the great fireplace.

I met the man. He was still so handsome, I could well imagine what he must have looked like in his younger days. And he had a liveliness, humor, and gentleness that made him immediately attractive beyond physical considerations. My first thought was, "This could have been my father." But my second was, "This could not have been my father. Had he and my mother had children, David and I would never have been. Other children, but not the two of us."

That hesitation on the top of the stairs and then the steady steps on: by such small measures is all of human history written.

He was not the only pilgrim. We find them quite often. They are of various ages, but they all share that abstracted air of looking not only at the ranch as it is, but also at things that cannot be seen by the naked eye.

Just a few weeks ago, I found a wiry old man on my

doorstep. He is, by his own admission, eighty-nine, and he added, "I have lived too long. I don't understand the world anymore. But I understand this place. It looks just as it did when my parents came here."

He was an adult when he spent time here with his parents, in the thirties, and he remembered that Grandma had not liked his mother and had asked her not to return.

"My mother was given to putting on airs," he reported with a blend of affection and resignation. "She floated around in silky dresses and talked about the famous people she knew. Mrs. Campbell didn't like that."

"That sounds just like my grandmother," I conceded.

He seemed to believe there was a special honor in being despised by Mrs. Campbell, at least as high an honor as being liked by her.

People drift through who were once small children here, brought out to the country by their parents or grandparents decades ago. Sometimes they bring their own children to show them how it was. Older couples come to remember the romantic days they spent when they and their marriages were much, much younger. Some people come back because they worked for the ranch and remember what it was like to be part of a different sort of life.

I hope we will find some way to preserve the history and the beauty of this place, but there is no certainty of that.

In the end, the story of the ranch, nineteenth century in so many ways, has become the story of the late twentieth century in the Far West. Commercial and residential developments are spreading like toadstools that spring up overnight.

The part of the ranch sold to the state in the sixties is preserved in the park, but even that is at risk because the county administers it and funds are not appropriated for the biological care it needs. Flocks of starlings are settling in the nesting sites of the songbirds. The wetlands are drained and filled at random so that the wildlife that depends on the environment is constantly at risk. The dogs and cats that stray from encroaching residential communities wreak havoc on the native fauna. Poachers hunt on land that is supposed to be a refuge. Off-the-road vehicles tear up the hills and the river bottom. The rare creatures, the kit foxes, the bobcats, and others, grow more and more rare.

Another part of the ranch is designated green belt and is in a flood plain. It cannot be used for other than agricultural purposes. But, ironically, it increases the developmental value of the land behind it because it provides a buffer.

The hills behind the ranch buildings have been sold. There was no choice. The land has become the one crop that increases in value, but it is only valuable for the ways it can be destroyed, scraped clean of native growth so that when the wind blows, the air looks like the dust-bowl years in Oklahoma, and cut into tiny pieces for tiny houses or stacks of apartments.

There is no easy answer. Some land had to be sold to preserve other acres. And people do need places to live. But I would counter that by saying that not everyone can live in Southern California. It is simply impossible. And if more care is not given to the land and the plants and creatures that inhabit the wild spaces, then everything that once made this stretch of earth unique and beautiful will be gone.

Even the dead demand their tenancy. The old graveyard that guards the road has expanded beyond recognition from the simple "boot hill" of the past, and there is another cemetery on the other side of town. I have not checked to see if there are any peach trees there.

When I was a child, moonless nights spilled darkness as far as I could see. Only one light glowed across the river, and it was on the house of friends. The stars were bright, distinct, sparkling against black velvet. Now it is never dark. The glow of "civilization" bleaches the night; the stars are pallid.

Graveyard Peaches

Children born here now do not know that it was ever different. But I mourn for them. I mourn their loss of black nights and bright stars. I will live backwards for them, telling the tale so that they will know how it was once upon a time.

—August, 1990.

LEGEND

1 **Jack's House.** Early 1900s. Always named for current resident.

2 **Stone House.** ca. 1900. Originally a creamery.

2A **Play Barn.** 1870. Originally a bunkhouse for cowboys. Used for square dances, etc., in the heyday of the guest ranch.

2B **Storage Barn.** Latter part of 1800s. Originally probably a regular use barn, for sheltering feed and livestock.

3 **Red House.** 1867. Originally a hotel located somewhere in the north pasture.

4 **Grey House.** Early 1900s.

5 **Aunt Lura's House.** Probably late 1800s, early 1900s. Originally a carriage house.

D **Dairy Barn.** 1940–41. Concrete replaced a wooden dairy barn.

OB **Old Barn.** Where the Old Barn used to be. Mainly for hay storage and livestock shelter.

6 **Donna and Joe's Old House.** 1953. Constructed of two old houses hauled in from out on the ranch.

7 **Mom and Dad's House.** 1951. Much of the work was done by my father. The house was designed by John Byers.

8 **Lugo.** 1946. Designed and named after the Lugo house in Los Angeles.

9 **Cat House.** 1930s. Named for Walter Catlett.

Pool and Tennis Court. 1930s. Grandma built these with money earned from trying industrial accident cases, work she detested.

P **Playhouse.** 1931–32. Built by my mother's generation, a summer project directed by Grandma to teach the children how to make adobe bricks and tiles.

10 **Main House.** 1927–1929. Designed by John Byers. Wings added in the 1930s—10AN, the Annex, 10M, the Montereys (the second story added above the Annex, 10AD, the Addition, 10C, the Cloisters).

10AN **Annex**

10M **The Montereys**

10AD **Addition**

10C **Cloisters**

11 **Apartments.** 1948. Grandma had them built and lived in the first one for years.

HC **Horse Corrals**

12 **Donna and Joe's New House.** 1970.